T0042079

Far Journeys

Also by Robert A. Monroe

JOURNEYS OUT OF THE BODY

Far Journeys

ROBERT A. MONROE

HARMONY

BOOKS • NEW YORK

Copyright © by Robert A. Monroe

All rights reserved.

Published in the United States by Harmony Books, an imprint of the Crown Publishing Group, a division of Random House LLC, a Penguin Random House Company, New York.
www.crownpublishing.com

Harmony Books is a registered trademark, and the Circle colophon is a trademark of Random House LLC.

Originally published in hardcover in the United States by Doubleday in 1985. Subsequently published in paperback by Broadway Books, an imprint of the Crown Publishing Group, a division of Random House LLC, New York, in 2001.

Those interested in the activities of the Institute may write
The Monroe Institute
Route 1, Box 175
Faber, Virginia 22938

"The Out-of-Body Experience A Phenomenological Typology Based on Questionnaire Responses," by S. W. Twemlow, G. O. Gabbard, and F. C. Jones. *The American Journal of Psychiatry* Vol. 139 4, pp. 450–55, 1982. Copyright © 1982, the American Psychiatric Association. Reprinted by permission.

"The OBE Psychophysiology of Robert A. Monroe" from *With the Eyes of the Mind* by Glen O. Gabbard and Stuart W. Twemlow. Copyright © 1984 Praeger Publishers. Reprinted by permission.

The Library of Congress Cataloging-in-Publication Data has cataloged the previous edition as:

Monroe, Robert A.
Far Journeys
"A Main Street book"
    1. Monroe, Robert A.   2. Psychical research—
Biography   3. Out-of-Body experiences   I. Title.
BF1283.M582A29   1985   133.9'01'3   85-1633

ISBN 978-0-385-23182-4
eBook ISBN 978-0-8041-5371-3

Printed in the United States of America

First Harmony Books Edition

DEDICATED TO:

Nancy Penn Monroe, much more than a wife,
whose constant and consistent love, support,
sharing, and understanding were the indispensable
elements in the writing and completion of this
record.

The literally hundreds of others over the past
fifteen years who freely gave their time, energy, and
interest in so many different ways and without
whom very little would have been accomplished.

Flow Sheet

Prologue

There seems to be an easy way to do—and a hard way. Given the choice, all of us take the easy route simply because it's more efficient, saves time and energy. If it's too easy, some of us feel guilty. We get the uncomfortable sense that we're missing something if we don't go the laborious, tried-and-true pattern. If it's that easy, it must not be good, might even be sinful.

But after a while, the easy way becomes the ordinary way and we forget the old road. When you've lived in an area long enough to have traveled between two cities before the interstates and freeways were built, try the old familiar highway just once. You'll find once is enough. The start-and-stop congestion, the total disorder, the growing frustrations far overshadow any remaining nostalgia you may have harbored. You have enough of such local traffic at the beginning and end of each run on the Interstate.

Now the problem. Suppose you met someone who had never driven on an interstate. All his life, he has driven only in local traffic. He's heard about such superhighways. He might even have seen one from a distance or heard the rumble of vehicles or smelled their exhaust fumes. He rationalizes any number of reasons why he hasn't and won't go interstate; he doesn't need to, he's satisfied the way he is; they travel too fast so it's not safe; you have to go out of your way to get on it; it's full of strangers from all over the place so you don't know whom you'll meet so you can't trust them; your car isn't in very good condition and it might break down and leave you stranded without anybody to help, in some lonely spot you never heard of. Maybe sometime you'll try it, but not right now.

Suppose you happened to see a construction order from the state highway department to begin demolition of the old highway so that all local traffic will have to go interstate eventually, like it or not. What do you do? What *would* you do? Nothing? Suppose the recalcitrant is an old and dear friend. Then what? Your friend knows of the order but refuses to believe it. He can see the work crews beginning to form at the end of the old highway and he ignores their existence. Thus you know the intense trauma he will undergo when the old road is shut off, and he will be carried kicking and screaming onto the Interstate.

You decide to do something, anything you can. After your decision, weeks, months—years—pass due to your own inertia. You have your own rationale. You don't know how to proceed. You don't know how to describe the interstate in local traffic terms, and your friend understands only local traffic. Someone else will come along and do it *for* you, for your friend.

Finally, finally—you discover the stupidly simple answer. You and your friend suffer from the same affliction but from different causes. It *is* inertia. Back in the old railroad days, a locomotive could pull only four or five cars at a time because if more cars than that were added, it would simply spin its drive wheels trying to get started. Inertia. Then a smart young thinker came along and invented the sliding coupler, which let the locomotive pick up the slack—and inertia—one car at a time. Ask any freight conductor what it was like to be in a caboose on the tail end of a 100-car train when he highballs the engineer. Instantaneous zero to thirty miles per hour. It's the same with automobiles. The transmission is there to provide big torque in low gear to overcome inertia. Once under way at cruising speed, power is required only to overcome wind resistance and road friction—and very little of it relatively. The hard case is the catapult launch on an aircraft carrier, which does the job in a hurry and not too gently. Guns are inertia-overcoming devices for bullets.

It's doubtful that explosive or catapult methods to full-speed interstate in a different form will be less than confusing and bewildering, even with modification to local traffic standards. Take this as an illustration:

. . . I can't get the stuff under a null point, there ought to be a better way to do this!

(Your uncontrolled emotion of anger is using much of your energy. A very human response.)

A better way to do it . . . stuff can't help being what it is, you kick a stone in your path and it hurts your toe, why get angry at the stone, you can't be angry at it for being on the path or being harder than a toe . . . yes, now let's see if it works.

(It is focus of attention, of consciousness, which is without diversion or deviation. No other energy available to you as human is as powerful. As a lens will direct energy you call light, so you can use consciousness.)

Each time I hear something like that, I realize how far I have to go.

(You are doing very well, Mister Monroe. Your own recognition of such percept is an indication.)

Hey, I got it! It's under the baseline . . . uh, except for this one saw-tooth, can't seem to hold onto it, and there's a smaller waveform on the sawtooth, can't get it put away.

(It is another form of rote, as you call it. Take it if you so desire. It may be interesting to you.)

Sure, why not!

(Click!)

Going from local traffic to interstate does indeed require an entry or acceleration lane to merge into the flow. If you can make the tools supplied by local traffic apply in the design and building of the ramp, so much the better. You need to remember especially the inertia factor—pick up the slack on one loaded car at a time, start in low gear so you don't stall the engine, then shift smoothly; automatic transmissions don't know when *you* need to shift. If the design is correct, your friend is cruising along the interstate long before the old highway is closed down.

You do the best you can.

Robert A. Monroe
Faber, Virginia
1985

Part I
Near Reaches

1.
Old Local Traffic

If there is a first and obvious point to be made, I can report that I am still alive physically after twenty-five years of exploring personally the out-of-body experience. A little timeworn, but still more or less operational.

There were several moments when I was not so sure. However, some of the best medical authorities have assured me that the physical problems I have encountered have been simple cause-and-effect of living in the culture/civilization of mid-twentieth century America. Some take another position. I am still alive as a *result* of such OOBE activity. Take your pick.

So it would seem that one can practice "going out of the body" regularly and survive. Also, after having been tested periodically by experts, I can still make the statement that I am reasonably sane in a not so reasonably sane world. There are many people who do strange things and get away with it. A century ago, it might have been going over Niagara Falls in a barrel.

What is the out-of-body experience? For those who have not encountered the subject as yet, an out-of-body experience (OOBE) is a condition where you find yourself outside of your physical body, fully conscious and able to perceive and act as if you were functioning physically—with several exceptions. You can move through space (and time?) slowly or apparently somewhere beyond the speed of light. You can observe, participate in events, make willful decisions based upon what you perceive and do. You can move through physical matter such as walls, steel plates, concrete, earth, oceans, air, even atomic radiation without effort or effect.

You can go into an adjoining room without bothering to open the door. You can visit a friend three thousand miles away. You can explore the moon, the solar system, and the galaxy if these interest you. Or—you can enter other reality systems only dimly perceived and theorized by our time/space consciousness.

It is not a new phenomenon. Recent surveys indicate some 25 percent of our population remembers having at least one such experience. Man's history is full of reports of such events. In earlier literature, it was commonly labeled "astral projection." I began by refusing to use this term, as it had an occult connotation and was certainly nonscientific by our standards. Charles Tart, a psychologist friend, popularized the term "out-of-body experience" when we were working together in the sixties. In the past twenty years, it has become the accepted Western generic term for this particular state of being.

Without any obvious reason, I began to "go" out of my body in the fall of 1958. In the light of later historical events, it is important to state that no drugs or alcohol were involved. I was a nonuser of the former and an infrequent imbiber of the latter.

Several years ago, I attended a conference not too far from our former home in Westchester County, New York—the site of my first out-of-body experiences. As we drove by the house, I commented that the reason why they began was still obscure.

A psychologist friend riding with me took one look at the house, turned, and smiled. "The answer is easy. It's the house. Take a good look at it."

I stopped the car. The house looked the same. Green roof and stone. The new owner had maintained it nicely. I turned to my friend. "I don't see anything different."

"The roof." He pointed a finger upward. "It's a perfect pyramid. Moreover, it's covered with copper just like the tops of the big ones in Egypt before the looters took over."

I stared, dumbfounded.

"Pyramid power, Robert," he went on. "You've read about it. You were living in a pyramid. That did it!"

Pyramid power? Well, maybe. There are reports and books that make claims about strange energies therein.

That the out-of-body experience frightened me then is a quantum understatement. When it recurred, I was filled with panic-driven visions of brain tumors and oncoming insanity. This led to extensive physical examinations, all negative, followed by recommendations of psychotherapy for "minor hallucinatory dysfunction." I discarded this diagnosis automatically. Some of my best friends at the time were psychiatrists and psychologists with their own problems, albeit certainly more orthodox.

Instead, I stubbornly began a search and research into the phenomenon out of self-preservation and, as the fear and panic subsided, out of growing curiosity. The trail took me beyond conventional scientific circles (total rejection), religions ("It's the work of the devil"), parapsychology ("Interesting. Sorry, no data available"), and Eastern disciplines ("Come study at our ashram in northern India for ten years"). This was chronicled in my previous book, *Journeys Out of the Body.*

One thing is certain. The purpose of the previous book was many times fulfilled. It brought thousands of letters from all parts of the world and among them many hundreds of people wrote their personal thanks for a reassurance that they were not mentally deranged, were not so much alone after all with their "closet" secret experience that they could not explain, and, most important, that they were not necessarily candidates for the psychiatric couch or mental hospital. That was the stated purpose of the original book: to help just one person avoid such needless incarceration.

I personally am bemused at the changes in these twenty-five years. In most academic and intellectual societies, it is now quite acceptable to talk about OOBEs. However, I'm sure that the great majority of people in our culture are still unaware of this facet of their lives. In 1959 or 1960, I certainly would have derided the idea that I might give a talk on OOBEs at the Smithsonian Institution. Or papers on the subject would be presented before the American Psychiatric Association. But they happened.

One of the most frequent approaches I hear reminds me very much of the old and worn-out show-business routine about the question a producer usually puts to the job-seeking performer. He is listening to what he knows already, that the actor appeared in *The Great One* in 1922, starred in *Who Goes There?* in 1938, won the Critics Award for his lead in *Nose to Nose,* and in 1949 played the role of Willie in *What Makes Willie Weep.*

The producer interrupts and puts the very simple question: "That's great, but what have you done *yesterday?*"

And so it is. What have I been doing (out of body) since the publication of *Journeys Out of the Body?* The answer I usually give is this: Beginning in the seventies, I began to experience a frustration, a limitation in my out-of-body activities. It is hard for some people to believe, I suppose, but such travels actually became boring. The early excitement had long passed. It became an effort to participate in controlled tests, and because it was an effort, I began to sense that the particular theme of "proof" was not part of my mode of operation. Moreover, when free of such testing limitations, there didn't seem to be anything exciting to do.

My deliberate inducement of the second state also became tedious because I had found a simpler way to achieve it. I would wake up after two or possibly three sleep cycles, or approximately after three or four hours, and find myself already relaxed physically, rested, and completely wide awake. In that state, I found it ridiculously easy to "unhook" and flow freely out of the body. This, of course, posed the question of what to do. Everyone else was asleep at three or four-thirty in the morning. There seemed nothing to be gained by going and meeting people while they were asleep, not any easy prospect for validation because of the hour. So with no particular goal or attraction, I usually would drift around a bit, then slip back in, turn on the light, read until I was sleepy again, and that was it.

This compounded the frustration, as there was still the compulsion. All of the effort to work in the out-of-body state had to have some meaning or importance beyond what my conscious mind (or those of others) thought to be important.

In the spring of 1972, a decision was made that provided the answer. The limiting factor was my conscious mind. Therefore, if OOBE decisions were left up to that part of me, as they had been, I would remain just as I was. I was too much in control—this left-brain "I." What would happen if I turned this decision-making process over to my total self (soul?), who was purportedly conversant with such activities.

Believing this, I then put it into practice. The following night, I went to sleep, went through two sleep cycles (about three hours), woke up, and remembered the decision. I detached from the physical and floated free. I said in my conscious mind that the decision to *do* is to be made by my entire self. After waiting for what seemed only a few seconds, there was a tremendous surge, a movement, an energy in that familiar spatial blackness, and there began for me an entire new era in my out-of-body activities. Since that night, my nonphysical experiences have been almost totally due to this procedure.

The results have been of a nature so far removed from anything my conscious mind could conceive of that a new problem arose. Although my physical here-now consciousness is always a participant, better than 90 percent of such events seemed to me impossible to translate into the time-space medium. It is as if one were to try to describe music, such as a symphony orchestra with choir, and do it in words without the use of such technical descriptions as notation, instruments, intervals, tonalities, and so on. One can use such words as "nice," "compelling," "frightening," "awe-inspiring," "warm," "loving," "beautiful"—and be nowhere remotely near the actual description.

You do the best you can. Which, I suppose, is what will happen as the attempt is made. I'm sure reporting Niagara Falls barrel-cruising was easier.

My here-now activities posed another problem. None of the exercises and techniques I had been designing and providing for others would work for me. Psychologist friends have offered many reasons why they are ineffective in my case. The simplest one is that I just cannot get my left brain out of the way. I have been so deeply involved in the production process that my critical and analytical faculty simply won't let go of the here-now-attention-focusing material contained therein. Also, in order to produce these exercises in an audio mode, I have had to listen with an intense form of concentration in the recording and mixing of the various sounds that we use. Evidently, I have had to shut off the effect. Even a simple one-frequency tone causes me to analyze the frequency and attempt to determine that it is stable.

Perhaps there *is* an effect I am not aware of. But it is a strange place to be, looking over the fence at a garden you have planted and fertilized, watching everybody else have such a good time.

The here-now portions of recent events are relatively straightforward. For example, I had become painfully (literally) aware that my body has taken to rejecting chemicals. This includes alcohol, prescription drugs, caffeine, and evidently anything else my body says is unnatural for its operation. The rejection or allergic reaction takes the form of profuse sweating, vomiting, and/or severe abdominal cramps. This may be constructive, but it also has its disadvantages. I never was a consequential drinker, but even a glass of wine begins the rejection process.

During surgery, it is something intense to cope with. I begin to reject the anesthesia, and awake on the operating table to feel the surgeon sewing me up (I am sure to the surprise of the anesthesiologist). In recovery, under intense pain, a shot of Demerol only brings on extreme vomiting. You can imagine my frustration when others are using a system we developed that permits excellent nondrug pain control in the postsurgical period. In my hospital visits during the past ten years, only once has the system worked for me. I was sorely disappointed when it was not effective on the last trip. It was a nearly unbearable event. Yet I knew if I consciously went out of body, I would not have the courage to return to that sea of scalding pain.

A psychologist friend back in the early days was skeptical of this drug allergy. Further, he was interested in what the effects of what are now called entertainment drugs would be on my type of personal and physical makeup. We tried "laboratory"-quality mescaline and LSD on my system. Nothing happened.

Another item: I asked a nonphysical friend if I had been in a physical life existence in the recent past. It was one of the few clear verbal answers that I received:

"Your last human life was spent as a monk in a monastery in Coshocton, Pennsylvania."

I looked at the map of Pennsylvania and there was no Coshocton indicated. I knew there was a Coshocton, Ohio, because I had lived in the state. Therefore I asked again to be sure that the state was right. It was Pennsylvania. I didn't give it much thought because I personally am not deeply interested in who I was, if I was. I mentioned the event to a Catholic monsignor friend, and he offered to look it up in his records. Some weeks later he called to say there really was a monastery in a place called Coshocton, Pennsylvania. He thought it would be interesting to drive up there some weekend and see if I responded to any memories. Perhaps, someday.

Item: The money-pants pocket. For years, I have kept this as a closet secret because no one believes it. I have shown it to my wife, Nancy, and she still is skeptical. It seems that if I leave a certain pair of pants hung in the bedroom closet, it generates paper money. Real money, not new and crisp, usually fairly well worn. It is never a great amount; the maximum I have ever found in the pocket is eleven dollars. Usually there will be only two, three, or four dollars. Time does not seem to be a factor. I can ignore it for a week, and there will be perhaps three dollars. I may not go near it for three months, and there may be only six dollars. There seems to be no particular format for the generation or the amount of money. I can take the pants to the cleaners and return them to the closet in their plastic bag. It makes no difference. We have theorized that I may walk in my sleep and insert money in the pants pocket. The unopened plastic bag dispelled that idea. One rationale is that it is an ongoing result of a very urgent need for a few dollars back in my teenage period. (There was a strange event back in that era that might relate to it.) Some part of my system still remembers that urgent need and attempts to provide for it. Too bad that when you reach another stage in life, five or six or eleven dollars does not go very far! Very few people really believe it, and I don't blame them. I wouldn't if it didn't happen to me.

Item: In our house at Whistlefield Farm, there was a screened porch off the living room. To get to the porch, one had to go through two double doors and down a series of flagstone steps that led to the porch at a lower level. These steps were quite steep, the difference in floor height being approximately four feet.

One morning, with my arms full of books and papers, I walked out the entrance to the porch and stumbled. My left foot crossed over in front of my right, and I dove headlong in the direction of the flagstone floor of the porch. As I fell I was unable to get my arms out in front of me. I remember thinking, "Well, this will certainly end up with a fractured skull and a broken neck."

About six inches from the floor, my fall was suddenly arrested and I landed on my head and shoulders very lightly on the flagstone floor, no heavier than if I had simply put my head down very carefully. The rest of my body then draped down afterward, drifting as gently as a feather. I lay there for a moment wondering what had happened. I felt my head and my shoulders and there was no pain, no mark, no bruise, nothing. I stood up, picked up my books and papers, looked at the place from where I had fallen, and tried to figure some answer. Something had cushioned my fall, but I certainly was not consciously aware of what it was.

Some months later in the middle of winter, a similar event took place. I was walking down the front steps, which had been reportedly cleaned after a snow, slipped, and started to fall. This time I was not quite so surprised when I again landed very lightly. There have been only two such events, and I don't think I will deliberately try to fall experimentally. Just another one of those "as yet" unexplained moments.

Item: One of the more puzzling events took place as a result of a very direct communication—or so it seemed. Early one morning in the mid-seventies, about three o'clock to be exact, I went through my customary lazy man's way of rolling out of my body. Almost immediately I was accosted by a vaguely formed individual who gave me this very specific instruction:

"Mr. Monroe, be at Eaglehill at 7 A.M. on July fourth." Surprised, I asked for a repeat of the instruction. It came exactly the same: "Mr. Monroe, be at Eaglehill at 7 A.M. on July fourth."

Before I had a chance to ask why or what it was all about, the form faded and disappeared. I then rolled back into my body and sat up and wrote it down very carefully.

The next night when I performed the same act, almost immediately the form was there again with the same message. It was very definite—almost a command—and again the figure faded before I had a chance to query further. I tried the third night to see if it replicated again, but there was no response. What was so impressive about it was that the instruction was very clear. And it was repeated exactly the second night. Most important, "they" actually called me by name.

This instruction elicited a great deal of curiosity from me and those of my friends and family to whom I related it. We speculated in many ways about it but the big question was: "Where is Eaglehill?" It was about April when the instruction was given and there seemed to be plenty of time to find out what the message meant. But try as we might, we could not find any place called Eaglehill. After a few weeks, I more or less forgot about the idea.

An event changed all that. While visiting friends several hundred miles from home, we were having dinner out on the patio of their house. My host had a radio receiver that automatically scanned various frequencies such as police, fire, and so on. We were sitting there chatting when suddenly over the radio came someone saying "Eaglehill." It jarred my attention immediately. I excitedly asked my host what the radio was tuned to. He replied that it was the FAA aircraft channel for instructions to and from aircraft. I waited eagerly for something more on the radio. My host asked curiously what was so important. Needless to say, I didn't feel that I could tell him. A couple of minutes later the radio came to life loudly and clearly: "This is United 351 over Eaglehill at twelve thousand feet."

The next day, after a long drive home, I went to the FAA facility at our local airport and asked the FAA man where Eaglehill was. He replied instantly that it was a holding point in a neighboring state, a radio marker beacon. He showed it to me on the airways sectional map, and sure enough, there it was—Eaglehill. There evidently was some type of small village by that name, although it did not show on any of the road maps we had.

This put a whole new prospect on the message. Therefore, on the afternoon of July 3, I left home for the long drive over to Eaglehill. I drove into the small town nearest to the supposed site, checked into a local motel, had a casual dinner, and went to bed early.

At exactly seven the next morning, I drove into the crossroads called Eaglehill. It consisted of two or three houses, a garage, and a store, all situated around a small country crossroads. Not a very impressive place, to say the least. It looked like it had not changed in the last thirty or forty years. I pulled over to the side and stopped the car. Several local citizens sitting outside the garage looked at me curiously as I sat and waited.

I waited for over an hour and nothing happened. No one approached me. I didn't feel anything except first excitement and then disappointment. Finally, sometime after eight o'clock, under curious stares, I started the car and drove up through Eaglehill and into the countryside beyond. I drove about two miles further and there was nothing but farms. I returned to the crossroads and turned west and drove several miles. Again, nothing different, no one signaled me, nothing except country and farms. I turned around and drove east. It was all the same. I returned to my post at the crossroads, sat in the car, and waited. When it got to be twelve o'clock, I decided that it had all been an illusion, returned to the motel, checked out, and had lunch. It was either the wrong Eaglehill, or I understood it wrong, misinterpreted, or it was all a hoax or a dream.

After much contemplation, I finally decided where my mistake was. The invitation or request was not that I go to Eaglehill physically: it was that I be there in an out-of-body state. What the invitation did not take into account was how difficult it is for me to go directly to a specific place, rather than a person.

Adding fuel to the fire: Years later, in encountering a government official, I asked him about that particular site, without reference to why I was interested. He related to me that it was a special federal research installation. It was being constructed just about the time I was there. Evidently it is still not common knowledge, or at least I don't want to take that chance. Therefore, the location as indicated in my retelling is not the correct one. I still like to speculate as to what might have happened if I had kept the appointment in the out-of-body state.

Item: My company had received the franchise to install a cable television system in Charlottesville, Virginia, and we needed a receiving antenna site on top of a hill just outside of town. The owner of the hill was Roy, a small, balding, bright-blue-eyed energetic little man with a dry and subtle sense of humor. His face was wrinkled and tanned from many years of supervising the work in the twenty-thousand-apple-tree orchard atop the hill. As he was a true Scotsman, the negotiation was elaborately casual but came to a very reasonable and fair end. And we became friends.

After lunch one Friday, he looked at me with a twinkle and asked, "Do you like to play cards?"

An old familiar surge rose in me. "What kind of cards?"

"Well," he said, "some people don't call it poker because we play so many wild games, but you can have a lot of fun at it. It's only ten- and twenty-cent games, so you can't expect to make any money. We hold it at a different fellow's house each Friday night and the only thing is, we don't have any drinking. It's the oldest, continuous poker game in the city of Charlottesville. Must have been going on steady for seventy years—and that's a long time. If you would like to come tonight, I'll pick you up, wherever you are, about seven-thirty. You'll have a good time at choir practice."

I looked at him blankly. "Choir practice?"

He smiled. "That's what we call it here in Virginia. Some fellows say that they are not sure whether it's legal or not and we've heard of other games being raided for gambling. Course, we aren't doing anything like that."

I smiled. "No, of course not. See you at seven-thirty for choir practice."

I became a regular member of choir practice. I did not attend every Friday, but I did show up at least two Fridays per month. Again, it was a welcome change from my daily work in cable television and the participants were strictly local businessmen who had, for the most part, lived in the Charlottesville area all of their lives.

They also were totally unaware of any strange research or other activities I might be involved in. Even when my first book was published they knew nothing about it and I made no mention of it. To this day perhaps one or two are remotely aware of what I now do.

The first indicator that there were unusual factors involved in cardplaying choir practice came about two years later when there were six of us playing a game of seven-card stud. The deal began normally. My two hole cards were a three and four of clubs. Among the face-up cards dealt to me were a five and seven of clubs. The betting was quite strong; there were pairs all over the table, including a pair of aces showing on Roy's face-up cards. After I stayed in the betting, which I had no statistical right to do, trying to buy an inside straight or a flush, the final, seventh card was dealt to each of us face down. I did not look at mine. Suddenly, without any question, I knew that the card dealt to me was the six of clubs. It was very strange, simply a "knowing."

"Roy," I said, indicating the untouched down card, "that's a six of clubs and that will make me a straight flush. And that will beat your aces full."

Roy looked at the card and looked up at me with a sly grin. He had already looked at his last card and he knew he had aces full. "I got five that says you don't have it. That's not the six of clubs."

I reached for the pile of chips and said, "There it is, Roy."

He smiled and matched the stack. "All right, show me." I turned it over and it was the six of clubs.

Roy smiled. "That doesn't beat my full house." He turned over his aces full, which beat the other hands on the table. "I have another five that says you don't have the three and four of clubs in the hole."

I smiled. "I don't want to take your money, Roy."

"A straight flush will beat my aces full." He pushed another stack out. "I don't think you got it. You somehow knew there was a six of clubs there and you ought to quit while you're ahead."

I smiled and said, "I don't want the other five, Roy." And then I turned over the three and four in the hole, making the straight flush in clubs.

He just looked at it and said, "Isn't that something!"

On the very next hand, with Roy doing the dealing, the feeling I had was still there, very strong, the "knowing." I didn't even look at my hole cards. Of the four cards dealt face up to me there was a five and seven of hearts. I knew. That's all I can tell you, I knew.

"Roy," I said, "you see that five and seven of hearts?" Roy nodded. He didn't have the aces this time. "Well," I said, "this last card you are going to deal is a six of hearts and that will make me a straight flush in hearts. You see, I haven't seen my bottom cards yet, you notice?" He nodded, watching. Roy had been the dealer. The rest of the players were watching intently, expecting me to lose. Roy was an exceptional card player.

The last card was dealt to me face down, and before I could pick it up, Roy said, "I got another five says it's not the six of hearts. No, as a matter of fact, I'll make it ten." He shot a pack of chips forward.

"I don't want to take your money, Roy," I said, smiling.

"You are not taking it from me and I am not giving it to you," he said. "Put it up."

I did.

"Now turn over the card," he demanded. I did, and it was the six of hearts. He looked at me with utter astonishment. He was doing the dealing. No trickery was at all possible in his frame of reference.

"Moreover," I said, "those two hole cards that I haven't looked at yet are the three and four of hearts."

Roy looked at me. "I have twenty that says that they aren't."

With utmost casualness I said, "I don't want to take your money, Roy," and turned over the two hole cards. They were the three and four of hearts.

Roy looked at the straight flush, the same one as before except in hearts. "Sometimes you are about the luckiest fellow I ever met."

The others at the table agreed.

That particular run of "luck" was talked about for several months. The odds against two successive straight flushes of the same denomination held by the same person in a six-handed card game are about 5,780,000 to one. How did it happen? I don't know. How did I know? Very simply, a sureness. I suspect a lot of high rollers have made a lot of money on such dealings and lost also because the "knowing" was not right.

2.
Hemi-Sync et al.

With the publication of *Journeys Out of the Body*, we began to receive surprising inquiries, information, and cooperation from many unexpected sources. A book intended for the general public was attracting interest in scientific and academic circles. Our laboratory west of Charlottesville, Virginia, opened on an entirely voluntary basis. Originally named Whistlefield Research Laboratories, this was later changed to the Monroe Institute of Applied Sciences. Using the name Monroe was not an ego factor, but simply the quickest way to clear the title officially. The "Applied Sciences" part was quite specific. We felt that the understanding of OOBEs could be achieved on a level compatible with our Western sciences and that the greatest service we could perform would be to apply any discoveries or information that we encountered.

The laboratory consisted of a one-story building designed for the purpose, and included two offices, a lounge, and a research wing. In the wing were an instrument or control room, three isolation booths, and a briefing room. All three booths were connected independently to the control room for both physiological monitoring and the delivery of various types of audio and electromagnetic signals to stimulate a response from a volunteer subject in a booth.

The booths themselves each contained a heated water bed, thus providing a comfortable condition in total darkness. They were also environmentally controlled in air, temperature, and acoustics. A subject in the booth could be wired to transmit to the control room a wide array of physiological signals. These included eight-channel EEG (brain-wave electrical patterns), EMG (muscle tone), pulse rate, and body voltage. As things developed, we were able to determine most of what we wanted to know simply by reading body-voltage changes.

Aside from visiting participants from out of town, we had a local volunteer group consisting of several M.D.s, a physicist, an electronic engineer, several psychiatric and social service workers, plus assorted friends and family. Most research and experiments took place at night or on weekends, as all of us were employed in other occupations. In retrospect, the immense contribution that this group gave freely was a major factor in helping the whole process get started under these new conditions, and for this I will be forever grateful. It took much patience and dedication to paste up with electrodes, then lie hour after hour in a darkened booth and report subjective results of various tests—results that could be correlated with instrument readouts in the control room to the point where a consensus could be achieved.

Our first studies were a continuation of the sleep research begun in New York. The demand for a solution to a problem brought one of our early results of significance. Because so much of the reported out-of-body states, including many of my own, revolved around the sleep state, we still believed some answers would be found in this area. However, most of our subjects arrived at night after dinner, and with long, boring periods of being wired up with electrodes, they were either too tired to stay awake in the booth or too restless to be able to relax enough to report any subtle and subjective responses. It defeated our purpose to use any types of medication or drugs to control these states, so we looked for a method within our own frame of reference.

The old truism held. Necessity *is* the mother. It was through this need to help our subjects stay awake, get into a borderland sleep state, that we began to try utilizing sound. This resulted in the discovery of Frequency-Following Response (FFR), which permitted us to hold the subject in a certain state of consciousness between wakefulness and sleep for extended periods of time. By introducing certain sound patterns in the subject's ear, we determined that there was a similar electrical response in the brain waves of the subject. By controlling that brain-wave frequency, we were able to help the subject relax, keep him awake, or put him to sleep. One of our engineering participants suggested that we patent this unusual process, and we received a patent on the method and technique in 1975.

By cross-referencing the various effective frequencies among subjects, we slowly began to evolve combinations of sound frequencies that created FFRs highly conducive to OOBEs and other unusual stages of consciousness. Among these, of course, was a very effective means of moving into what is commonly known as a meditative state.

All of this did not come quickly. Only a few words cover hundreds of hours of putting together different sound patterns and testing for responses, with subjects patiently lying in a booth as sound warbled in their ears, slowly changing in pitch, while the technician in the control room looked for changes in the monitoring instruments.

During such sessions, our volunteer subject participants learned to report verbally on any changes in their mental or physical condition. This became a very important ability, to speak and perceive when the normal pattern would be to lose consciousness or be "asleep."

One of the first solid points of identification was a state that we began to label Focus 10. There was no particular significance to the number 10, and I am not sure where it originated. Also, we wanted to be sure it was not confused with other forms of consciousness. Therefore it became simply TEN. We were able to identify this state very specifically and to return to it again and again with our subjects. Easily defined, Focus 10 is a state where the mind is awake and the body asleep. All the physiological responses are those of one in light or deep sleep. However, the brain-wave patterns are different. The EEGs show a mix of waves ordinarily associated with sleep, light and deep, and overlying beta signals (wakefulness).

Gradually there developed a very special group, a total of some eight subjects completely familiar with the Focus 10 state. Verbal communication in Focus 10 through the microphone/headphone system became as normal as if we were sitting across from one another in a conference room. We could tell easily from the instrument readout when they were and when they were not in Focus 10. It could not be imagined or faked, even if there had been any remote desire to do so. There were many times, of course, when they were unable to get into the Focus 10 state because of external pressures and stresses in their daily lives that they could not abandon easily. In such cases, they simply reported that they could not "do it" that night or canceled the appointment. This saved much time and effort.

With the constant stream of visitors we began to determine that others, totally untrained, could be assisted into Focus 10 without a great deal of trouble. The process of learning to communicate verbally would take much longer. To see how far this would go, we sent a tape of the composite signal to a psychiatrist friend in Kansas. In an experiment, he tested it on four completely naïve subjects and with no suggestion as to what to expect. He reported that one of the four subjects quit the test because he found that he was bouncing against the ceiling of the room looking down at his physical body.

Our next step came as an interesting proposition. With the body asleep —i.e., the physical senses turned off or reduced—why not develop frequencies that would enhance perceiving by means other than the five physical senses? With the insertion of higher-frequency beta signals, our subjects began to find much more than the usual blackness. First came light and color patterns seen visually in the blacked-out booth, with eyes either closed or open. Next came sounds heard in the head, not a part of the synthesized sounds, but voices, music, sometimes loud explosions that startled the subject completely out of Focus 10—something that has still to be explained.

These phenomena were gradually perceived in a pattern, as somewhat of a band preceding a change into the out-of-body experience. There were also preliminary physiological responses—lowering of blood pressure and pulse, slight temperature drop (0.3°), loss of muscle tone. Subjectively, there were reports of a heaviness in the physical body, sometimes catalepsy, and a strong sense of heat followed by coolness. As the induction of the OOBE state was examined further, one key element did repeat consistently. Subjects began to locate within their nonphysical perception a pinpoint of light. When the subject learned to "move" in the direction of the light until it became larger and larger, and then move through it, the OOBE state was achieved. In slow motion, it "felt as if one were going through a tunnel to get to the light," a classic description that has been brought forth by many who performed the OOBE inadvertently or in a near-death situation.

One new development was the key that opened many things for us. We now call it the Hemi-Sync process.

Science has long known that your brain is divided into two halves, or hemispheres. But only in recent years has it been discovered that these two halves are entirely different in the functions they perform. There is still controversy about the theory as to details. Most of the time, we think only with our "left brain." When we use our "right brain," it is primarily to support the action of the left. Otherwise, we do our best to ignore it. In function, the nerve signals from these brain halves act in an X crossover. The left brain controls the right side of the body, and the right brain controls the left. We are primarily a right-handed civilization, dominated by our left brains. Only in the last fifty years have left-handers been accepted as "equals." In many ways, we still discriminate against left-handers. Did you know that a pair of scissors is a right-handed tool?

We use the left brain to talk and read, to do mathematics, to reason deductively, to remember detail, to measure time, among many other facets—the source of logical, rational thought. It "knows" nothing else.

Our right brain is the originator of ideas, spatial sense, intuition, music, emotion, and probably much more than we now realize. It is timeless, apparently with a language all its own.

One of the best descriptions given to illustrate the difference is with a reel of movie film. To determine the content, the left brain will put it on a projector, show the movie on a screen, and thus be informed. The right brain will pick up the roll of film, hold it for a moment, then put it down and say, "Oh, I understand."

Ridiculous! That's your left brain's reaction as you use it to read these words. It simply doesn't compute—by left-brain standards.

Basically, we are a half-brained society. Virtually everything we consider valuable is operated or controlled by our dominant left brain. Even if it originates in the right brain, such as an idea or music, the left brain takes over and puts it to use.

How did we get this way? No one is absolutely sure, but one of the better guesses is that the left-brain dominance came about because of a basic need to survive in a physical world. Through thousands of years, our forebears added to left-brainism because that was the way to get things done. Our entire system—books, schools, colleges and universities, industry, political structures, churches—is fundamentally left-brained in learning, application, and operation. We have generally regarded right-brain thinking with amused tolerance, suspicion, disgust, irritation, distrust—and awe.

Then why bother! Why not stay half-brained and let it go at that. Who needs the right brain!

We do. Recent studies show we use our right brain throughout our daily lives in many subtle ways. For example, the left brain remembers the name, but the right brain remembers the face. (How many times have you spotted a familiar face but couldn't remember his name? Left brain, watch out! Studies of world leaders throughout history indicate they thought with far more than their analytical, intellectual minds. All great decisions by mankind have been made with the left brain *plus*. Plus the right brain? Evidence supports it, based upon what we now know. Moreover, it's a good guess that the right brain pulls the voting-booth lever in presidential elections. Current theory centers around the idea that we shift brain-hemisphere dominance many times during our daily activities. Such a shift takes place instantly, depending on the mental or physical need at the moment. This seems to limit even more rigidly the already minor use of our brain/mind potential. How we got smart enough long enough to climb down out of the trees and survive as a species was either dumb luck or a miracle. Or something else.

How do we then go about using more of our brain power? There have been many ways attempted over the course of human evolution. Virtually all of them have had drawbacks or limitations in one form or another. The Hemi-Sync process offers promise and potential in this area. It can be utilized with relative ease, does not require years of intensive training, and is not limited to a narrow band of application.

Hemi-Sync (short for hemispheric synchronization) uses patterns of sound to help create simultaneously an identical wave form in both brain hemispheres. This means that when your ear hears a certain type of sound signal, the brain tends to respond or "resonate" with similar electrical signals. Knowing that various electrical brain waves are indicators of states of consciousness (such as awake or asleep), you thus can listen to a similar sound pattern and it will help you be in the desired state of awareness.

Hemi-Sync takes the process an important step further. Each ear sends its dominant nerve signal to the opposite brain hemisphere, following the X pattern. When separate sound pulses are sent to each ear (using head-phones to isolate one ear from the other), the halves of the brain must act in unison to "hear" a third signal, which is the difference between the two signals in each ear. For example, if you hear a sound measuring 100 in one ear and another signal of 125 in the other, the signal your whole brain will "generate" will be 25. It is never an actual sound, but it is an electrical signal that only can be created by both brain hemispheres acting and working together. The signal so generated is narrow-band in frequency and often twice the amplitude or strength of a typical EEG brain-wave form.

If the 25 signal (above) is one that produces a certain type of consciousness, then the whole brain—both hemispheres—is focused in an identical state of awareness at the same time. Most important, the condition can be changed at will by changing the sound pattern. It also can be learned and re-created from memory when the need arrives.

Once the researcher or clinician is exposed to some of the potentials of the Hemi-Sync process, his first thought is application within areas of his own interest. One illustration of this is in the field of psychiatry. The use of Hemi-Sync in analysis apparently opens the patient to levels of memory that may take years to achieve using standard interview methods. Another experimental use has been in reduction of stress tension in patients. Sometimes the change is so subtle that the patient himself is unaware of it. One of our psychiatric associates was treating an Air Force colonel for stress-related problems. After two weeks working with Hemi-Sync and the psychiatrist, he angrily wanted to give up.

"It isn't doing a damn thing for me," he reported. "Everything's the same. I don't feel any different, not a thing." He hesitated. "Well, I did take my wife out for dinner the other night for the first time in six months. And, oh yes, I finally took my son out fishing for the weekend, which I had promised to do for a long time. But that's all. Nothing else. Not a single thing!"

Our psychiatrist friend simply nodded.

There has been much talk about the use of Hemi-Sync with terminal cases. However, in spite of the broad interest and numerous requests, very few have actually utilized the system with specific patients. One example of this took place with another psychiatric associate, who was treating what might be labeled the hard-core terminal case. His patient was a psychologist who had been ill for two years and had become drug-addicted in order to handle the pain of his illness. Thus the problems doubled up— the patient was supposed to know all the answers and would automatically resist all normal treatment, with the added drug dependency. Our psychiatrist began working with him daily, utilizing the Hemi-Sync process. By the Wednesday of the second week, a simple but very significant event took place. The patient was able to go to sleep at night for the first time in two years without any pain or sleep medication.

At the end of two weeks, the patient returned home. He died several months later, and the final report came from his wife. The psychologist patient had spent a very calm and quiet last week of his life, completely free of pain, without any medication, and had a pleasant and peaceful last few days with his family. Our psychiatrist who treated him believes that his exposure to Hemi-Sync during treatment made this possible.

Another psychiatrist friend, active in research with schizophrenics, found that under certain Hemi-Sync patterns one patient lost many of the symptoms of his illness. When taken off the Hemi-Sync sound, he reverted back to his typical psychotic condition. This was only one particular patient. However, it does beg for further investigation, to determine if the patient can be trained to replicate the conditions created by Hemi-Sync, plus some form of encoding or entrainment that would let him remember and use it in his daily life.

Certainly one of the most successful applications of Hemi-Sync is a training series we call Emergency Treatment. This is designed to help an individual through the process of serious illness, accident injury, or surgery. One of the earliest examples comes to mind.

A psychiatric counselor visited our lab, having heard of some of our work, and in the course of conversation we discovered that he was at that time the second-oldest living kidney transplant recipient. He had undergone some fifteen successive operations over the years to correct the effects of the chemicals that he had to take in order to avoid rejection of the transplanted kidney. He was due to go in for surgery for the sixteenth time on the following Thursday. We suggested that he try this Emergency Treatment series. He readily agreed.

His case was important in that, because of the many previous operations, his doctor had a very precise history of his physiological state during surgery, how much anesthesia he required, what was needed to control his pain, and his rate of recuperation, among other items. Knowing this, his doctor agreed to let him use the tape series, which involved preliminary exercises and then listening to a Hemi-Sync tape in the operating room during the actual operation, during recovery, and again while recuperating.

On the scheduled Thursday, he went into surgery at eleven o'clock. According to the report, the surgeon very nearly canceled the operation because of his low blood pressure. However, it was steady, so he decided that this was not a serious risk. At four o'clock in the afternoon, the patient called me from his hospital room. He was sitting up in bed.

"I just thought I'd let you know how it went." His voice sounded strong. "They gave me one shot of pain medication before I had a chance to stop them, but I have not needed any since. The only problem that I had was that I tried to get up and go to the bathroom and I fainted. The doctor reported that my blood pressure still was very low. Is that normal?"

"Try counting yourself out from ten to one," I replied, "and then see where your blood pressure is. It would seem that the recovery tape didn't get you out of it completely. Call me back after your doctor takes your blood pressure again."

He did as suggested, and reported that his blood pressure had completely returned to normal. According to the records, his recuperation time was cut in half from what it had been after all of his previous operations. More important, he was able to control totally his problem of chronic pain, which had plagued him in the months and years previously.

Once out of the hospital, he began to develop actively the use of Hemi-Sync for pain control. He met with the State Rehabilitation Agency, as one of their major problems in rehabilitation is the control of pain which prevents many from living and working normally. The State Rehab people became interested enough so that we were invited to conduct a demonstration at the Federal Rehabilitation Facility at Hot Springs, Arkansas. As a result, we received a request for the cost to train personnel in our process at rehab centers in all fifty states. We provided this, but never received any further requests. Evidently it was too unorthodox to fit into a federal budget.

The use of Emergency Treatment during surgery has had varying degrees of success and no failures whenever it has been properly used. One vascular surgeon has utilized it with over thirty patients and still has difficulty in enlisting his fellow practitioners in its use. The president of a major corporation used it during surgery, and refused any postoperative pain or sleep medication. He evidently became so annoyed at hospital procedures that he discharged himself three days after surgery. A young woman had major abdominal surgery and was sky-diving one week later. The Emergency Treatment series has had a remarkable history. The biggest problem is gaining the consent of the surgeon and the hospital personnel to its use in their highly organized environment.

For a good night's sleep, Hemi-Sync appears as effective as prescription drugs. Executives on long airline flights use it to overcome jet lag. Others find it helpful in stress-tension reduction or in playing a better game of golf.

As a learning tool, it has a great ability to focus and hold attention. In a particular course in a government training school, it increased mental-motor skills by 75 percent. In another test, Morse code students improved their ability by as much as 30 percent. On the other end of the scale, primary-grade pupils in Tacoma learned in four weeks what ordinarily took a full semester.

These and other results led us to the beginnings of definitions of what we were doing and why we were doing it. It appeared to be something much different from finding ways to trigger OOBE states. This brought us to the following formal premise:

Stated simply, the Institute holds to the concept that (1) consciousness and the focusing thereof contain any and all solutions to the life processes that man desires or encounters; (2) greater understanding and appreciation of such consciousness can be achieved only through interdisciplinary approaches and coordination; (3) the results of related research effort are meaningful only if reduced to practical application, to "something of value" within the context of the contemporary culture or era.

This led us to the base that consciousness is a form of energy at work. The first step must therefore be to perceive the energy itself—no small trick when you are using yourself to measure yourself, as it were. Once it is perceived in its raw form, one can possibly begin to understand how it is naturally used. Such perception will permit a broader and more deliberate control of such energy fields. From control, it is a very logical step to apply it in new and expanded forms. This is all a very circumlocutory way to say that if you can find out the stuff that makes you think and be, you can use it in ways that you are not using it now.

3.
The Gateway Program

In the mid-seventies, a development took place that changed drastically much of our activities. Only in retrospect did it become discernible.

Esalen at Big Sur in California invited us to conduct a weekend workshop using our new methods and techniques. In a way, we took it to be somewhat of a recognition of what we were doing. Esalen was then known as a beginning source for many new types of psychological theory and practice, and somewhat a fountainhead of intellectual approaches to the human mind.

We accepted, and made the trip, not quite sure what to expect when we got there. We had never handled twenty-four people at one time in the consciousness states familiar to us. I am sure the participants really didn't know what to expect either, except that it had to do with the out-of-body experience. We had planned a round-the-clock program, with food available at all times, and breaking up occasionally for two cycles of sleep. I and an engineer associate, Bill Yost, were the only ones there to conduct this marathon.

Because we were dealing with unknown subjects, we brought with us an affirmation for all of the participants to memorize before they started the session.

I am more than my physical body. Because I am more than physical matter, I can perceive that which is greater than the physical world.

Therefore, I deeply desire to expand, to experience: to know, to understand, to control, to use such greater energies and energy systems as may be beneficial and constructive to me and to those who follow me.

Also, I deeply desire the help and cooperation, the assistance, the understanding of those individuals whose wisdom, development, and experience are equal to or greater than my own. I ask their guidance and protection from any influence or any source that might provide me with less than my stated desires.

The results of this first workshop were not spectacular, as far as we could determine, but we did learn much from it. It certainly provided a much broader base for our experimental testing. Basically we had introduced Focus 10 and various simple applications of the potentials of this particular state of consciousness. Our debriefing indicated that we had achieved this goal. The participants learned what Focus 10 was—mind awake, body asleep—and learned how to produce it within themselves at will. We returned to Virginia well satisfied that the method was a practical one.

Not long thereafter, we began to get requests from individuals and other organizations to conduct more such sessions. After reviewing our results, we decided that this would be a very productive way to conduct experiments on such a broad scale that we could certainly not afford to do otherwise. Thus we began to conduct weekend sessions on an occasional basis. We grandly called it the M-5000 Program, on the premise that we would have a magnificent statistical base and a highly sophisticated and well-tuned training system if we ran five thousand participants through it. The information and experience gleaned from one program would be used to modify each succeeding program in order to maximize the results.

This involved also obtaining trainers to conduct these sessions, no easy task, and converting the system into headphones so that the Hemi-Sync effect could be fully utilized. After the first few sessions, we realized that it was folly to presume that we would ever reach the five-thousand mark. We also began to recognize that we were creating for the participant a doorway, a window, a gap through which he could achieve other states of consciousness. Thus it became known as the Gateway Program.

We did little or no promotion for the training series. Those who attended had heard about it by word of mouth from graduates. Because it was experimental, each participant signed a statement to that effect and was obliged to report results beyond the session itself. This is not to say that all did so, but enough did to give us significant statistics. Earlier programs were held over weekends at motels, conference centers, and special meeting facilities throughout the United States. Participants met in a large room where a distribution system we devised provided the taped training exercises via headphones. In retrospect, it was astounding that the program was effective at all, because often the meeting place directly adjoined the motel lounge and bar with a live orchestra playing at nighttime. To get around this problem locally, we wired a small motel some five miles from our laboratory where we had two-way communication to each room. The major problem there was that the motel had no restaurant, and all food had to be catered during the session. It was at this site that we tried an interesting experiment.

We developed an exercise whereby the participants simultaneously would be able to move this special mental energy into a visible pattern of light some one thousand feet above the motel. In the latter stages of the session, late one night, we put them through the test. The idea was that the combined energy of some twenty-four individuals might provide something we could see. All external lights in the motel were turned out (the motel itself was out in the country) and by stopwatch timing we knew the exact moment when any light should appear above the motel.

Four of us went outside and looked up into the darkness. We had had plenty of chance to accustom our eyes to the darkness beforehand, so when the signal came at the proper time, we looked very eagerly. None of us saw anything.

Suddenly our electronics engineer yelled excitedly, "Look higher, look higher!"

We did. Most of us had been looking just above the roof of the motel. We now looked far up into the sky in astonishment. Against the starlit night there were soft, red, neonlike waves. They resembled nothing so much as trickling water moving across an arc of the sky directly atop the roof of the motel. At exactly the time that the exercise called for the light to shut off, it suddenly disappeared. Three minutes later the exercise was repeated on the tape, and the red waving rivulets appeared again and shut off at the appropriate signal. All four of us observed it and were tremendously excited by the result.

Later at a Gateway session in California, at a ranch north of San Francisco, we repeated the exercise. This time we had an engineer with a special Polaroid camera pointed upward to attempt to take a picture if the phenomenon was repeated. To ensure against the possibility of fogged film, two photographs were taken just prior to the signal for the light energy to be generated. During the exercise when the energy was supposed to be in place, two other pictures were taken. After the signal was turned off by the tape, subsequent pictures were also taken.

There were some five or six observers present. None of us saw any light phenomena. However, when we went in afterwards and conducted the debriefing we examined the Polaroid photographs taken. The ones preceding the light signal were blank; the two after the exercise were blank. The two taken during the exercise itself showed a round ball with a marbleized effect much like the earth seen from a distance. Why the Polaroid picked up a picture and we could not has been explained by several physicists and photographers. The film can "see" light frequencies our eyes cannot. The usual explanations of light leaks, film fogging, etc., have also been put forward as the source of the round-ball-of-energy photograph. The blank film before and after made the two energy photographs more significant, being in the center of the film pack—a most unlikely place to be pre-exposed.

What does the Gateway Program really do for an individual? It varies so much that each seems to find his own answer. Many, of course, have come on the possibility that they will have an out-of-body experience. Most of the time this expectation is not fulfilled during the session itself. Instead, they gain profound insights and understanding of the purposes behind their being and doing. Not at all unusual are life-changing peak experiences or moments of revelation never before encountered and which neither cannot nor need be repeated.

The program itself teaches the Focus 10 state (mind awake, body asleep). Participants also learn to move into what is called Focus 12, where all physical-data input is shut off and the consciousness can reach out and begin to perceive in ways other than through the five senses. The action really begins here, where perspectives and overviews change drastically. It is here where the participant truly understands that he is "more than his physical body."

The Gateway Program thus has evolved into a unique process of self-exploration and discovery. It first surmounts the Fear Barrier (of the unknown, of change), which seems to be the greatest cultural restraint on individual growth. Think of where you are now as a clearing in a dark forest—we call it C-1 consciousness. We then take you into the forest to a point where you can still "see" the familiar clearing. That point is a guidepost (Focus 10). After a sufficient number of runs between guidepost and clearing, the fear disappears. At the Focus 10 guidepost, you always know you can get back to the clearing if you get uncomfortable for any reason.

From the Focus 10 guidepost, another point is established deeper into the forest and probably "out of sight" of the clearing. This we call Focus 12. After several runs between guideposts 10 and 12, this too becomes familiar and secondary fears fade away. You know that even if you can't perceive the clearing (C-1) from Focus 12, you *can* "see" Focus 10—and from 10, you know the way back to C-1. The process is expanded to succeeding guideposts, each deeper and different, beyond ever-expanding limits.

With the Fear Barrier dissolved, one of the greatest gifts to the human species comes into full play. Curiosity. With the tools provided, the participant is then free to do as he wishes. He accepts the authority to do so —and the responsibility.

The individual, of his own accord, without suggestion but through direct experience, begins to know, rather than believe, that he does survive physical death. It doesn't make any difference what he does during his physical life, what he believes; he will go on after his physical body dies.

Survival beyond physical death is not a belief system, therefore, but a simple fact as natural as being born. There is no dogma related to the Gateway Program—except that when you begin the session, you should seriously consider that you are "more than your physical body."

It is inevitable that the borders between this and other reality-energy systems are crossed. Many of the results are reported as reunions with "dead" friends and family as well as encounters with other forms of intelligent energy not generally recognized or accepted by mainstream American cultural levels.

Again, if you are aware of the basic effect of the Hemi-Sync process, that of providing an access to many levels of consciousness simultaneously, something far different from the usual consciousness that we use for the most part in our daily lives, you can begin to grasp some of the potential results.

Through the Gateway Program, we have been able to conduct tests with the Hemi-Sync process with over 3,000 subjects over the past ten years. With a minimum of twenty individual test/exercises per subject participant, that comes out to 60,000-plus individual tests of the effectiveness of the method and techniques involved. That has been and is the basic value to us of the Gateway Program—a test base of 60,000. At the very least, we know that we have been able to put people to sleep 60,000 times and awaken them. That is a pretty good statistic for product testing, especially one that is noninvasive in its physiological impact.

Most significant is the analysis of the Gateway population—those who have attended the sessions over the past eight years. First, 41 percent are male. This is double the norm for the typical self-awareness workshop. Most researchers agree this is due to the scientific aspect of the Hemi-Sync process as against more esoteric origins. Second, 29 percent are what we label professionals—psychologists, psychiatrists, educators, scientists, engineers, etc. These attend principally to determine possible applications in their own areas of interest. Third, the average age is thirty-nine, which puts Gateway completely out of the age range of the faddist and "in" transient group. Finally, 83 percent attend for one basic reason and come away with another, more valuable result.

The best way that we can report the meaning of Gateway is to give you some of the reports that we have received relative to the program from those who have attended. Here are a few of these:

1,135-CM

"The most thrilling experience for me was with Focus 15 on increased vibrations: I felt the energy flow going slowly up on one side and down on the other side of my body, then faster and faster. I felt I would become a spiral, then a point, and so I did, and as a compact unit I was flying higher and higher. . . . But then I thought: I cannot go any further, any higher—and in a flash I 'hear': Hey, you limit yourself! Okay, then, I overcame, accepted, and off I was, I felt projected like a Sputnik into the universe, to the stars, another entity integrated in the all. Feeling this oneness was an indescribable joy and happiness!

"The deep lesson I took from this exercise was that although having

heard and read many times that we are what we think, that we limit ourselves by our mind, there I was experiencing something unique, at least for me, by overcoming doubts or limitations which I am solely responsible for."

1644-CM

". . . That morning, having lost interest in holding the solar system in my hands (can't believe I just said that!) as the tape had directed me to do, I visualized the Focus 15* blue 'door.' Finding nothing there, I proceeded through red, yellow, pink, green, purple, and finally into white. Using white as 'Level 21,' I continued to '26,' where I then (and have since) received messages for other people in the program. I later moved to '27,' where I had previously found my father. Feeling that he was busy, I decided to try uncharted (to me) territory.

"Devising a digital counter, I sailed backward through darkness as the counter flashed numbers faster than I could read them. Somewhere near where I perceived to be 100 (98?), I stopped and saw many people milling around: They looked like holograms, but conveyed the message of being 'alive.' Some ignored me, some moved away, but several approached me with great joy. I sensed that the latter felt that they were stranded and thought that I was there to guide them back. I asked about the others and was told that some were just exploring, and would return to their bodies when they felt like doing so, while others were waiting for their bodies to die, so they could be free. The ones speaking to me, though, said that they got there inadvertently, and were not able to return on their own.

"At this point, Bob, I heard your barely audible voice saying, 'You will now return to Focus 10.' In panic, I felt I needed your voice to find my way back. I tried to piggyback someone, but was not able to, and returned to my CHEC Unit† in what I felt was the nick of time. With a great sigh of relief, and an expletive or two, I reexamined the experience, and am doing so again at the moment of this writing:

* "No time" consciousness.
† Controlled Holistic Environmental Chamber.

1. *I don't believe that it was a dream. As I type this, two weeks after the event took place, I'm still overcome with a feeling of profoundness.*
2. *I don't believe in coincidence. Although the implications are not clear to me, I feel that there is a reason I experienced something I had never consciously thought about before.*
3. *Fact: There are people in various institutions who are catatonic or comatose and whom medical science has not been able to reanimate."*

4659-CM

"I am now considering what to me is the strong possibility that almost anything that can be formed into five physical senses, language, oriented thought is an illusion. Extraphysical feeling is as close as I can come to describing what is ultimate reality for me now.

"When I seek to perceive ultimate reality for me, (what I think you are referring to when you use the word 'home'), I experience blankness and bliss. Blankness, not because it is blank, but because I attempt to experience it with mental processes that are geared to the five physical senses and that are in the habit of perceiving illusion. I am trying to use my biological illusion computer to perceive beyond the apparent limits of illusion. Like trying to smell a flower with your ear. I experience bliss because emotional feeling is the only perceptual tool that I am able to use to sense beyond the illusion. If there are other perceptual tools that are available to me, they are either atrophied by lack of use, and must somehow be reactivated, or they must be initially activated.

2312-CF

". . . During one 'Rebal' breathing exercise I experienced what was the beginning of some rather puzzling happenings. For reasons unknown to me I was suddenly in a black box—a void of total blackness. It was like being juggled from one extreme to the other—from total sensation to lack of sensation. Frustration began to invade me, for I found it was somewhat difficult finding a way out of this vast blackness. In my next tape I began to experience the blackness again, and that's when I started

to worry. At our next meal I mentioned what was occurring to our trainer, hoping she might offer a solution.

"During our discussion, my problem was overheard by a few males at the table who had apparently been listening in. Later one of the men took me aside to explain. He told me that a few of the men in our group had found themselves fantasizing about me during their own tape experiences—hence all the sexual thought vibrations I was picking up. He also told me that, having a hard time dealing with their sexual attraction, they were putting me in their 'energy conversion box' (a place to leave problems behind) before embarking into their other states of consciousness. They had all helped put me in my black void so as not to distract them! At first I was annoyed at this. How dare they influence my experiences! How dare their sexual energy have that much control over me! I still marvel at how powerful thoughts are, and three men's directed at me was overwhelming. At the same time I felt somewhat naïve for not having picked up the signs earlier, but I was much too wrapped up in how the workshop was changing me to fully get into what others were thinking.

"But this was not the end. . . . I transformed my annoyance at being used as a 'sex object,' even if only consciously projected, and started wondering what growth could be gained from this experience. It started me thinking along other lines and what was to follow would change the course of my life.

"And it happened simply because I asked the divine forces in all sincerity for me to be able to experience spiritual love. I asked not for me to be the recipient of it but that I might learn how to give to others to my fullest ability. My request was granted:

"As I went into the next tape I kept that thought in mind—I wanted to feel what it would be like to feel a part of the love in the universe, to in a sense actually be making love to a part of me, a part of everyone. I left my own CHEC Unit at that point (nonphysically; OOBE) and felt an urge to visit my other Gateway participants. Straying into one room, I called softly to one of the people. He seemed taken aback to see me and I told him not to be alarmed, that I was only there to send him love and then left after blowing him a quick goodbye kiss. (Later this person recalled that he heard a soft voice in his ear calling his name. He said *that he had felt a surge of love upon hearing it but wasn't sure where it came from.)*

"*Then quite unexpectedly I was suddenly drawn by a powerful force to one room in particular—to one CHEC Unit in particular. It took me by total surprise, for the man in that unit was someone I didn't know very well. In fact, he was the only one at the workshop I had never really had a chance to talk to. He was a young, good-looking psychologist, yet for some reason we seemed to be purposely avoiding each other.*

"*All at once I had an all-knowing, as I seemed to float over him, that his vibrations were my vibrations. I had an overwhelming desire to meld, to feel a part of him—to become one. It was truly one of the sharpest and clearest of experiences.*

"*I gave to him both my body and soul until there was this tremendous energy surge that rocked and exploded in us. It was an experience that is beyond words, for love, total and absolute, surrounded us more strongly than can be earthly experienced or imagined. The more I gave, the greater I received and I didn't want to let go. I wanted to give him even more. It was like two energies in perfect unison becoming one at last. (I can remember thinking how physical sex paled in comparison.)*

"*Memories of past lives together came rushing in like flashes of light. We talked in this state and I came to realize this experience could only have happened at the end of the workshop as it did, for each of us would have been distracted had we 'met' earlier on—perhaps hampering other growth experiences that week. There was a meeting of both our minds with this experience and I knew our meeting had been more than coincidence—it was predestined.*

"*I truly experienced everything I asked for and more, and when I came down to the meeting room after the tape there was an unusual heightened energy where people seemed to be flying. I saw 'him' as I came down the stairs to join the group and he looked at me excitedly, ecstatically, as if something totally incredible had happened to him. I hadn't said a word yet, as he quietly repeated a number of times, 'Thank you. Thank you.' I felt elated—I had made contact. We compared our individual experiences, making sure each of us was not coloring the other's story. It didn't matter—our stories fit like puzzle pieces, matching per-*

*fectly and interlocking. We both had also had the use of all our senses—
the strongest being touch.*

*"After this experience we were later reunited to share others together.
We've been with each other for the past two years now—growing and
loving together.*

*"So much did I learn at my Gateway experience—but I was truly lucky
to get it all. I not only got the icing—I got the whole cake!"*

Today the Gateway Program is held for a full seven-day period at our
Center facility in Virginia. The Center is designed specifically to handle
the Gateway Program. No longer does one have to lie on the floor for
taped exercises. Instead the Center now provides what are called CHEC
Units (Controlled Holistic Environmental Chambers), which provide isolation much as we had in our original laboratory booths. Not only are the
taped exercises conducted by headphones in the CHEC Unit, but the
participant actually sleeps in these during the night. Because it is much
like a Pullman berth on the old railroad trains, some people initially feel
they cannot sleep in there the first night, because of a sense of claustro-
phobia perhaps. With the environmental treatment in the CHEC Unit—
fresh air and temperature control plus sleep sounds that are available—the
main problem after the second night is to wake them up, the isolated sleep
has been so productive and restful. It helps achieve such a complete sleep
that a number of participants have built CHEC Units in their own
homes.

Because the Gateway Program is so difficult to produce and conduct
properly, each year we question the value of continuing it. All things
considered, it is certainly not a financial success, although supposedly we
are the only research facility that charges for the privilege of being a
volunteer. Each time we consider closing it down, we receive just coinci-
dentally another report from a graduate who states how meaningful and
how constructive have been the results of his attendance.

So we schedule another year of Gateways.

4.
Explorer Team I

Amid the diversion of Gateway sessions, visitors ranging from psychologists and electronics engineers to ex-flower children with backpacks, mail response to the original *Journeys*, we continued our research program with our volunteer group in the laboratory. The group became consistently more proficient in achieving other forms of consciousness, including the out-of-body state. However, personal events in their lives (such as moving to another city) brought the regular weekly group down to six. These were the physicist, electronics engineer, social services executive, transpersonal psychologist, office manager, and psychiatric counselor. I would have liked to use actual names, but several felt their employers would take a dim view of it all. Therefore, no names at all.

One of the most peculiar aspects was that their experiences paralleled my own only in the preliminary stages. They could and did replicate my own near out-of-body experiences but from that point on there seemed little similarity. Possibly because of the confidence factor of a monitor with whom to communicate, in some respects they had freedoms that I had never experienced.

So that the picture is clear: The subject lies on a water bed in a darkened, acoustically and electrically shielded 8-by-10 room (usually booth 2, everyone's favorite for some unknown reason). The booth has its own air-conditioning and heating controls. Electrodes for monitoring physiological states are glued to head, fingers, and body. A sound microphone hangs about four inches above the face. Audio headphones completely cover each ear. Most important, the subject has just gone to the bathroom to be sure the bladder is empty. Too many sessions had been aborted because the subject reported a "problem" in the physical body, only to find upon a hurried return that it was nothing more than a distended bladder. Evidently the total physical relaxation encourages this body process.

In the control room twenty feet down the hall, a human monitor (I or one of several others) communicates vocally through a sound system with the person in the booth. The monitor also feeds Hemi-Sync sound into the subject's headphones, either to test responses to new frequencies or to aid the subject in achieving desired states of consciousness. Finally, the monitor observes and notes changes in instrument readouts on the subject's physiological condition. Often an assistant is present to help in the processing.

Here is a typical "entry" report, the beginning of an OOBE, transcribed from an early file recording during an experiment:

SS/ROMC (OFFICE MANAGER) 7 MINUTES IN—TEST #188

"I am going rapidly now through a tunnel—I was standing straight up and now I am just sort of sucked up through this tunnel. It is very narrow and I am rapidly shooting through this tunnel. Now I can see a point of light at the other end. I am traveling rapidly to this point of light. It is like I am on some type of light beam that is helping to propel me. I am coming out. I am going into a different dimension and I have just completely slowed down. And I am right at the opening of this point. And now I am gently coming through and everything is green. It is so bright that it is almost blinding because of coming out of a dark tunnel. It is a different feeling. Now it is a real strong energy that seems to be pressing against me. It is a great feeling now. This is a new energy level. I feel a strong—everything around me is green. It is so bright that it is taking me a minute to adjust and to absorb where I am."

There was one "small" problem. Once our subjects passed through the light or achieved the out-of-body state, they were not particularly interested in hour after hour of dull searching for new effective sound frequency patterns. They would still perform the tasks, but beyond the tunnel and into the light was Paris! Keeping them on the farm was certainly no trivial problem. So we had to play a little.

And play we did. We sent our subjects to explore the moon, which they found a very dull place. We went to other parts of the solar system, the other planets, and found them, as far as we could determine, nothing but mile after mile of craters and mountains or simply layers of turbulent matter—no vegetation, no sign of life, nothing to truly attract our human attention. We did find that in such a state as the OOBE, a different kind of consciousness seemed to exist. The overview of the subject was different. For example, what to us in the control room was a minute could become hours or timeless to the volunteer in the booth. It was at this point that we began to call them our Explorer team.

Like most humans, we were possessed with the idea or hope that there had to be intelligent life somewhere among the billions of stars that we could perceive physically. So in our play we took to sending our Explorers out beyond the solar system at what appeared a near-instantaneous change of locale. The instruction was to keep going until he or she perceived something worthwhile. They passed by the other suns, found other planets, but no intelligent life. It seemed to us a sterile universe.

The change came in 1974. It took place in all of our Explorers within several weeks. Some had never met one another, so there was no cross-communication. In looking back to examine the reason for this massive change, the only thing that we could find was: we had inserted the affirmation developed for the Gateway Program at the beginning of each experimental session in the lab. Other than that, we made no significant changes in Hemi-Sync frequencies, basic environment, or methods of presentation. It may have been the second part that was the catalyst:

> . . . *Also, I deeply desire the help and cooperation, the assistance, the understanding of those individuals whose wisdom, development, and experience are equal to or greater than my own. I ask their guidance and protection from any influence or any source that might provide me with less than my stated desires.*

It was suddenly as if a curtain had been lifted. Almost every time one of our Explorers went into the out-of-body state or simply into an advanced Focus 12, they encountered intelligent beings who were more or less willing to communicate—and could do so. After several years of finding only barrenness, the effect upon us was overwhelming. We sometimes had difficulty knowing how to handle it. Here is a portion of the transcript from the file recording of one of these early meetings.

ss/tc (physicist) xal—8:12 min #332

"Back into regular 12. Had two encounters—the first with an unseen intelligence who replied to a general query for communications. Sort of an 'I'll talk to you,' but it was obvious that he (I guess I say 'he' because I got the feeling of a 'he') wanted to listen and said 'O.K., what do you want to talk about?' And as I tried to put the burden on him or it for some information about itself, about its environment, I got the feeling it was angry for being bothered. Sort of like bumping into a busy New York pedestrian. The second was much more interesting. The second communication, I didn't just get an intelligence, but got a complete visual image. Female, late thirties, and she was very pleased to communicate and offered to show me around and showed me a lot of the facility. I don't know what else to call it that she was in. We walked up to this wall and two big doors swung open and there was nothing there that seemed impressive at all, but she thought that these markings and irregularities of the surface were quite something. I don't know why. I didn't relate to it at all. I asked her if she was in any way familiar with physical matter existence as I knew it and she asked me to explain. I really didn't know how to explain physical matter, so I asked if it was all right if I came back and that I wanted to leave to report in. She seemed a little dismayed that I was taking off after getting partway through the tour, but she said, 'all right,' and that brings us up to the present moment."

Monitor: "Very good. In your return, try and understand the type of energy being utilized there."

(time lapse: 3 minutes)

"O.K., I thought I had better report back again before I forgot much of what went on. Reestablished contact with same female. She was quite surprised that I did return. Pleased. At first, I began to wonder what this intelligence really looked like to itself. Was I just imposing my own image of female humanoid form? And we discussed this, realizing that I *was creating this image of her and could not really tell whether this was her own image of herself or not. She, likewise, was creating an image of me in a likeness to which she was familiar, and whether or not these likenesses were similar, mine and hers, there was no way to tell, so we left that question. Then I got an itch of some intensity that began on my neck and tried to explain that I existed in another reality besides the one I was sharing with her and that I had a physical body elsewhere and that the physical body had an itch on its neck and was disturbing the focus of my attention, and that is why I seemed to be fading in and out as my attention wavered. She seemed to think that was quite incredible. I don't believe she believed me at all. She just kind of ignored that statement like one might ignore somebody who says an irrational thing. I asked about her physics. She took me to another place where there was another entity. This one male, and there was a writing surface, much like a blackboard, but not a blackboard, whereupon he attempted to explain the nature of things there. We had no success at all with his writing. The marks he made on this surface, this blackboard, were totally unintelligible to me, and after a few efforts we gave up. We tried to go to pictures. All the time we could communicate telepathically. Pictures were O.K. He drew some pictures, and from the telepathic exchange, I felt that their science, indeed their concept of their existence and reality was in many ways similar to our own, in that they were fixed in that reality and could not travel out of it, as I had traveled out of physical reality into theirs. I do not know whether they even believed that there was another reality other than their own. They had a physical science much as we do, in that objects in their reality obeyed specific laws. I tried to see if any of their laws were similar to ours, such as gravitation. It was very difficult to tell. I could not separate what was their concept of their reality, all I could do was translate into my own concepts, meaning I did not see them floating around in air, but whether that was because they experience a thing like gravity like we do or whether that was a function of my own experience, visualizing humanoids not floating in the air, I could not tell. But I did feel that they had a basic physical science that ruled the objects of their reality. They did not move things around by thought processes or anything like that. It seemed like an earth-type physical reality to them, although I don't recognize many of their devices and structures—seemed very foreign, but they seemed to be fixed and isolated within those de-vices and structures. Somehow I appear to them as one of their own kind, whether that's humanoid or not, I don't know. Maybe I should have tried to find out where they think I came from or who they think I might be."*

Here is another, to give you a feeling for a different point of contact:

SS/JCA (SOCIAL SERVICES EXECUTIVE) 6:27 MIN #356

"I am talking with my green man and practicing going up and down to where they are . . . and found out why he has this green robe. He said that he did not need it but that I needed it to make me more comfortable with him. And he said that I still have some fears, so he still wants me to feel more comfortable with going in and out of my body. . . . I want to sit and talk with him some more. . . . he just kind of sat down and talked about me and where I am. And he told me that he is kind of my overseer. And he is responsible, somewhat responsible for my growth and development. Overseer in that contact and responsibility. Apparently he has been through a lot of lives and different lifetimes . . . and I don't know if they are a part of him or not.

"I feel very comfortable here, like this is where I belong and I have felt like this before. Think I made some progress, because this time I did not need any folks to help me. I was just there seeing them. More like a vote of confidence than anything else. I asked him what he was doing here and he said, 'Here, that is something that you are trying to pinpoint. Here isn't . . . here does not matter.' I don't know why but I really feel very tired. I feel like I am ready to come back all of a sudden. I noticed it before, that it was like a flash, but it was dark in here. There was a surprise because it was just like a flash of light that came on."

Far more significant were the instances where our Explorers quickly "made friends" with a being or beings (entities?) who seemed to have no special interest in or connection to or with our Explorer. Here is a sample of an Explorer response to one of these:

SS/BY (ELECTRONICS ENGINEER) 26:20 MIN #325

"I recontacted the source and asked the source about his pointers and perspective and asked him if he was familiar with the earth and his reply was 'Yes, that is my territory.' I got the idea that the earth was sort of his assigned beat. I also got the idea that he and other entities are made available to us to help us maximize or get through our earth experience. I don't mean 'get through' like 'get it over with.' I mean to help us get as much out of it as possible. They are there like explainers or helpers and not particularly assigned to earth duty. I then asked about geological conditions in the next ten years. He picked data up from my mind and knew what I was thinking about and said, 'I didn't know that information was available.' He was surprised that this information was given out or had been released. He was not aware that such information was being released."

Another type occurred in this fashion:

SS/SHE (PSYCHIATRIC COUNSELOR) 16:14 MIN #314

". . . Point of light. Other than that, I don't perceive anything."

Monitor: "How does the light feel?"
"It feels like a star. When I focus on it, I begin to float."

Monitor: "Experiment with the light."
"Now they are getting closer, now I am getting closer to them."

(TIME LAPSE: 2:55)

New Voice: *"How are you?"*

Monitor: "I am very glad to meet you. I am very thankful that you came."

New Voice: *"It is hard to get here."*

Monitor: "What is the difficulty?"

New Voice: *"There are many layers to penetrate."*

Monitor: "We are very, very grateful that you did penetrate the layers to us. We will help in any way that we can."

New Voice: *"Her color pattern is very good. We must find a way to help her let go."*

Monitor: "Do you have any recommendations?"

New Voice: *"There needs to be a period in which she goes very deep."*

Monitor: "A longer preliminary period, then, would you suggest?"

New Voice: *"Possibly. It will get easier as the trust builds. There is still a lot of fear."*

Monitor: "I am very grateful for your concern for her."

New Voice: *"Now she is feeling a lot of disharmony. I have taken her to a place where she can rest."*

In this case, the subject had no memory whatsoever of the event or encounter. The last that she remembered was working with the colors. Changes in voice quality and monitoring instruments supported the idea of another "presence" or personality in the body of SHE. We had much discussion of the advisability of continuing along this route, in spite of the immense interest and excitement it generated among our group. The fact of the matter is, I suspect, there was at that stage no actual means that we knew of to "turn off" such communication. I suspect also that no one wanted to anyway, at the least, myself.

One Explorer developed a very close relationship with what appeared to be some four or five beings, one of whom acted as a spokesman. Here is the transcript of the recording of a major step in that relationship.

SS/ROMC (OFFICE MANAGER) 8:05 MIN #306

"I was watching what happened and experiencing at the same time. The four helpers just helped to lift, as this energy body just came to my physical body. The four helpers helped to lift my energy body out, and I just felt real light and really, really good and got the sense then that this energy form that was then sort of implanted or just, in other words, it was in my body then. It was just energizing my body. It was just light and well protected, and I felt good being out and felt very light and then I could sense that energy of being. One person was just talking about how they could or would like to experiment in trying to use my body sort of like a transmitting set between dimensions. I'll be able to step out and feel very safe and confident with these helpers and light and happy and still be able to observe, if I would like, what's going on with the energy being."

Monitor: "Do they want to perform any other experiment now?"

"O.K. The feeling that maybe they would just like to experiment a little bit with talking maybe through my vocal cords, but I still am not out far enough that I might get out of the way. It will be with practice and experimentation, and then as I learn to be less, I mean be more relaxed and just let it flow and go along and not let my mind stop it. The more they practice, it will be able to flow more rapidly, so they just want to experiment for just a short time with trying to come through with some thoughts through my vocal cords and my mental faculties, so to speak. So we will just see what, we will try to see what happens here."

Monitor: "Right. I will be here if you need me."
"O.K."

(TIME LAPSE: 3:23)

New Voice: *"Greetings. I am speaking through these vocal cords and I would like to speak to this young lady as she observes what is taking place. Her physical body is seeming to heat up very rapidly. Sometimes it will be in a cool stage, but other times it will be in a heated stage, and the molecules of the energy body, which is working through her physical body, is working at a more rapid rate and, therefore, right at this time, there is a feeling of heat surrounding this body. This young lady will understand what is happening when we first come into her aura. There will be the feeling of warmth, and as she gets more relaxed and is able to begin her float above her physical body, she will experience as the coolness and feeling of relaxation, complete relaxation, the feeling of complete calm, complete peace, and complete security. And then there will be the light stage and the coolness that will come over her and she will know that she is gently going out of the body, but will always be in complete control if she so chooses. She is always there to observe, to speak at any time, or can always even choose to step into other dimensions; and there will be those who will help her into those other dimensions, and while this is taking place, we will work with trying to bring through information through these vocal cords. This is a special experiment of stepping into knowledge dimensions, and this could never be done were it not for you with the knowledge that you bring and with the great light and confidence that you surround this whole project that you work on. I have worked with others who will come in as we reach different dimensions and levels. We will not say higher or lower—they are light dimensions as we break through into the various levels. It is easier to bring through the knowledge. I am working now on the level where this entity is presently, but we will work together through various levels. There are others who are working with her. I speak in terms of 'we' because each time that I come, we come as a group, there are the others who are the assistants and will always be there to bring the energy levels up and to work. And we say that you are doing exactly what is necessary to help the situation to be in that perfected state whereby the energies can be released into other levels of consciousness. And now we will step out and allow her to step back fully into her own body. It is a privilege. Thank you, dear friends."*

Her confidence in the group was so great that their assistance was very much standard operating procedure. For example, in order to help her get out of the body, four of these beings would position themselves, two on each side, and simply "lift her out." This made it all the simpler to get on with what had to be done.

An interesting sidelight to this particular routine took place some months later. The Explorer ROMC usually had a lab session at five o'clock on Wednesdays. On this particular Wednesday she had canceled several days in advance. By coincidence on that Wednesday, a female psychologist from the Washington area dropped in to visit. She was quite skeptical of what we were doing, and we spent several hours that afternoon going over our methods and techniques. Finally, in order to help her understand a little better, I suggested that she go into booth 2 and lie down and listen to some of the Hemi-Sync patterns and find out for herself if she had any response to them. She agreed, fully expecting that there would be nothing unusual about what was to happen. With her skepticism, I was inclined to agree.

After about five minutes in the booth with the Hemi-Sync sound in her ears, her voice came through the intercom speaker.

"There is someone else in the booth with me."

I pushed the microphone button. "Are you sure?" I asked.

"Of course I am sure. As a matter of fact, there are four of them."

I made contact again. "Are you sure there are four?"

"I can perceive them very clearly. There are two at my feet and two at my head."

I pushed the mike button again. "What are they doing?"

"They are trying to lift me out of my body, if you can believe that."

Suddenly I knew the answer. I looked up at the clock. It was ten minutes after five—on Wednesday afternoon. ROMC's friends can get trapped in routines, too. I burst out laughing. I was about to reach for the microphone and explain it to the woman in the booth when I thought better of it.

I pushed the mike button. "What are they doing now?"

"They have stopped trying to lift me out of my body," her voice came back. *"And they are arguing."*

It was difficult to keep a calm voice as I responded. "What are they arguing about?"

"The four want to lift me out, and now there is a fifth that is arguing with them that they should not."

"Do you want them to?" I asked.

"I don't think so," her voice came back. *"Now they have stopped arguing and they are going away, so I guess there is no problem."*

I smiled as I pushed the mike button and said, "Well, just relax a bit and I'll get you out in a few minutes. Are you comfortable now?"

"Oh yes," she responded. *"I am fine."*

I left her in the booth for some ten to fifteen minutes and watched as the gauges showed that she was relaxing into a light sleep. After a suitable time I awakened her and brought her out much refreshed. She was somewhat bewildered by the experience and made a valiant attempt to stay skeptical. I showed her the appointment schedule that usually called for an experimental session, then I played a recording of the actual "lifting out" techniques as described by the Explorer subject.

She finally left, a very puzzled and preoccupied individual.

Things like that are hard on belief systems when they happen to most people. The problem was that so many were happening to *us.* There were many suspenseful moments.

It should be noted here that reaching this state of trust and communication and/or association with these friendly entities and beings took hours and hours of preliminary contact, plus "third party" communication discussions. It did not happen overnight to the degree indicated here. A great mass of material provided through such beings had to do with information of a philosophic nature or suggestions and advice regarding the personal well-being of the Explorers involved. In no case was any drug or any other medication used in any of our experiments.

Moreover, there are indications that a magnetic field is generated of a type with which our science is unfamiliar. One of the results of this is to set up magnetic fields in nearby electrical loops as well as audio cables. Another is to affect nearby magnetic tape to such an extent that a "print-through" takes place from one layer of tape to another. The recording industry would like very much to know how to do this at a commercial level. However, of course, the results that we have are not significant enough to be commercially viable. Not yet, at least.

One night, when we got into our cars parked outside some twenty feet from booth 2, we found that the batteries were dead in all three cars. They jump-started quite easily, as it was a summer night, and stayed in charge afterward. Cars parked on the other side, or sixty feet away, were unaffected. Thus we learned we had better not park too close to booth 2 during certain experiments with specific Explorers. Exactly why this took place—and still does so—we don't know.

In the current Explorer group, only two remain from the original team. The tide of personal events has moved the others away from the area, their lives visibly altered by the experience. The original material is still being processed. Meanwhile, more is entering through sessions in our new lab facility.

Perhaps we need a few more doctors, with other credentials.

5.
New Associations

In hundreds of hours of Explorer communication to date, about one-third consists of those instances where, with the Explorer's permission, their friendly entities take over their physical bodies and speak using the Explorer's vocal cords. The other two-thirds are contacts made by the Explorer, who then converses with the nonphysical third party and reports the conversation. In both cases, the monitor in the control room (living physical domain!) becomes a part of such discussions.

What we call the Explorer Material is a combination of fascinating, baffling, awe-inspiring, thought-provoking, sometimes boring data that is certainly much in conflict with many of the belief systems that we have within our culture and civilization. The most important possibility by far is the reality of the Explorer Material, their experiences, and especially these friendly entities who assist them. Second to this is the fact that the process is ongoing, expanding.

To resolve that possibility one way or another will take some doing and some capacities far beyond the limits of our organization.

In examining the Explorer sessions in consensus, certain elements repeat themselves:

1. Whatever they may be, such nonphysical third parties have the ability to radiate a warmth of friendliness that evokes complete trust—even with their lives—on the part of the Explorers.

2. Such beings are first of all totally solicitous as to the well-being of the Explorer and spend much time in attempting to advance the best mental and physical state of the human being with whom they are "associated."

3. A being usually appears to the Explorer in the form of a hooded figure whose face is hidden in shadow and apparently invisible to the Explorer. Once the Explorer becomes completely familiar with the

"feel" of the entity, the hooded robe is discarded and the Explorer can perceive nothing, but still senses the radiation that is the entity.

4. In speaking to the Explorer, the being is limited in vocabulary to that in the memory bank of said Explorer. Therefore it often shows hesitation in searching for the correct word to express what needs to be described—and often there is no such word in the memory of the individual.

5. During visits by certain of these beings, especially when they use the physical body to speak through, there is a change in body voltage and other biomonitoring data in the Explorer.

Without further comment, here are excerpts from various sessions.

SS/TC (PHYSICIST) 22:30 MIN #372

"I've gotten all kinds of things, and I've been trying to sort them and put them into some kind of rational order. First of all, I had the impression that physical matter reality—inasmuch of I guess what is normally called reality, not only physical matter, but also a certain amount of our daydreaming and our imaginative intuitive qualities—is part of a, sort of like a large daydream or thought from a higher consciousness. Just as we can daydream and invent characters and situations, we are characters in a situation that was invented or dreamt, quite consciously dreamt by a more advanced sort of consciousness. The part that we have to play in this daydream is one of education, one of learning and bettering ourselves, striving to become more. Now, I'm not clear why this kind of over-consciousness or over-soul is having this daydream, but I have the feeling that it is for its own education. It learns as we learn. Anyway, we have such limited consciousness to begin because if you are going to set up a situation where you expect certain processes to happen—these processes, of course, are our education, our learning—you don't set up the most complex and involved experiment or situation. You set up a simple one that you can produce, that still has the qualities to get the results that you want. This is the reason that we are seemingly of such limited consciousness. But the reason that we have an option to develop our consciousness more fully is part of the experiment itself. We are to learn and grow and evolve and become and learn through experience in doing, and as closely

as we can come to understanding and being a part of, our understanding a part of our creator, our over-soul daydreamer, if you like, then sort of the more power to us. The more of that we can understand, then the more learning that we've acquired. So it's not really—well, I take that back. It's not so much that we are driven to expand our awareness or that we should be, other than it's available, and being available makes it a direction in which we can evolve if we so choose. That's a little jumbled to myself, but that's the way it's coming out."

SS/SHE (SOCIAL WORKER) 18 MIN #366

"I've been on a, almost like a vortex I was caught in. Twenty-two is not physical in any way. Twenty-one can be either physical or nonphysical, depending on where you choose to focus the energy.

"It's neither up nor down nor forward or backward. Twenty-one, all appear very comfortable, but very different. The sense I have like a rainbow going before me of colors, and they are like the colors that Miranon has described, but they are all going at different beats and moving. It is like I see a spectrum of 22 through, I don't know, through 28, something like that and they are all interwoven. I think I could draw it for you. I like 21, so I have just kind of stayed here and the sense that I have, it's like, when you asked that, I got the illusion of looking at a sunset and having it sense that the horizon is the end, but that it's only an illusion because as you go forward in the levels, new levels arise."

(TIME LAPSE: 1:22)

Other Voice: *"I apologize for being so late, but I need to thank you and to tell you that I am glad you received my message. If you would like to explore these levels, I would be very happy to do so with you."*

Monitor: "I would appreciate it very much."

Other Voice: *"As I have said to you earlier, plants exist on levels one through seven. They are on a vibrational rate on the levels one through seven. It is the same pattern. Animals exist on the levels eight through* *fourteen, and when a person attains, when a consciousness attains level fourteen, it can no longer go any higher unless it is willing to change its form of consciousness. Levels fifteen through twenty-one are what you call human life on this earth. When a person progresses to level twenty-one, he then has the choice of going higher or staying within the realm of human form, but he cannot go higher unless he is willing to give up human form."*

Monitor: "Give up being human?"

Other Voice: *"Levels twenty-two through twenty-eight are your bridge. They are your levels that you enter upon death. You are on level twenty and because that is an ascending level, you can enter into the realm beyond physical life, but you cannot stay there unless you are willing to give up your human form. Is that clear?"*

Monitor: "That much is clear, yes."

Other Voice: *"And then once a person or a consciousness—we are talking about consciousness—reaches level twenty-eight, the bridge is crossed, and from that point on for a consciousness to evolve higher, it would not again assume human form of any kind, not even as a learning experience. I will never incarnate again as a human—as another form of life, yes, but not as a human. The words are very hard because your plane of existence is not the same. Perhaps I can explain it by asking you to image seven of the circles, which would give you the forty-nine levels. The first three levels are physical matter as you know physical matter. They are your plants, your animals, your humans. The fourth circle is your bridge, your realm, your center for that overall plane. It is the time in which a consciousness can choose whether to go back into the lower levels or to transcend into the higher levels, and many consciousnesses do choose to go back into the lower levels in physical form. The upper three circles are the realm that in your consciousness is called the spiritual realm, and here much of the work is done. I could not help someone who was not on the eighteenth level very much because my plane, my vibrational rate would be different. This is why it is hard for me to help you with specific problems. I can give you ideas, but I cannot give you the direct guidance I could if you were on level eighteen. Our planes do touch since yours is an ascending spiral—an ascending, what is your word for that? It is an ellipse. It is an ascending ellipse, and therefore I can cross and communicate with you, but not as directly. Once I reach level forty-nine, which I will, I then leave all of this realm of existence. It does not mean I have reached the highest point by any means. It simply means I have left this group of seven, this overall group of seven. Imagine, if you will, the seven circles enclosed in an even larger circle upon which seven more circles are stacked, which is in turn enclosed in even a great circle. Then you can have some idea of what infinity is. It does not ever stop."*

Monitor: "Well, I must confess that 'it' is kind of hard on my tiny, poor physical matter consciousness."

Other Voice: *"That is true. I must—it is very hard on my consciousness also. I feel at times, because I am very near to completing this circle, that I have accomplished a major evolvement for my consciousness, but then when I try to explain it, I realize just how far I have yet to go and how little I have actually gone through. Because my level of consciousness is one of love, I leave you with love. Good day."*

SS/SCA (EXECUTIVE) 34 MIN #402

Monitor: "Ask him to describe this interactive unit that is you now and your physical body. What is this relationship between this energy form and your physical body?"

"Part of my energy that I have when I'm out of body is used to build my body. When I use this energy to build my body here on earth, it blocks . . . or curves my thinking processes so it doesn't go out of body. The thinking process needs to be curved to communicate with the other personalities here on earth again. This is one type of communication when I'm out of body. I take most of that energy that is used for my body with me but enough to keep the body informed is left here. It permits me

to open up my mind and allows me to communicate with other personalities, other brains so to speak, to communicate with, to learn from, to talk to."

Monitor: "At what point do you first enter to become a part of this physical body?"

"Apparently when, although fertilization is a mechanical thing, a chemical thing . . . the personalities out of body are very much aware of when things happen and choose at that time to develop the fetus or not to develop. So part of my energy at this moment may be used to develop a personality and I may have several personalities going on at the same time, being developed at the same time."

Monitor: "At the same time in the physical kind of reality?"

"Yes, yes. They tell me right now, one is old, one is crippled, one is male, and where they are I am not ready to know. . . . and I could feel being old and crippled but I could not feel being male."

Monitor: "Is this entering of the physical body limited just to the planet Earth or other planets?"

"We go to other places. There are beings on other places and our energy is aware of all these other places."

Monitor: "Do we inhabit physical bodies in these other places?"

"Not like human Earth bodies . . . but . . . other forms of things or beings."

Monitor: "What are some of the other forms on planets? What are these other forms?"

"One's like a gelatin kind of thing . . . slimy kinds of things."

Monitor: "Are these located anywhere near the planet Earth?"

"Thousands of light-years away."

Monitor: "In this energy, is there a set of rules in which one operates?"

"I'm not sure what you are asking."

Monitor: "Is there a set of rules in which the body operates?"

"No, the energy itself decides if the energy itself makes a wrong decision, then it destroys itself. If it makes correct decisions it builds or strengthens its personality. It is possible for the energy to destroy itself."

Monitor: "What is classified then as misuse?"

"When it has not added to its present knowledge, when it has not gained anything more than it had learned previously. It is more than just a question of good or bad or good or evil. For example, killing by itself would not mean that it was destroying the energy by killing the animal or another human being. Not just adding to the knowledge, but enhancing the personality, the deed actually enhances previous knowledge or understanding that is used as addition . . . strength. If the killing was for the sake of killing, if nothing was learned, nothing gained, then it could destroy the overall personality. But there also seems to be a hierarchy of understanding and as the energy is strengthened it moves up a hierarchy of knowing."

Monitor: "Then where does this hierarchy of knowing lead to?"

"It's very important to become a move toward a unified whole like there is one on the top. . . . As the personalities move and merge the more knowledgeable . . . the level of understanding increases as they move up. It doesn't make sense verbally but visually it makes a lot of sense."

Monitor: "All right, then I think you have given us a lot of material to think about, so thank your guide and ask if there is a name that he goes by."

"He doesn't want to give a name right now because he doesn't want it to interfere with the training that we are doing . . . be too concrete, I need to be more and more aware and he can do his work better right now without me giving him a name."

Monitor: "Ask him if there is any other training exercise that he would like you to perform before we close this session."

"No, he thinks I've gone . . . further than he really anticipated."

SS/MSL (PSYCHOLOGIST) 8:22 MIN #375

Monitor: "Ask your friend how we got here in the first place. How we got on the planet Earth and in space-time."

"I felt like I was being taken back in time and could feel a bombardment of particles . . . of matter . . . and actually seeing the bombardment of particles. Some particles that fuse together actually became a working mechanism. I guess the only thing that we can understand and relate it to would be like a computer. And as a fusion of these particles occurred, they actually started communicating with one another by the heat of the light or the energy that they were radiating. And once they knew they were communicating with one another, and that is trying to communicate on the same level. And there were lots of these things. And they wanted to find out what they could do with this communication— how far they could go, could expand, could see, could think. They developed Earth and actually built Earth. They took a part of themselves, played around with animals, people, and they realized the number. How many they could produce just from one. Like one of these things could have thousands of people, parts of them, situated everywhere. The problem after a time, though, they created better minds, or thinking ma-

chines, and the event that the original should die or disintegrate. They are not long-lasting, in the sense of thousands and thousands of years, they are not forever kinds of things. Our spirits seemed to be an improved model of the original. The original has disintegrated."

Monitor: "Did the spirit originate in this process?"

"The spirit was a result of that. The spirit resulted from the fusion of these particles. The particles were matter fused together. That was spirit also. It was and that spirit lived for thousands and thousands and thousands of years and it disintegrated and before it disintegrated it rebuilt something that was better and it knew that it was going to die. It was going to disintegrate and it created the spirit that I now communicate with. So in a sense, they both can be called spirits or super minds. But your spirit could be and is different from my spirit."

Monitor: "How many such spirits are there such as the one you are communicating with?"

"Only a thousand."

Monitor: "Did they remain in the vicinity of Earth?"

"They don't know that term 'vicinity.' Vicinity to them is, as long as it is within millions of millions of miles of their reach it is in their vicinity. To us it means very close. Their minds can reach out over millions of light-years."

Monitor: "Are there communications with other spirits or other intelligent entities?"

"They have created them. If they have created them, yes, there are."

Monitor: "Why do they give so much attention to man?"

"They are creation. Like I said before, months ago, we are experiments. We are the tester to see how far this spirit can think, can fuse particles together. Can see what its potential is. They are still experimenting to see what their own potential is and we are one part of that experiment."

Monitor: "Are we an important or a minor part of this experiment?"

"They are afraid that all the brains that they created could fathom it or could take it. It is like some of the brains that they have developed would short out."

Monitor: "Have they created all of the human brains that are on the planet Earth?"

"Yes."

Monitor: "I see."

"They know everything that is going on. To clarify one thing, when humans have offspring, they don't necessarily control the offspring but it is part of the experimentation to see what results from the mating. When two parts of a spirit or two different spirits actually mate, what happens? . . . they don't know and that is part of the experimentation."

Monitor: "Can your spirit be in touch with my spirit?"

"Yes. Anytime."

Monitor: "Ask your spirit to see if he can be in touch with my spirit and see if there is any special message that my spirit has for me."

"I am feeling uncomfortable about going to other spirits and he was laughing at me for doing this, for feeling uncomfortable. Even though I did it with my mother. I just better come on back."

Monitor: "Right. And then, thank your spirit."

"O.K."

SS/NVP (DECORATOR) 92:30 MIN #388

"Blessed are they who seek me. In seeking me, their long period of forgetfulness is coming to an end. They are awakening to who they truly are—a living part of me, manifesting life and radiating love.

"You have forgotten to look for me, much less gaze upon my countenance, oh, ye of little faith. There are countless numbers who live in the expectancy of my coming. In truth, I never left.

"Let him who has ears to hear, let him hear, now.

"You seek me amidst your blindness. You look upon me without recognition. You touch my hand and know not whom you have touched.

"You proclaim my name and my teachings as it suits you and the occasion. Awaken, behold the reality of my being that is among you.

"I am the earthquake, wind, and fire.

"I am the still small voice piercing the thunderous tumult.

"I am the peace beyond all understanding.

"I am the light that guides all men to the Father.

"I am the love that overcometh all things.

"I am the light that illumines the minds of men. I am the sustenance of men's souls.

"I am your life and you are my own.

"I am the very breath you breathe.

"We are one in the Father.

"Do not despair, I will never leave thee nor forsake thee, nor can you truly forsake me, for we are one.

"Let the old way be gone. It must die and its ashes be blown to the four corners of the earth. The new is emerging but you must change your perspective. Do not look for me in the form of a man. The time is not yet. But look for me in the life that speaks to you in your everyday activities. You have looked amiss.

"I have no limitations and am not bound by physical dimensions.

"I defy logic and am beyond your conceptual imaginings.

"I live and move and have my being in all there is. You have sought me amiss.

"My countenance is seen within each face of my Father's creation. Look upon your brother and see my face.

"Bend over a still pool. Do not be deceived. The image that you see reflected is my own.

"Do you not see the truth now?

"Learn of me. Take within your hand a leaf, a stone, a drop of water, and know that nothing exists that does not contain me.

"Have you not known that I am eternal life and therefore recognize neither the past nor the future? Only the now, that is. Live in the now, with me.

"I stand in the light, as you stand in the light. But you do not know of your light. I am here to show you that your light and my light are one and the same. Once you recognize this divine light to be a part of all that is, will you then begin to understand your own relationship to life, to your creator, and thereby to your own sonship eternal.

"I neither slumber nor sleep and you must learn that your soul neither slumbers nor sleeps. Once you realize this, you are aware of your spiritual vitality and wakefulness to your high consciousness. In so knowing you will understand that I am truly closer than your hands and your feet. In this knowing, in this knowledge, we are one.

"Live in truth. Be truth. Live in beauty. Become an artist in living.

"Live in me and let me express you.

"I reside in all space and no space, all time and no time.

"Once you turn and become a part of my reality, all power is restored unto you. This is the power that makes you one with all things. This is the power that will set you free.

"My children, abide in me."

All of the Explorer Material has one characteristic in common. They pose more questions than they answer.

As they say, we have a problem here. We thought our "new" associations would provide answers. But for every answer, at least fifty new questions arise out of the Explorer Material.

Therefore, it became time to stop counting the trees and look at the forest instead.

And so we did.

6.
Segue

Not being at all loath to borrow a word or term from one cultural context and apply it aptly here, "segue" is defined as a proper interlude of musical melodies and harmonies that moves from the conclusion of one composition to the introduction of another. "Proper" infers a transition that smoothly loses that previous theme or mood and sets the stage for what is to come.

So this is a segue. The movement from what we have labeled "local traffic," i.e., events and activities that relate directly to here-now time—space, filled with much congestion, motivations, devious highways and byways, misconceptions, overwhelming emotions, detours, road repairs, confusing and conflicting signposts, inaccurate road maps, baits and lures both subtle and obnoxious—and dreams, ideas, learning, love . . .

To "interstate," where virtually all of the rules, patterns, illusions, and the rest of "local traffic," with few exceptions, are nonexistent.

To begin the segue, here is the mix of premises and conclusions we had reached by mid-1984:

1. All humans move into the out-of-body state during sleep. Going, falling, dropping asleep is simply a process of moving out of phase with physical time-space. As the event takes place, the various stages of sleep are readily interpreted if viewed from this perspective. Thus deep or "delta" sleep represents the point where consciousness is completely detached from physical reality, and the physical body is operating on an autonomic basis with preprogrammed alert and alarm systems to recall consciousness if needed. The fact that most human consciousnesses do not or cannot recall or remember these nightly excursions is insufficient proof that they do not take place. A night of OD'ing on booze can provide the same degree of amnesia.

2. A form of dynamic energy yet to be identified and measured by main-

stream human civilization is present in all carbon-based organic life. It is this essence in organized form that enters the physical body prior to birth and departs at death presumably more educated and with a minimum of wear and tear. The difference between the human version and that of a cow or a worm is only a degree of complexity of such organization.

3. The dominant waking consciousness that Man considers of paramount importance in the scheme of his existence is but a part—and perhaps the lesser—of the various forms thereof used by and/or available to him. The addition of other parts can be made systematically, albeit carefully, to the dominant without danger or destruction. The result may be of a magnitude beyond the comprehension of the present dominant, therefore engendering, at the least, anxieties—at the most, total rejection.

4. Human consciousness is but a manifestation of a system generated under (2). As a vibrational pattern—multilayered and of many interacting and resonating frequencies—it responds to and acts upon like patterns from external sources. The key to greater utilization thus may be the creation and application of external vibration at appropriate resonating frequencies so as to enhance a desired or needed specific.

5. Human and other patterns of consciousness are inherently nonphysical. As such, they are not time-space-dependent. Once released from physical restraints, they move into ambience and environment in accordance with the then total energy matrix generated by each and the complexity contained therein. No belief system, illusion, action, or thought incurred during a sojourn in time-space can alter this basic process. In short, like it or not, you're going to continue to do and be after you can no longer hang in there physically. There is no rest not only for the wicked but for everyone else.

6. In the awe-inspiring cloud of cosmology that has emanated from the Explorers and their contacts, almost unnoticed is an underlying mosaic of action that becomes an astounding potential when examined separately. We would not have become aware of it ourselves except that we were exposed time after time to various details of its use.

It is the display and application of a science—call it technology—which is totally absent from our human culture. We simply don't know anything about it nor do we have any accepted means by which to begin to gather information as to its nature or content.

Here is a series of excerpts from different Explorer sessions. They are even more startling when the actual report is heard, taken out of context just as we are doing here:

ss/romc 6:45 min #322

"Two discs came to me. At first it looked like two big eyes. I was put on one of them. I am spinning around and there is a light being put on me. I had a pain in one part of my body and they are working on that. They are spinning me around on this disc and shooting a light beam on me. My body is heavy because of this physical pain I had when I woke up this morning. I feel sluggish today and not as clear as before, so they are trying to help me. I say 'they.' I feel there is someone there, but it looks like two discs and a light. I was put on one disc and I don't know what happened to the other disc. I am still lying on one disc. It is getting more light. There is light over all my body. I think the light is coming from the other disc which is up over me. It is as if I am between two energy discs."

Monitor: "Ask who they are."

"O.K. I just got the answer back that 'we are a source of light and energy which your body needs right now!' "

Monitor: "Do you feel any results from the energy?"

"At first I was feeling out of it, but I am starting to feel a little more consciously energized."

Monitor: "Report when you have any change."

"O.K. I am supposed to tell you what is happening, because it helps. I keep sort of sniffing a little bit, and I get the feeling that it is going to help lift the vibration with my voice to keep on the level. I went onto that disc that I had gone on before, and I felt like it was twirling around very rapidly. It is sort of a balance—an energy balancing—and then I sensed from the center with this light beam that was sort of centering down on

me. Then they were working on an area of my body that shows up dark. So I felt that it was like they were putting some little, I don't know what you call them, like little stakes into my abdomen. They were being put one by one right across my abdomen And after these little stakes were put in one by one, then I felt that they were working with different colors, especially a violet and a blue. The beam came from the back of me, through my spine and through these stakes that had been put right across my abdomen. They were doing some healing work. I'm being taken off this disc now. They are going to start working to help me to go into the next level."

SS/MJL 11:23 MIN #351

"When I go up I have to leave that energy ball back down with my body. What I'm supposed to do is put the energy ball right down my spine and when I take off. I will try it on and this will keep protection on my physical body and I feel then that they are saying then at that point, they will be able to talk through me and work through me and I will feel completely comfortable, and that I am in control, that I had left my energy ball which I have been working with as part of me, that I will have that there in my body to keep the protection and also that I'm going to be out exploring other things and they will be able to talk through my vocal cords."

SS/ROMC 9:30 MIN #385

"I'm just floating up now. Now I'm supposed to stand and observe what is going to happen. My ear is ringing now but someone is working on my face. They are helping to exercise my throat muscles to talk by getting me prepared."

Other Voice: *"We are trying to show that she is multidimensional, and this is why she is able to see as a great circle of self, of many forms, of the self. It appears to her to be like many selves extending from a circle and between. We are trying to show her there are many, many dimensions of one human self. As she can see and understand that she is much more of that conscious self that she sees in the mirror, and that she experiences in her waking state. She will be much more prepared to go into the multidimensional levels of the consciousness, and this is why we are working on various levels, and not only the visual. This is very important to work on the visual, but also we are working with the other senses as well."*

SS/JCA 39:30 MIN #396

Monitor: "Ask him if he can help you communicate with some other mind on some other planet."

"He did, and briefly when I was talking just a second ago, he showed me and I quickly went to this other place and . . . I saw a person, not really a person, a being and a . . . a place that was a yucky kind of green. That had a bright sky, but was kind of cold. And people live under mounds. That's weird . . ."

SS/TC 21:30 MIN #392

"I went back to where I had been before and the entity there did something to me. He came over to me and did something to me and my perception began to change and since that time I have progressed through half a dozen or more altered states, each one being different than the other. I tried to strike up other conversations with this entity and he seemed more inclined and he seemed more to say, 'Well, do these things and we are not ready to discuss things yet.' He didn't seem in a very talkative mood. He was more interested in my performing these exercises than discussing. He came over and his, what I perceive to be hands, in what I perceive to be head, although this was not really related to a physical body. When he did that I could immediately feel these changes in awareness. Some of the states I went through were very specially disoriented to where I really could not determine up from down to sideways or anywhere else. Where I seem to be twisting and kind of rotating specially. Until I just lost any kind of sense of orientation. The fact that I was aware that the states were changing and relating them to my changing internal states seemed to be the lesson. Just to observe this."

SS/JCA 7:45 MIN #318

"I have just experienced being sucked in a long tube and pushed the other way. I'm like in a cocoon. My hands feel they are clasped up tight. Remember doing that before. Feels kind of neat. Now I'm standing on my head. Now on my side . . . darkness. But now I'm floating but I'm in something. I feel someone looking at me. Watching over me. Several people rode watching over me. They are looking down. Looking down but they came to see me. No figure, just communication, just his presence. I can see where we are going, or can I see the rest, or can they come here? He said no, they want to watch me. They want to watch me in this limbo. Now they are all circled around, bending over, and now they are touching me. But I didn't see them. Feel them. They are nice, warm friendly folk . . . friendly hands, but they were hands leading me someplace. Their presence was all around me leading me someplace. He . . . it cares about me. The first thing that came is that we're part of one another. But we are kind of lost in communicating with one another. It's there on the tip but it's not out in the open. The white presence is trying to help us or pushing me. It's kind of a transparent, feeling me. . . . You're going to laugh at this. I've been practicing going in and out of this tunnel, back down and up there. They thought it was kind of important to practice that. So I've been zooming up and zooming down. My body looks like, you know, through a telescope the long way and you kind of zoom in and then you zoom out. A hug and I said, 'I'll see you later.'"

SS/MJL 10:10 MIN #367

"They are working on my feet now. Two at the end . . . each of them are taking my feet and just giving me a real good foot massage. And as their hands touch my feet I tingle on my feet. These are energy light beings. And they are just very gentle and they are working on a different level than my physical foot. They are working on my other body. My energy foot and so they are doing some special kind of a touching of my feet now. They are working on my toes. Barely touching my toes. But I can feel a lot of energy between their touch and my energy body. It feels

good . . . it is a tingle . . . they are going to work on little spots on my feet. My toes. My big toe. Their fingers now are just working on my big toe."

If one cuts through the purely subjective reporting, even with this small sample, much becomes apparent:

· Notice how easily any potential anxieties or fears are overcome by simply a pattern of radiation emanating from strangers. If you were feeling your way along in an environment new to you, would you accept so eagerly the appearance of an unknown being?

· The color patterns. Our Explorers interpret them as visual patterns of light. This is the best that they can do to report the presence of some unknown type of radiation. Purple, blue, and green light will not create this effect on the human. With our sophisticated knowledge of light frequencies and our use of them, we would long ago have observed such effects.

· The use of what appears to be specific devices, such as the counter-revolving discs, which produce an effect totally beyond our comprehension.

· The ability to remove the energy essence of a human from his physical body without disrupting his biologic systems. This technology does this with a casualness and certainty that indicates standard operating procedure. They know what they are doing because they have done it many, many times.

· The ability to enter such a vacated human body and operate it to some degree—again, without disrupting said body's normal functions.

· Not only can they utilize the vocal cords and the breathing apparatus, but they have total access to the memory storage lodged in the individual.

· They can at will change the temperature of that visited human body, make it either hot or cold (which is reflected quite accurately on our remote-reading body temperature gauges).

· The ability to move that extracted human essence, once taken from the body, to various other sites (realities?), and return, all under perfect control and what seems to be absolute safety. The trip can be instantaneous or in "slow motion," and can penetrate matter as if it does not exist.

· Although this technology does not seem to have the ability to directly affect matter, by some method not visible it can create changes in matter. In other words, there is no evidence that it can produce matter (that is not to say that it cannot; it simply has not as yet). But it can affect an energy structure, which in turn connects to our neurological system, which in turn affects the physical structure.

· Perceiving our thoughts, as flickering as they are, is absurdly easy for this technology, but for the most part they apparently don't find it worth doing.

· Time and space become our phenomena. This technology understands them from a viewpoint about which we can only speculate. Even the best of such speculations do not begin to cover the nuances implicit in their approach to the vital conditions under which we exist.

· The entire history of humankind and earth is available to them in the most minute detail, if needed. Where and how such information is stored and retrieved is a part of such technology, a seeming unimportant part. Implied also in such information storage is data on the entire physical universe, if there were any reason to require such detail.

· This technology can produce a beam of energy, which is first translated as light, through which the human energy essence can travel back and forth, information can flow, and the operators of such technology can enter time-space/earth environments. Once properly perceived, they can endow the human mind with the ability to create (enhance?) such a beam of energy.

These observations are based on several hundred encounters with such technology. With our limited contact, the implication is certainly there that we have learned so little about so much. Our attempts to learn more in a specific sense have been severely hampered by the knowledge and experience of the Explorer through which the information is being translated. Also, there is a polite inference in the response to our queries that we would not be able to understand it in any event.

It does not take much speculation to recognize the potential revolutionary changes in our science and culture if but a part of such technology were actively introduced and applied in the months and years to come. Any serious consideration of all of the above hinges on one question: How valid is the entire project? To this end, responsible parties who wish to replicate such experiments are welcomed.

Who are the beings who know and use this technology? (Some have admitted that they never have been a human being in physical life existence; others were here thousands of years ago. Some have been in physical life existence in other parts of the universe in nonhuman form.) Why are they interested in human life on earth? Are there thousands of them, millions, billions? (They apparently do have individuality of a sort.) How did such a technology begin? Who developed it? Is there some restriction on our learning such technology and applying it here in time-space/earth? Is this technology being applied constantly in other ways on earth and in human affairs that we don't know about and certainly of which we are not consciously aware?

We do seem to have one answer. In all of our contacts and communication, the application of this technology seems totally benevolent. There also seem to be rules and restrictions in regard to its use.

For this we are humbly grateful. To contemplate any other possibility could lead to mental disaster. I don't think we could do anything about it whatever our stance.

A key point has surfaced, however. The sum of all my own personal experience, that of our work in the laboratory and the thousands of Gateway experiments, indicates that all other intelligent species, either in the physical universe or in other energy systems, use a form of communication that is total and certainly nonverbal. When words are used in such communication with us, this is a tight narrow-banded tuning, so that they can be understood at least in part.

I cannot stress this too much. All other intelligent species use what we now call nonverbal communication (NVC). It is something far more than what we label body language, telepathy, remote viewing, and the often mystical or religious connotations so commonly applied to a tiny part of NVC. We say that a picture is worth 1,000 words. A color picture is worth 10,000 words. A moving color picture is worth 50,000 words, perhaps, and a talking moving picture is worth a 100,000 or more words in the transmission of information and/or communication.

NVC takes a quantum jump beyond a talking moving color picture. It is direct instant experience and/or immediate knowing transmitted from one intelligent energy system and received by another. The content can be only a two-digit number, or the actual reliving of an event not a part of your own life patterns.

Why did we evolve along our particular path so differently from the rest? I like the explanation which attributes it to the very rare characteristic of the earth environment—we could see the sun and moon, planets and stars. This presumes that most life-generating and -sustaining planets have thick cloud covers that blot out all of these. Their suns visually are no more than a haze of light. No more, nothing but blackness at night.

Our species, able to see the physical universe from the beginning, took the route of astronomy, gravity, electromagnetics, particle theory, quantum mechanics, etc., which we call our sciences.

Lacking this clue of a visible physical universe, other species learned NVC.

If I were proficient at NVC (which I am not), and you asked me what was the matter because you detected (unconsciously by NVC) that I had a problem, I would be able to transmit into your sensory system how it felt to have the sore big toe that I had. You would momentarily have a sore toe, just as I had, still understanding that it was my big toe that hurt, not yours. Thus you would know, far better than by means of any possible words that I could say, what I was experiencing or feeling or wanted to communicate.

Instead of my wife calling by phone to say that she would be late for dinner and that she would arrive at nine o'clock, I would get a picture "in my head" of her driving the car with the headlights on, with the number 9 flashing simultaneously in the picture. She would also show me a picture of the right rear tire of the car, flat and being changed by a local state trooper. All of this could be transmitted superimposed with a signal of warmth and love in the space of perhaps two or three seconds, no more.

If I were proficient at NVC and my son also was trained in the technique, I could pass along to him, in very short order, all of the education and experience that I have gathered that he might desire or that might be of use to him. It would not be the absorption of words simply received in serial form, but an instantaneous, or nearly so, transmission absorption of the entire event—including my emotional reaction, what my five senses perceived, and the interpretations and conclusions that I gleaned from the experience.

Take this starting point, and draw any extrapolation from it, then understand the limitations of our semi-intelligent species.

NVC implies a control of mental processes so alien to our present standards of being that I doubt that there is a single human or group of humans on our planet who have mastered the technique. If there are, they are very quiet about it. On the other hand, if it were the case, they certainly would have had to develop some type of mental shielding to survive the cacophony of unorganized thinking that is so common here.

Before man can communicate (and associate) with intelligent species at all levels of reality, he must become proficient at NVC. I am sure it must bemuse if not amuse other intelligent species when we spend millions for huge radio telescopes in the attempt to receive electromagnetic signals from other intelligent life sources. This is much like another culture measuring the exhaust gases from our cars or our pollution to perceive communication via this loose discharge of energy residue. At the other end, animals do most of their communication by scents and smell.

It would be easy to give hundreds of illustrations of attempts to cope with NVC problems. We have faced them in so many different ways that we are probably much more aware than the average group or facility. We still grope with the rudiments of NVC type of training and mental processing. The only statement that we can make at this moment is that we recognize the existence and the need.

From this segue, the material following goes "interstate"—an attempt to translate and transpose the NVC perspective into the written word. Due to such conversion, the question of validity always will be present. Some "thought balls" are easier to unravel serially than others; the time-space humanizing is bound to create distortions. It always has.

You do the best you can.

Part II
Far Reaches

7.
Surveys and Schematics

The following is a deliberately free translation of nonverbal communication. To compound the rendering, most if not all represents the transposing of non-time-space events and ambience into replicas of conscious human physical experience. Thus a "humanizing" process is used extensively in the retelling—which may increase comprehension and simultaneously reduce accuracy.

To abet the method, a few specific words are utilized in a different context to provide a connotation not so totally unlike their common definition. You can't report "he said" or "he walked" or "she smiled"—because it wasn't that way, the physical equipment wasn't available.

Instead, here are parts of the "replica" vocabulary:

Time-Space Illusion (TSI): An anomaly among the "standard" energy systems, which includes the entire physical universe

M Band: Part of energy spectrum commonly used for thought, not electromagnetic, electrical, magnetic, nucleonic, etc. *M Band noise* is caused by uncontrolled thought.

Ident: Mental name or "address," i.e., energy pattern of item

Rote: Thought ball
> A "packet" of thought/mentation, total memory
> Knowledge
> Information
> Experience
> History

Run the rote: To recall portions of Rote after receipt of total

Percept: Insight
> Intuition
> Understand

Open: Receptive

Closed: Tune down (or out) external stimuli
Flickered: Uncertain
CLICK!: Instantaneous change in consciousness
Blank: Don't understand
Turn in: Consider, think over
Vibrate: Show emotion
Smooth: Get it together, in charge of self
Dulled: Lost interest
Lighted: Happy, idea, enthusiasm
Rolled: Amused, laughed
Curl: Organized energy, usually intelligent, local slang
Plied: The way things are, goes with the territory

One of the earliest discoveries made in the new mode of Let-Somebody-Else-Do-the-Driving was that I had more than one nonphysical body. Upon return, I began to notice it took a small additional effort to get back into the physical. Initially, I assumed this to be nothing more than some minor misalignment as I tried to reenter. On one particularly difficult attempt, I pulled back slightly, stopped trying, and examined the problem. My physical body appeared to be not one, but two—much as when your vision is slightly impaired by astigmatism. They seemed very close together, no more than three or four inches apart, one slightly behind and fainter than the other. I approached the nearest of the two slowly, slid into it very easily. I held this position for several moments. It seemed as if I were partially interspersed with the physical, yet not quite in phase. The condition had a familiarity that took me all the way back to the vibration I first encountered and the physical paralysis that went with it. The sensation was near-identical—without the panic.

From there, it was easy to reenter the physical with a simple twitchlike movement, akin to a shrug of the shoulders. Thereafter, I began to take particular notice of physical reentry and found that I did indeed reenter a second form just prior to the physical body. In appearance, it was identical to the physical, only less dense. However, upon return this second body appeared more real, the more solid of the two. Upon entering the second, the actual physical then seemed more definite. Also, I began to observe more closely my separation process, presuming that if the premise were valid, I would be able to perceive the release from this near-second body. I found it was very real. I could stay in the second body, hovering near the physical, but could move no more than ten or fifteen feet away. It was reminiscent of my first limited out-of-body activities. It also brought back the memory of the many frustrative attempts in those early days to move away farther—and the moment I found the release point. Without being aware of the reason, I had provided subsequently to others in training the key to such release—the mental "security repository box," where one can place thoughts that get in the way.

Once I had become aware of the actual process, it became automatic, and both separation and return contained these elements—leaving the second body in "orbit" close to the physical, moving and being entirely apart and separate from the physical in a "third" body, or an energy essence (without form?). I no longer concerned myself with the details. Understanding it functionally—if not the reason—was enough for my purposes.

Another early result of my new navigator (my total self?) was remembering the going-to-class format. This came after my usual out-of-body separation process, releasing to such guidance, and without much movement finding myself among a crowd of gray forms. "Crowd" means so many they seemed to fade into the distance. All were focused in one direction, and none seemed to notice my arrival—except one, brighter than the others. It approached me and stopped.

It opened—with words! In my consciousness. *(Glad you're back, Bob. You've missed quite a few sessions.)*

I flickered. *(Well, uh, I've been busy.)*

The form focused. *(You're different. You haven't been on drugs or alcohol, have you?)*

I opened wide. *(I've lost a lot of rote, or I can't pull it out. Where am I?)*

The form rolled. *(I guess you have! You're back at sleeper's class.)*

I turned inward, and the percept came out bright and clear. Sleeper's classes—attended by countless humans during a portion of their deep sleep, during the sleeping out-of-body period. The only limitation was that such sleep could not be distorted by chemicals, it had to be natural. How many times I had been here long before I knew it, before I knew anything about OOBEs and the like! I just didn't remember when I woke up, like everyone else. If anything leaked through, it was attributed to a dream, inspiration, idea, or imagination.

And I knew my instructor. *(Hi, Bill.)*

Bill rolled. *(Took you long enough. Want me to plug you in?)*

I flickered. *(Well, I don't know. You see, I think I am different. I'm not asleep.)*

Bill blanked slightly, then lighted. *(Oh, you're one of those. How did that happen?)*

I plied. *(I don't know. It just did.)*

Bill turned inward, then opened. *(That means you don't belong here anymore. Too bad. You were one of my star pupils.)*

I flickered. *(You're sure about that? About my not belonging?)*

Bill smoothed. *(I've had them before. It doesn't work out. Your type gets impatient, bored. The biz kids, the OOB-ers, busy, busy, busy.)*

I smoothed carefully. *(How about plugging me in one last time? As long as I'm here.)*

Bill dulled. *(You probably know it already. Can't change the program.)*

I opened wide. *(Try me.)*

Bill flickered and tossed me a rote. I opened it easily.

CLICK!

The anti-ulcer, anxiety-lowering, tension-reduction, get-it-together formula:

The major underlying cause of human worry relates to the Law of Change. All human conflict relates to this law. Some worry that change *will* take place, others that it will not. Wars are fought to resist change or to accelerate it.

At the individual level, this translates into various forms of indecision. Fear enters into the pattern, fear of the consequences of any decision or action. The pressure builds up, intensifies as the decision is put off, delayed. The result accumulates toxins in all parts of the human system until there is failure or severe reduction in operating efficiency. Indecision is the killer.

Consider the statistics of decision, in general and simplified. In any abstract decision, there is a 50 percent probability that the correct or constructive choice will be made. If the correct path is taken, obviously no problems will exist. If the incorrect selection is made, it will become evident. When it does, there is a 50 percent probability that the choice can be reversed and the constructive path substituted in its place.

Therefore, there is only one chance in four, at the most, that an irrevocable direction may be taken in decision making. All vital decisions in the history of man have been made on much worse odds than three to one. Some were as high as one in twenty and came out positively.

To move away from the null point of indecision, take the position that *any* action or decision is better than none at all, based upon the odds of three to one. To get the process underway without trauma, perform the following:

Make up an A list. Place on this list all of your worries, anxieties, and concerns about which you can do absolutely nothing. You cannot do anything about tomorrow's weather conditions. It will rain, snow, be cold or hot, and there is no action you can take to prevent it. If there is absolutely nothing you can do *today* about such items, place them on this A list.

Make up a B list. Place on this list all of your worries, anxieties, and concerns about which you can do something *today*, take action, large or small.

Make up a C list. Place on this list all of your needs, hopes, and desires, large or small, which have yet to be fulfilled.

Today, perform the following functions:

1. Take the A list and destroy it, and in so doing, dismiss all items contained therein from your consciousness. Why waste your energy worrying about that which you cannot control?

2. Take the B list and take some action, however small, to begin the resolution of each item contained therein. Several may be concluded immediately and thus can be released and dismissed from your consciousness. Others will be reduced in pressure because the flow has begun, a decision has been made.

3. Take at least one item on the C list and perform one act, large or small, that moves you in the direction of such goal.

Perform this entire process each day until you have no A list, no B list, and all of your energy and consciousness are devoted to items on your C list.

You then will complete serenely your human life purpose.

CLICK!

I folded the rote and tucked it in me, turned to Bill. *(That's pretty good. Seems familiar.)*

Bill plied. *(It ought to. You must have picked it up a couple hundred classes back.)*

I opened. *(Bill, if I don't belong here, where do I go?)*

(I don't know. I don't have the slightest percept on that.)

(There must be classes for, uh, mavericks like me.)

Bill plied. *(I'm sure there are. I got to go make my rounds now. Drop in for a visit if you feel like it. I'm two rings out.)*

I opened wide. *(Sure, Bill.)*

He turned and faded into the host of gray forms, and with nothing better to pull me, I rotated and dived back for the physical. Reentry was normal.

The next early absorption was a series of demonstrations—live guided experiences—of the old saw about fools and angels. I cannot conceive of the latter having fear, just selective. As to the former, I had ignorantly rushed in many times in the early period, so I certainly qualified. I began to call it the Defooling Treatment.

The presumption I made was that my Greater Self (soul?) always knew what it was doing. I had learned from it how a homing device loosely called ident was utilized; this was like a signal you could follow to the source of that place or being. In this one instance of Defooling, I had rolled out of body in the early morning, and after releasing the second, I expressed the mild observation that it would be nice to visit a near-human culture that was in time-space and that I could understand. Immediately the ident Z-55 flashed into me, so I reached and stretched. There was a slight sense of movement and I was in front of a slightly glowing figure. Other, similar figures were in the background. Beyond, nothing.

The figure opened. *(Well, Robert, we meet again.)*

I flickered. *(Uh, yes.)*

(Still digging out the secrets of the universe?)

This wasn't what I expected. It definitely wasn't any near-human culture, and this being seemed to know me. Some mistake in the ident, but the radiation did seem familiar. I didn't want to ask the obvious, but I had to. *(Where am I?)*

The figure smoothed. *(Outermost ring, Robert. One more final cycle in-human and that will be it. For me.)*

I flickered. *(I don't have a percept on the Z-55 ident, but I know you.)*

Z-55 rolled. *(After all those hours putting music together . . . The run to Cuba back in the fifties to record in Havana . . .)*

The percept came bright and sure in me. Of course I knew him. Even then I called him an old soul! I vibrated strongly. *(Lou! Sure! The Z-55 ident threw me. You seem different. It's great to be with you again!)*

Z-55/LOU smoothed. *(Well, I've had a couple more in-human runs since we were together, so Lou is sort of covered over a little.)*

I turned inward. Lou, one of the most gentle of persons I had ever met . . . musician, arranger, orchestra conductor . . . quietly living through his life and his work . . . hours and days we spent together . . . working far into the night developing melody lines . . . chord progressions, orchestrations . . . then our paths diverged . . . and I heard of his early death . . . the diabetes I knew he lived with . . .

Z-55/LOU opened. *(You're still in-human!)*

I smoothed. *(Yep.)*

He flickered. *(Oh, a sleeper. You got out this far? That's pretty good. Too bad you won't remember it.)*

I opened more. *(It's not quite that way, Lou. I, uh, here.)*

I tossed him a short rote covering the out-of-body beginning. He took it in and closed. Then he opened and rolled lightly. *(One of those. You never told me.)*

I plied. *(I didn't know myself when we were working together.)*

He flickered. *(So how do I fit in? You come looking for me. More music?)*

I plied again. *(I'm not sure. I asked to visit a near-human culture, got your ident . . . and here I am.)*

Z-55/LOU lighted. *(You want to visit my . . . uh . . . hometown, so to speak?)*

I rolled. *(Not Kentucky. I've been there. It's too human!)*

He rolled with me. *(No, no . . . my original home. It's just what you want, that's why you got my ident. . . . It's, uh, different, but you can understand it all right.)*

I turned inward.

If you've never been to a particular exotic place—or to a locale that at least to you seems exotic and exciting from your distant viewpoint—there is much anticipation. You can conjure up any number of possibilities as to what you will do and experience.

In your eagerness, you are willing to accept all sorts of limitations, restrictions, that seem unimportant from the outside. Also, you forget one most important factor. You take along as hidden extra baggage your own enculturation as a comparative tool of measurement.

Z-55/LOU lighted brightly. *(To really get the feel of it, you ought to go there just like a regular tourist, limited amount of assets, and stay through the regular historical event we, uh, they call the surge.)*

I lighted, too. *(Great! Good percept.)*

(And so you can truly experience it), he went on, *(cut off communication with here until after the surge. A little like the in-human training but without rote erasure.)*

I opened wide. *(I'm all for it. How do we start?)*

(I'll be your anchor here. To get back, all you need do is home on my ident.) There was a whimsical radiation mixed in with his pattern. *(To get there focus in on ident . . . Zeer-surge . . .)*

I vibrated. *(Zeer surge.)*

I reached and stretched.

CLICK!

I was in a city, or what appeared to be a city. There were buildings in all directions, fairly uniform, none over three or four stories high. They were not particularly attractive or unusual, had openings in the sides that my percept took as windows and doors. The streets or spaces between buildings were not unusually wide, but contained only people, percept beings like me or what I was temporarily. No cars, trucks, vehicles of any type. No utility poles or overhead wires, no sidewalks. It was bright daylight, but I couldn't find a sun overhead.

As I walked and mingled with the population, people noticed me but didn't seem to react as if I were an alien. With each step, I felt more at ease and the population seemed more human. Each inhabitant was very purposeful and closed, as if preoccupied on a job to be done with not much nonsense in the process. If there was any body language present, no percept showed. Point of fact was I couldn't tell the males from the females, which was unusual for me, so I assumed there was no such difference.

Unable to attract the attention of those moving on the street, I entered one of the buildings and found myself in a large room which greatly resembled the lobby of a medium-sized hotel. There were people standing around, apparently in conversation. I approached a man (?) who appeared to be standing behind a desk. He looked at me expectantly. I knew I needed a reason.

"Do you, uh, do you have a restaurant here?" I tried to make it casual, but as he blanked I knew I had done it wrong.

I turned to my rudimentary NVC. *(Do you have the means for me to recharge?)*

The man lighted brightly, waved me off to the right. As I walked in the indicated direction, I felt smug. I had passed one test. They didn't vocalize but they understood me. Even my weak, nonverbal communication. From here on, it would be easy. I began to speculate as to the food they consumed. It was sure to be unusual. An archway, rounded, was in front of me, and it appeared dark beyond—no, not dark, just lit differently in a mixture of colors.

I strode confidently through the archway and into the colors. Just inside, the radiation hit me like a sheet of hot flame and I staggered back. This wasn't the restaurant, the man got it all wrong. From all sides came the overwhelming attraction of female sexuality, inviting, asking, offering, promising—it was too much. With great effort, I backed out through the archway, breathing heavily and trying to calm down. I had just about smoothed out when I looked up and the room clerk (?) was in front of me, accompanied by two other men—percept police, authority, KGB, etc.

One KGB moved in. *(Your ident, please?)*

I began fumbling in my pockets for my wallet, only there were no pockets in the one-piece cover I was wearing. But there was a belt on me with a small pouch attached to it. I reached in the pouch and there was a card in it. I pulled it out and it resembled nothing so much as a typical credit card. KGB took it from me, examined it carefully, then looked up.

(From Earth, huh? Never heard of that city. Over on the other side of the ocean?)

I smoothed. *(Why, uh, yes, you see . . .)*

KGB waved the card at me. *(Well, we don't particularly like you visiting here, but you got to obey the rules.)*

I brightened. *(Sure, I understand.)*

(Here, we don't go into private space and take without paying first. Always pay first.) KGB turned to the desk clerk, handing him my card. *(How much of it do you want? He hasn't got very much.)*

The desk clerk dropped the card into the pouch on *his* belt. *(That ought to about cover it.)*

I started to protest. *(But that's all I got, I can't . . .)*

(In that case we'll have to flag you.) The second KGB stepped forward and took my hands. *(Can't have you walking around upsetting things without any ident.)*

I flickered. *(What are you going to do?)*

The second KGB pulled a small flat box out of his pouch and opened it. *(Hold still, this won't hurt.)*

He took one hand and pressed my fingertips into the box. I thought, fingerprints, they're taking my fingerprints. But I was wrong. A black dye spread quickly up my fingers until it covered my entire hand. As I stared at it, bewildered, they stuck the fingers of my other hand into the box and I had two black hands. I tried to rub it off, but it had penetrated the skin.

The first KGB looked at my hands, satisfied. *(That ought to do it. At least the people will see you coming.)*

(And be warned,) the second KGB added. *(I'd advise you to go back home. Not much action for you here, the way you are. No ident to play with.)*

The first KGB looked at me hard. *(We'll be keeping an eye on you.)* Then the two turned and walked across the room and out into the street.

I smoothed at the desk clerk. *(Sorry, I didn't know it was a private space.)*

The desk clerk vibrated. *(What other kind is there!)*

I flickered. *(You mean all of these buildings are private?)*

The desk clerk dulled.

(Then what are all these people doing here? There must be a hundred!) I hit it strong enough to catch his attention.

(It's their private space, naturally.)

(All one hundred?)

The desk clerk waved me over to the desk and I followed. He pointed to the drawing on the wall behind him. It showed some five rows of large black dots that looked like holes, twenty to a row.

(That's our personal space.) He gestured proudly. *(Best in the city.)*

I stared at the drawing. *(You go into those?)*

He nodded. *(Only when the surge takes place. They're this big across the middle.)*

He indicated a width of about two feet with his arms. He was about to continue when there was a sound like thunder in the distance and the floor began to rock. Immediately, everyone in the room turned and hurried out through exits in the back. The room clerk ran to join them.

(That's the surge starting up,) he called over his shoulder. *(I suppose that's what you came to witness, but you better get to your personal space fast.)*

Then the room was empty and I tried to keep my footing as the floor heaved rhythmically. I staggered over to the entrance as the roar grew louder. In the distance and approaching fast was a mighty wave, not water but in the ground itself, lifting buildings and streets into a tumbling flotsam hundreds of feet high. Behind the first wave, I could see a second and a third wave, each larger than the first. There may have been more, but I didn't have a chance to find out, as the first wave came surging into where I was, and the building lifted and tumbled, me in it, bouncing, rolling, twisting, jarring . . .

. . . desperately, I tried to focus, ident what? ident . . . ident Z-55/ LOU . . . Z-55/LOU . . . reach and stretch, reach and stretch . . . closed tightly . . . tightly . . .

CLICK!

It was quiet, the pounding had stopped. I tried to keep from shaking long enough to open. I finally made it. I was in front of Z-55/LOU, and I got a percept of his polite expectation.

I smoothed somewhat. *(That's home for you? Where you were before starting human?)*

He plied. *(It's not Kentucky.)*

(And you're going back there?)

Z-55/LOU opened wide. He glowed very brightly, almost white. *(No, not there.)*

There was a sudden urgent signal to go back, and before I could reply, I moved away automatically and he faded. . . . I was back hovering over the physical, the return signal still strong. I slid into the second, then the physical, and sat up on the water bed. Body fine, no full bladder. No signal. What called me back? Nothing I could find.

The Defooling Treatment. They do rush in.

Releasing to my total self for direction and purpose provided what I now recognize as a crash program in comprehension of what I had formerly labeled Locale II. It began with hard basics at the inner end of the spectrum, with a modified hands-on process that forced inescapable conclusions. Simply put, I could observe but not participate. The purpose, I discovered, was multifaceted and determined in part long after the event itself.

One of the principal examples came one night when I rolled out of the physical, and before I could release from the second body, an overwhelming drive for sexual union rose in me. I was about to employ my usual not-now-but-later cooling technique when I moved away sharply with a sudden shift. The movement was fast and short. When I was able to perceive, I found I was standing a few feet away from an enormous pile of writhing forms. It reached up, slanting back as high as I could see. In each direction, right and left, it swept off into the distance. It reminded me of nothing so much as the interweaving of huge fishing worms in the bottom of a can after being left there overnight. The motion was continuous, thousands upon thousands, each wet slippery form wiggling in and out among the others in the pile, searching, trying to do something . . . but never achieving satisfaction.

Three perceptive shocks hit me simultaneously. The forms were not worms, they were human! Second, the incredible, staggering radiation of sexuality, both male and female, that emanated from the seething mass. Third, they all were physically dead. I wanted to turn and run, but some other part of me held me in place. I finally calmed down enough to become analytical. Did I want to join in? My whole being shuddered in rejection. No vestige remained of the sexual drive I found so important moments before. I had the strong percept that it would come again, but never where it would control wholly what I thought or did.

With this flash of knowing, another emotion washed through me—intense compassion for those trapped in the undulating mass, so focused and intent on seeking sexual satisfaction they were unaware of any other existence—anger at a system that could so inhibit, repress, and distort as to create the situation in front of me. Were these the castoffs of the human process, to remain so throughout eternity?

I moved forward slowly and stopped close to the edge of the pile. The moving bodies were male and female, of all shapes and sizes, glistening with wetness. A bare hairy leg thrust momentarily from the pile, and I grabbed it by the foot and pulled. . . . The leg pushed out blindly, trying to move more deeply back into the pulsating mass. I pulled harder, trying to keep my grip on the sweat-covered ankle. Slowly, I was able to pull the rest of the body clear of the pile. It was a man, small in stature, dark-haired, fine-featured, of indeterminate age. He lay there on his belly, his arms and legs moving crablike, attempting to pull himself back into the pile, totally oblivious to the fact that I was holding on to his foot and preventing him from doing so.

I easily held him in place, bent over, and shouted in his ear, *(Hey, I want to talk to you. Hold still for a moment!)*

There was not the slightest indication that he heard me. His face was fixed, a gleam of anticipation spread across it. He kept trying to move back and I held him in place, wondering what to do next.

I tried another approach. *(It's the cops, the police, they're raiding the joint! Gotta get out!)*

I waited for some response, but there was none. I couldn't provide him with the radiation that would get his attention. I released his foot, and he crawled back into the mass and was swallowed up in the movement. I turned away sadly and stretched for my physical ident, and returned without incident.

From that point on, I had a new technique to control any surfacing sexual drive. All I need do is think of that wriggling, writhing, mindless pile of humanity. That does it.

This episode was of the milder variety that may be encountered in the immediate postphysical areas. I soon discovered there was a pattern at work in my own guided tour through them—states of being I had previously passed through quickly to avoid confrontation. All of these forays started while in the second body, before I could release it and move outward. I felt safe and secure with my higher self doing the driving.

The feeling was right. But not the reason.

8.
Contact Point

The suspicion began where I thought I had a good perspective of the human experience. In retrospect, the whole thing may have been planned that way all along.

I had been moving in and out of OOB situations very blithely and calmly, always sure that my guiding total self knew the answers, would take care of anything and any problem as they arose. It had worked perfectly to date, and perhaps that was why the slight scent of suspicion began to form. However great my ego might think I was, I knew I wasn't *that* good.

Thus entered again one of my many questionable characteristics. I can't let a good thing alone and simply let it do; I have to find out why. In several succeeding OOB excursions, I tried to become aware of who *was* doing the driving and/or navigating. The contact was elusive in the beginning, no percept other than a gentle presence behind me, directing where I went. I turned around, but there was nothing—at the most a trace of a friendly presence. But it was there and it seemed definitely external.

I went back through my notes, all the way to the beginning. I was astounded that I had ignored what was so apparent. A hand helping me get out, a hand on my arm, a response to my anguished screams, and the more subtle clues apparent from my new perspective. I had called them helpers at the time and let it go at that. At the minimum, I had not turned my activities over to my "greater self," but to them, whoever "they" were.

Thereafter, during active OOBEs, I tried many times to communicate with these presences, singular or plural, to no avail. Correction: I thought I received no reply because no words were forthcoming, only pictures, sensations, and action. The change came about when I dimly began to realize I wasn't speaking their "language," as it were. Review of my early notes supported this, for the most part. Words and language, as we know them, are strictly human. The inference was obvious to me—being human. My deflated ego rose somewhat with the realization that whatever my communication method was, a response was coming from these—*non*humans?

With this awareness, I continued to ask and let "them" do the driving and navigating during my OOB states for one simple reason: the process had been working. Whoever they were, they certainly knew the territory far better than I. Each time, though, I attempted another kind of communication, and it began getting results. I directed wordless thoughts—pictures, activities, feelings, and emotions to the supposed presence behind me. Each time, there was an immediate response of like quality. It took some analytical and subjective attitudes combined to comprehend what I received. It was painfully slow on my side, astoundingly patient on theirs. Out of it came the rudiments of what we now call nonverbal communication (NVC). It was a milestone in my consciousness. I knew then that NVC exists and I knew the difference. Not too much more.

With the mutual recognition of such communication, the depth and extent of my OOB patterns shifted. I was escorted frequently to what might be loosely described as another kind of class, in that there was an instructor and there were students, including me. It was entirely different from the sleeper's classes I remembered. Here, freely translated, there was a brilliant white, radiating ball of light that was the teacher. I could detect radiation of others—presumed students—all around me, but nothing beyond that, no form or any indicators as to who and what the others were. Instruction consisted of a seeming sequential bombardment of packages of total experiential information to be absorbed instantly and stored thought balls, whose actual name cannot be translated into a word, which I called rotes. It apparently is a very common communication technique in NVC. What I could bring back, I attempted to convert into in-human usage, with mixed results. I have been unable to relate the vast majority of such information in any way to life here on time-space earth. It may be preparation for activity yet to take place here, for use in other nonphysical energy systems, or it is beyond my comprehension. The last is most likely.

Thus the relationship took on an entirely new aspect. I began to trust my unseen pilot(s?) as I never would have trusted myself. For example, in flying as a passenger on a commercial airliner, I never can trust completely the air crew up front—perhaps I know too much. However, I have to get from here to there physically in a short time, so I fasten the seat belt and fly the airplane with nothing but anxiety and muscle twitches. Sleep is unthinkable.

This was different. They knew how and where to fly *this* airplane over this route far better than I. With each "flight," my confidence and trust in them grew. Conversely, I realized how *little* I knew as the route became more complicated. I fondly began to call them INSPECS—short for "intelligent species," which presumes humans are not quite so.

Knowing of such assistance and help, I approached my visits into the cycling rings in near-earth environs with much more confidence and consciousness than before. I felt an absolute security. If I got in beyond my depth, THEY would pull me out to safety—although I found that their concept of beyond my depth and mine differed somewhat. I may have believed that I was going down for the third and last time, screaming for help, yet THEY waited until the eighth or ninth time before calmly extending a hand. All part of a learning process with built-in intensity.

A favorite quick and learn-forever method of theirs was simulation. It was based on their ability to create and place into a human consciousness —mine—an earth-type situation so real and so overwhelming that I could not tell reality from illusion. I don't know the limits of such simulation talent/technology. Nor do I know the extent to which they employ the technique. It may be only in my own particular case, but I doubt it. The potentials of its application in other ways begs for broad speculation.

In my own pattern, it was usually applied as in instant cleanup of minor emotional patterns that blocked or distorted my clarity of perception or my stability. Usually I was unaware of such dysfunction. THEY would note it and offer to take care of the problem. I would be informed that the lesson was about to take place with my consent, yet once into the simulation, it became absolutely and totally real—and I lived it. Most of them were short, single events that were the peak decision-making points under very adverse circumstances. The vital part—the lesson to be learned indelibly—was my constructive and reasoned resolution of the problem. If I did not come up with the desired action, the simulation would be repeated until I did. Even in the repetition, I couldn't break through the reality of the simulation. Yet once the training sequence was completed, I then knew it for what it was.

An interesting sidelight arose when our laboratory Explorers met and associated with intelligent beings who did accommodate to the use of words, some of whom closely resembled my percepts of the INSPECS. Further, they greeted me with familiarity and I felt the same toward them.

I had never asked the INSPECS exactly what their role was in the human earth pattern. I assumed THEY were simply a graduate school version of the ex-human helpers from the outer rings. Their mode of operation and purpose seemed very similar, except that the INSPECS had knowledge and technology far beyond that drawn from the human experience. The fact that THEY seemed to be independent of the recycling rings supported this belief. To pose questions about motives seemed—irreverent. Or perhaps I didn't want to endanger the good thing I had going for me. Thus I had no direct and conscious communication with them while in the OOB state.

But we fools can't let it alone. On a particular night, I had an idea and I decided to try it out. I had been developing a sense of familiarity with the radiation of the INSPECS and thought I could home in on the signal—the ident—just as I could others. I might learn much. Here is the event, as taken from my notes and expanded to a semblance of understanding:

Time: 2:17 A.M. . . . *bedroom* . . . After two sleep cycles, awake, rested, relaxed . . . went through unhook rollout method into second body, rolled out of second, and this time I did have a percept of the ident INSPEC . . . not much, but enough, I thought . . . homing on the ident . . . went through normal reach and stretch procedure . . . moved rapidly through ring system . . . and beyond, which did not surprise me . . . began to feel warm, more so as I went until it became almost too uncomfortable and was at the point of turning back . . . when I rammed headlong into something and collapsed, shaken . . . I reached out and there *was* a barrier, smooth in texture, rigid, impenetrable . . . still very uncomfortable from the heat, I pulled myself together, knowing this was the end of the line, I might as well turn back to the physical . . . and a bright light, very intense, glowed in front of me, first ovate, reshaping into a tall humanoid form, so bright I cringed from it . . . for what seemed an eternity, I shrank back, trying to shield myself from the brightness

. . . then I began to cool down until I was no longer uncomfortable, and I could tolerate the brightness.

(Is that better for you?)

"Better" was an understatement. Much longer, and I would have melted.

(Did you bump your head?)

Well, I guess I could call it that. Usually my head was out front when . . .

(It is nothing to be concerned about. You have a hard head, Mister Monroe.)

That turned me around. I never thought of God having a whimsical sense of humor. That and the Mister Monroe routine. I straightened, no longer cowering. I almost felt like reaching out and shaking hands in greeting.

(There are more significant and suitable ways.)

I was getting bewildered. I was just floating there, trying to figure out what happened . . .

(You encountered a condition similar to that which your scientists call a standing wave, where two like energies in phase appear to cancel one another to zero. Yet there is no zero, as energy does not cancel, it transforms into other dynamic states.)

So now I supposedly knew what happened. But that didn't explain where I was. If I asked . . .

("Where" is a relative term. The most reasonable explanation from your perspective is that you are just outside the portal, the gate to our reality, a conversion point. The ident you used brought you here.)

Well! There *are* gates to heaven, after all. I guess they could be construed as golden and/or pearly, if you thought heaven was beyond.

(You are correct in your assumption. It is all from within the observer.)

The percept finally came out. The communication was so natural and so rapid that I had missed it completely. There I was, casually talking—correction: communicating with this wonderfully glowing being just as I would a new friend. He/It was answering my questions before I asked them, so I must be using NVC better than I realized—no point in holding back any part of me, even if I wanted to. Whatever I was, It was reading every thought I had anyway. I opened wide, all of what I was.

(That is not necessary, Mister Monroe.)

And I immediately knew why. It/THEY had been a part of the process. My concept of an external intelligent energy source, helping, navigating, doing the driving, was accurate.

(With your present need for individuation, yes.)

The question arose automatically: How long had this been going on? I had become aware of it only recently, and had traced it back to the beginning of my OOB activity, but how about before then? Have they always been . . .

(You will become aware of such reality at an appropriate point.)

All I could be sure of was my own direct experience, but they must communicate with other people . . .

(With very many by different methods, very few as we are functioning at this point.)

I knew that was the best I would get, but I wondered about the It/ THEY.

(We are many, and you have known many of us.)

So THEY would be correct . . . I hoped they didn't mind the INSPECS label. Now, it seemed inadequate.

(It will serve nicely at this point, as well as any other.)

I wondered if THEY were the same as those we had met in the lab with the various Explorers . . .

(In some instances, but not all.)

So many questions, and now was my big opportunity . . .

(There will be others.)

The first question, the first, what should be the first? . . . Are THEY God or . . . ?

(We are created and we create, just as you. If God and creator are identical, then you are God to that which you create.)

I couldn't help the next one, even if it killed me. I had to know. Did THEY . . . ?

(It will not kill, as you put it, nor will it harm you. You are prepared for an answer by your very presence here, your curiosity, as you call it. The essence that is you and others in the human process was not our creation. As we, you exist before time-space human earth pattern, just as you do at

this point. The in-human experience is merely an addition to what you are. However, it is an important addition.)

I tried to sort out what was so important in being human that it would . . .

(How do you state it? A drop of water in an ocean cannot understand the seas or the wave that casts it up on a sandy beach.)

Wait a minute! That came out very human. Maybe THEY are only superhuman graduates, after all.

(Some of us have passed through the in-human. I was selected because I am one of those few.)

Few . . . I wonder how many are few. Five, ten, a thousand . . .

(It is difficult to assess due to the melding. More than the current in-physical human population, perhaps one hundred times as many.)

That would imply THEY have been involved since the very beginning of human life.

(That is correct. Before that, we are, just as you.)

And if several hundred billion are just a few, that must mean the total of THEM must be big numbers . . .

(We do not count the parts of the whole. It is not necessary.)

If there are that many parts of the whole, then there must be other important ways to learn, other non-earth human systems . . .

(No other precisely as you have found in-human physical earth. There are many other consciousness growth centers or schools, as you call them, throughout what you know as the physical universe.)

I could bet that they participate in all of them. They would have to if . . .

(A very safe bet, Mister Monroe.)

This was becoming an event not anything like what I expected. I was rapidly losing my sense of awe. It was replaced with a great feeling of warmth, of understanding, much on the order of old deep friendships, yet filled with intense respect, not the usual pattern of expected angels, if that is what THEY were.

(We can quickly grow some wings if you wish.)

No, no, please, no wings. No halos either, although I got the clear percept, staring at my INSPEC—friend? . . .

(At least that, for now.)

I could understand how humans with limited but definite momentary superconscious vision could add a halo to make the human-formed INSPEC stand out as different. A brightly radiant form? How often in human history has such perception taken place? Miracle workers, saints, local medicine men, and last-timers on their final run, no doubt.

(No doubt at all.)

I wanted to be very careful about this, that I had at least a faint comprehension, that I got it as specifically and accurately as I possibly could. They, INSPECS, were in existence before humans ever came into being, several million years ago at the minimum.

(By your time measurement, that is correct. As were you and all other energies that are now or have been in-human, if you use this perspective.)

Could that infer we as humans, the nonphysical energy part of us, actually are INSPECS and we don't know it?

(As we understand it, you are created by the same source.)

But we humans are not the same.

(It is difficult to express in your terms. Consider the structure of physical matter as various forms. Moving inward, you have named subconstructs as atoms. These in turn have many organizations of particles that result in distinctive patterns. Your scientists have begun to understand the energy relationship of these particles. They have begun to perceive the spinning of the particle itself. It is the creative force that produces such spinning which we have in common.)

Which could mean vast differences if I work outward through the structure from that base. Differences so profound there could be no point of reconciliation, even similarity.

(You are presuming a complexity which in our reality is very direct and simple. It is the distortion of time-space illusion that causes this in your consciousness.)

I would have to try again. There must be some ongoing relationship between such INSPECS and humans, else why would they bother with us? For some reason, they need us, we need them, they have been involved with human existence since we began. I'm drawing a blank.

(All of your percepts are correct within certain limits.)

I began to receive a discomforting signal to take care of something back there . . . Back where? Where? The signal, annoying, persisted, and I tried to ignore it. What I was doing was much too important to be interrupted. I wanted to concentrate on my next thought-question, but the signal got in the way. I turned to dismiss it, and realized it was a need to return to my physical body . . . Of course, my physical body! I had to go back, but I didn't want to, the chance might never come again . . .

(We can meet often at this point. We understand your need. A stronger ident homing signal will be provided that you can do so.)

The radiation was warm, understanding friendship and much more, and I gratefully responded, and reached for the ident of my physical body and stretched. The feeling of movement back seemed short, and I automatically slipped into the second, then into the physical. By habit, I looked at the clock. 2:23 A.M. Only six minutes? By comparison, the problem that called me back was frustratingly minuscule. My thoughts were filled with the dazzling import of those six minutes as I got out of bed and went to the bathroom to empty my bladder.

I slept very little, if at all, the rest of the night.

During the next several weeks, the press of daily physical activity plus the eagerness and excitement in my anticipation kept me from another meeting. I had difficulty in getting into the required pre-sleep. However carefully I approached the OOB release point after I did get relaxed, I couldn't get into the OOB state. After repeated effort, I did no more than fall asleep. I realized I was forcing it too strongly, but it was hard to control. Finally, I gave up trying for the moment—and it happened easily.

Time: 4:45 A.M. . . . awake and rested, although far past my usual cycle, I went into the unhook rollout, and moved easily into the second body state . . . moving out of the second was easy, and I reached for an ident to home in to . . . It was there! I held back my excitement, stayed calm . . . reached and stretched, following the signal. The feeling of movement was short and quick and I stopped. Before me was the shining form. Several others were behind it. Trying to remain calm and casual, I focused on the radiation that had been so distressing before. Now it was very tolerable—or I was getting used to it.

(A little of both, Mister Monroe. We did modify it somewhat for you.)

I had gone over many times how I would resume our communication, the questions I would ask, the order of priority in case the pattern was going to be broken off again suddenly. And the first one, the first one . . .

(Your interest lay in our relationship with those in human experience prior to your departure to . . .)

To go to the bathroom! What an incongruity! Well, this time I made absolutely sure it wouldn't happen, no coffee, very little liquids . . .

(Cause and effect, in which you place such great belief.)

Belief relief! That's a good one, I'll have to remember it. But the other ones behind my friend, I don't remember their . . .

(As you have noted, there are others of us also here at this point. They have been present throughout our meeting. It is your ability to perceive that has changed. They are, how do you call it? . . . interested . . . "curious" is a better definition, which you understand very well.)

I'm sure I'll need all the help I can get. Here I am, consulting with a being or beings whose penetration into human life activity has been interpreted to be God, gods, angels, the devil . . .

(It was not our intent. Certain . . . adjustments had to be made.)

Now it is UFOs and flying saucers, which is more in keeping with current cultural concepts.

(You would have lost that bet, Mister Monroe. Such are manifestations of another pattern, of which you will soon become aware.)

I'd better let that one stay where it is and stick to the main point. Why adjustments, whatever that means?

(Because free will is such a vital part of the human learning experience, deviations from the design are frequent and predicted, as you would express it. Such adjustments are no more than . . . the exact term is not there . . . fine-tuning, yes. Fine-tuning.)

I got a percept of an immense machine . . . infinitely complex and complicated . . . with INSPECS climbing all over it, in and out of it, turning a knob here, a valve there, taking off a filter and cleaning it, matching waveforms on an oscilloscope, checking materials-input flow . . !. Flow! That was it! Their concern was the flow of energy through the human experience. The idea of a machine wiped away completely and there was the physical earth with the human energy rings encircling it, dreamlike in its quality . . .

(Your last percept indicates good progress.)

But if they created the process in the first place, they should have been aware that it would need . . . maintenance, modification.

(We did not create time-space as you know it, nor the physical earth, nor the human process, nor the energy flow itself. That is not our department, as you put it. Our concern is the output and the . . . quality of such. To this end, we adjust the internal flow as needed.)

I would have to let that one pass by, too. Try to keep from any deviation . . .

(You will learn of the basic or original design.)

The greatest of virtues, patience . . .

(You are intended to walk before you fly, as you put it. Those who fly first must reach back and remember they have already learned to walk. This was necessary for you.)

Now came the first of the high hard ones. Why me? Why did I learn to fly first?

(You had the latent capability to perform an important function of a very minor nature at this point in the development of human consciousness.)

What possible capability could that be! What function! It must be so minor I can't perceive it.

(You need but examine yourself, as you and only you know what you are. As to function, you are performing it very well, as expected.)

With a little help now and then, I hope, whatever the function is . . . Can't pull it all together instantly, have to sort it out . . . even to the beginning of my flying. Did they help on that one?

(You were given some assistance. One facet of your capability was the actual instigator. It should be obvious to you. It directs your actions so frequently you have become conscious of it.)

The percept flared instantly. I always felt the trait was of dubious quality. It always created more problems than solutions. Curiosity.

(That is correct.)

And the old saying, curiosity killed . . .

(A different species. It may kill cats on occasion. You are alive in many forms.)

Now, if I could just get a percept on this function business, I might be able to perform more efficiently.

(We will attempt to bring you into an awareness of the totality of which your function is but a part, in other meetings. Until that is accomplished,

*you are unable to obtain a clear percept or any rote you receive will distort
the function you are performing.)*

I held on to the promise of that statement, feeling very humble and
inadequate . . . and astounded that I remained as calm as I had in the
face of the encounter that was taking place . . . the effrontery of my
probing, the extent of my ignorance . . . Their radiant response to these
flickers of thought was so profound that I nearly broke down and lost
control, no patronizing, no compassion, no feeling of superiority . . . but
beyond friendship, beyond brotherhood, beyond father-mother-parent, beyond endearment, beyond words . . . If they had told me they were my
God-creator, I would have settled for that.

(But we are not, Mister Monroe.)

They even knew how to pull me together, the Mister Monroe stuff. If I
had been physical, I would have laughed uproariously in relief. Or: Thank
you, I needed that!

(We have another name for you. We can use that if you wish.)

I was happy to leave it the way it was, for the moment. There was
nothing formal or reserved the way they used their ident for me. But I
wondered how it started.

*(One of us began to use it in a meeting in your work area . . . yes,
laboratory. Thereafter we applied this ident to you among all of us.)*

I knew instantly which one, and it came as no surprise. I wished that
they would give him my greetings.

(We have done so.)

But the problem, the basic question still remains unanswered. If I don't
know where I'm going, what I am supposed to do, I might go in the wrong
direction again. I know I already have done this several times . . .

*(We will help you become much more aware very soon in terms of your
time. There is a facet of your particular process that must be accomplished
first. It is all coming together rapidly. The time, as you put it, is growing
short.)*

With their perspective of time, that could mean a million years. By that
time, I'll be long gone, and humans, too.

*(We refer to the span within your present physical life. So that your
awareness can be accelerated, we recommend that you use only the ident
homing signal, as you describe it, that we provide. If it is not there, you may*

*draw the inference that you need to focus on your physical manifestation
until the point that it is present.)*

In other words, if it comes, play time is over, now back to work.

*(There are certain patterns you must undergo before you proceed. We will
be with you through them, but not in your physical consciousness. We have
prepared an exercise for you that may help you through such experiences.
Do you wish to use it?)*

I had a percept of the kind of exercise, but not its content, and knew
that it would be rough. If THEY say it will help, of course I wish it.

(Turn inward and close tightly.)

CLICK!

I am flying a single-engine Navion over a large city. Bill is in the seat
beside me. We are about two thousand feet up, and we are just below the
overcast. Turbulence is minor. Gauges look good. It's a borrowed aircraft.
I need to keep an appointment in the city below.

Bill leans and yells in my ear, *(You're going to have to land now if you
want to be on time!)*

I look around. *(I don't see the airport.)*

(Never mind the airport.) Bill points downward. *(You have to land now.
Down there!)*

I nod, nose the Navion down, throttle back, low pitch, gear down, three
in the green, gentle spiral, trying to decide where to set it down . . . the
street, full of cars . . . there's a wide, flat roof, I turn to look at Bill for
approval, but he's gone! Gone! I look back quickly, I'm below one thousand, airspeed seventy, 500 down. Have to decide fast, opt for the roof, at
least if I get it stopped I won't kill anybody else, while in the street . . .
line up the roof, full flaps, nose over steeply . . . drop her in right on the
edge of the roof . . . stall warning yelling its head off . . . chop throttle, switches off . . . let her drop out, drop out . . . she's down, brakes,
stand on them . . . other edge coming up fast, now slow, she's going to
make it, she's down and stopped! I sigh and stop shaking. It's hot and I
open the canopy and climb down to the roof. I stand there looking at the
Navion, it's all in one piece, not a scratch. All I have to do is find the
stairway down and I'll be on time for my appointment. But how will I get

the Navion back to its owner! It will never be able to take off a 200-foot roof. Have to remove the wings, lower it to the street by a crane, what a stupid decision, why did I have to . . .

CLICK!

RESET.

CLICK!

. . . the street or the roof . . . the street, cars will see me coming in and clear a path down the middle . . . full flaps . . . nose down . . . watch that taller building . . . that's it right over the street, straight down the middle . . . watch for turbulence, crosswinds at the corner . . . flare out, hold her off . . . get out of the way, get out of the way, can't you see me! . . . stall warning yelling . . . she's quitting on me, too quick . . . flash of light, heat, terrible heat.

CLICK!

RESET.

CLICK!

. . . I am flying a single-engine Navion over a large city. Bill is in the seat beside me. We are about two thousand feet up, and we are just below the overcast. Turbulence is minor. Gauges look good. It's a borrowed aircraft. I need to keep an appointment in the city below.

Bill leans and yells in my ear, *(You're going to have to land now if you want to be on time.)*

I look around. *(I don't see the airport.)*

(Never mind the airport.) Bill points downward. *(You have to land now. Down there!)*

(Not this kid!), I yell back. *(The appointment will have to wait. If it costs me the deal, so be it. Now, where's the airport?)*

CLICK!

RESET.

CLICK!

. . . It's a borrowed aircraft. I need to keep an appointment in the city below.

Bill leans and yells in my ear, *(You're going to have to land now if you want to be on time!)*

I look around. *(I don't see the airport!)*

(Never mind the airport.) Bill points downward. *(You have to land now. Down there!)*

I laugh, swing the yoke over in front of Bill, clip the parachute harness across my chest. Then I unsnap my seat belt, open the canopy.

(You fly it home,) I yell as I jump far enough to clear the tail assembly, pull the D ring, feel the jerk of the chute opening, and start to float down.

CLICK!

RESET.

CLICK!

(. . . Thanks for the offer of a loan of your Navion, but that's playing it too tight, couldn't possibly make it on time, so I called and put off the appointment . . .)

CLICK!

The haze was very thick and Bill was beside me. He was rolling lightly. *(It took you long enough!)*

I blanked, then rolled with him. *(You certainly weren't any help!)*

He smoothed. *(Use it in good health.)*

I spun a little. *(Where's, uh . . .)*

(I got the assignment. You better go back now. You have many things to put together.)

I plied. *(I guess so. See you.)*

I turned, dove inward, ident physical body, and reentered without incident. I sat up in bed, then got up, put on a bathrobe, and went out on the deck. It was a clear night, quiet and warm. I was still unsure as to how or why it happened, but I had no doubt as to the reality of the experience. If I encountered it and knew it, how many more thousands of human beings living right at this time-point on earth also have gone through the same or similar pattern? If they have, to whom would they tell it? And the other training centers on planets circling those billions of stars, tied to us by an intelligent energy field common to all of us. Were they as unaware as we?

I felt very small, looking at the stars—and beyond. But not alone. Never alone.

9.
Rainbow Route

At this point, I began to accept my new role, whatever it was, and no longer pushed hard for further adventures or activities in the other energy systems I knew to exist. I did realize that in my sleep state much was taking place which affected my conscious thought and action. I made no effort to investigate this, believing that it would take care of itself and was supportive of the course I was following. If I had resumed the sleeper's classes, hopefully I was applying what I learned in my daily life.

Spaced through several years of time were periodic meetings–instruction sessions with the INSPEC. I still used this ident because I knew of no other appropriate one that was not tainted with cultural-philosophical connotations. The most recent INSPEC event precipitated the gathering of all of my notes on the interim adventures, and the pieces filled in the mosaic.

The following is no more than a survey of the salient or critical parts of the sequence. In the interests of brevity and a feeling of get-to-the-point-ism, the usual preamble and closure as to going OOB and returning to the physical are omitted except when highly relevant. Each of the following events began at the point in non-time-space near the edge of INSPEC "territory," with at least one of them present.

CLICK!

If I have a desire, curiosity—no, more than curiosity—it would be to know, not believe, but know what is beyond this point . . . where THEY are . . .

(It is a question of remembering. As you are at this point, you cannot— the word?—tolerate a visit among us. We can prepare you for it, if that is your wish. The preparation is not simple.)

When THEY state it's not simple, I knew it was an understatement from my perspective. But it was what I wanted . . . yes!

(We will make the adjustments necessary in your space-time belief. The perception must be yours alone.)

CLICK!

. . . I am playing out in the front yard, riding my tricycle on and off the sidewalk and into the grass . . . the sun has gone out behind a cloud but it hasn't started to rain . . . I think if it gets dark, I can light the candle in my tin-can headlight, but I'll have to go in the kitchen to get some matches . . . when I get bigger, I'm going to have me a blue car that goes AAAAARRRRR, AAAAARRRRR . . . then I'm going to have an airplane, that's what I want most, an airplane, so I can fly up through that dark cloud, up where the sun is shining behind it, then I could go up and dive through the cloud, WHEEEOOO, WHEEEOOO . . . oh shoot, it's starting to rain, I'll have to go in the house, just one more circle in the yard . . . I have my airplane, WHEEEOOO, WHEEEOOO . . . big flash of light . . . white light, lightning! . . . bang! . . . I am off my tricycle . . . in the grass, grass is wet, got to get up and get in the house, get my tricycle on the porch so it won't get wet . . . but I can't move, I can't move, what's the matter? . . . it's dark, I can't see . . . can't feel anything . . . I'm not hurt, I don't hurt anywhere but I can't see, can't get my face out of the grass, got to get up, my bike will get wet and it will rust, got to get it on the porch . . . but I can't move, I can't move! . . . what? . . . what? . . . just beeloon it and I can go the porch, how could I forget *that!* How could I forget to beeloon! What would make me forget something so basic! Yes! Beeloon, can do it without thinking how, anybody can beeloon! And . . . yes! Three-way . . . I could do a three-way and it wouldn't be dark . . . why, any curl can do a three-way without turning, you need to three-way if you want to keep your spiral going, what happened to me that I would forget such a simple thing as *that!* . . . I could pull a skip and . . . skip? Skip! And there's more, it's all coming back, I remember it all and those important fundamentals that I never thought about forgetting because it was impossible, it is as basic as who you are, how is it possible that I forgot

these, and all the rest that I know? I am astounded that I could forget!
. . . forget, forget . . . I'm getting wet, it's raining hard . . . I'm getting muddy . . . that big bang was thunder, hurt my ears, but I can hear,
and I can move . . . I feel but I don't hurt, so I guess I'm all right . . .
got to get my bike up on the porch and get a rag and wipe the water and
mud off . . .

CLICK!

Now I remember! I was very young, playing out in front of the house
before a thunderstorm . . . the lightning hit a power pole near the
street, not me, my father told me . . . the concussion or something
stunned me . . . and he carried me up to the front porch. I was all right
in a few minutes . . . but the rest of it, I had forgotten completely, even
now I just remember the knowing, not the details . . .

*(A glimpse of who you are before you undertake the human experience.
How it took place is not important. Such momentary recall occurs frequently during the physical process but is obscured and discarded amid the
more immediate consistent impact of physical information input. Yet the
event is retained, below the surface of consciousness, and therefore affects
your subsequent action. It is significant that thenceforth you did not fear
lightning and thunder, as you call it, but found pleasure in such manifestation. This is one effect of such pre-human recall brought near your physical
conscious level. Another, more cogent, was the subtle alteration in your
physical life process that led you unknowingly to your present state.)*

I hope that doesn't mean that everyone has to get almost struck by
lightning to begin to wake up. It wouldn't be a very popular method . . .

*(Most such events are so gentle as to remain unnoticed. Yet they are there
if recall is necessary. We have another episode for you, if you desire it.)*

How could I forget these things! . . . Yes, yes.

*(Here is another area of your perception that is a part of the emergence
you have long forgotten. It is completely your own. We do no more than
assist you in your recall.)*

CLICK!

. . . I want to hear the music . . . I want to hear the special music
. . . I know how to make the Victrola play the music because I learned
how, I learned how just from watching, and then she watched me show
her how I could play it, then she said I could play it but I had to be real
careful so I don't break the records . . . so I'm not being bad if I play it
. . . I pull the chair over close to the Victrola so I can stand on it and put
the record in the top . . . I have to lift up the heavy lid, but I do it . . .
I turn the shiny crank in the side, more and more until it won't crank any
more, but I don't crank it after that because it might break the spring
. . . then I open the front doors of the Victrola, and there is my special
music record on the first shelf just where I left it . . . pull the record out
and be real careful to don't break it, and put it up on top. Then I climb up
on the chair. I pull the paper cover off the record and put the record on
the wheel . . . then I put the shiny fat arm part with the sharp needle in
it down real careful on the edge of the black record . . . now everything
is ready . . . I move the little shiny finger and the wheel with the black
record on it starts moving, and I hurry down off the chair to where the
music is . . . the music starts coming out of the Victrola and I feel real
quiet, so I close my eyes . . . it is blank for a long time as I listen to the
music, but then I feel a surge way down at the bottom of me, and it feels
like tingling when my foot goes to sleep, but it doesn't hurt, it feels good,
and with it I hear raining, just like rain on the roof, but it comes and goes
. . . and the music gets so soft I can't hear it anymore . . . then it's
quiet and I can't hear or feel anything . . . there it is again, coming up
from the bottom of me more, the tingle and the rain surge, and it feels
better than anything I ever felt . . . and I wait for it to happen again
. . . here it comes again, stronger and bigger, and it feels so good it starts
to hurt, but I don't mind the hurt because it feels so good . . . then it
fades away again . . . I know it's coming back, and it does . . . much,
much stronger and bigger, up through me, the best and happiest feeling I
could ever have, so happy I want to cry, and the hurt is so strong it's
cutting me right up the middle in two pieces . . . then it goes back
again, down out the bottom of me, and I know that there is nothing,
nothing nicer I will ever feel than what just was, no hurt could hurt more

than what I just felt . . . and I feel it rising again and I don't think I
could stand it if it was any stronger, but there it is getting bigger and
stronger, the good, good, good tingle and the rain roar and the hurt so
hard, coming right up to my head, terrible, terrible sharp hurt . . . this is
so good and so hurting there can't ever be anything that feels so good and
hurts so much, never never . . . then it starts to go away and I know that
I will always remember this bright, bright good and the big, big hurt and
nothing will ever be as good or hurt so much . . . but there it comes
again, no, no! . . . I can't stand it again, I can't, I can't! The good makes
me cry, it's so good, and the hurt makes me cry, it hurts so much, it can't
be more than the one before, it was the biggest there is, it can't be any
bigger, the good and the hurt . . . but it is, and I scream with joy and
pain and I know this is the greatest of all there is, the exquisite joy, beauty,
that transcends any thought or consciousness . . . that the pain is merely
the anguish of physical structure attempting to contain energy beyond the
ability to do so, that one day I will experience it again without the pain
because I will understand better, one day it will take place, the great glory
of . . . I feel hands picking me up and I am crying a little, not too much,
and I open my eyes and raise my head. The music in the Victrola has
stopped and she, my mother, is looking at me and saying something . . .

CLICK!

. . . Yes, yes, I remember what a great privilege I felt it was to have
been given permission to play the Victrola, and I proudly never broke a
single record . . . symphonies, operas my mother liked, plus some saxo-
phone jazz records the college student who roomed upstairs gave me,
which I played when no one was listening but me . . . and I remember
the same sequence when going under anesthesia before surgery, the identical pattern . . .

*(The acceptance of pain as a condition of joy is the symbol of conflict
within physical life existence. The pattern of the present is not consistent
with the promise of the future as you perceive it within time-space illusion.
A conflict of realities, from your aspect.)*

I remember so well . . . if that is the joy, I will take the pain again, if I
can stand it . . .

(It is not necessary. Your present consciousness now has a beginning point of reference. It is possible for you to perceive the destination of the rays of pure energy you have called loosh/love as it penetrates into your earth space in several segments of what you call time. We will assist you in your placement within the event. The delineation, the decision to distinguish must be yours solely. Are you ready to do this?)

I don't know positively what I will be looking for, but I will never forget again. If that is what I seek, I will find it.

CLICK!

The sun is setting and I am sitting alone in the sand outside our tent. The desert is cooling now, and soon it will be dark and it will become very cold. I have built a fire from camel dung so that we will be warm . . . yes, I am Shola, and my woman and our two offspring, a boy and a girl, are in the tent behind me. We are dying. I can see the village in the distance and the cooking fires are glowing in the twilight. We came with goods to trade but they would not let us enter. They cast stones at us to keep us away. We could not go across the desert to another village because we had little water and we are ill. Now after these many days, we have no water and no food. We have survived this far only by eating camel dung, something only a dog would do. Our two camels will live and we will die. They cannot catch the illness, the plague that brings the open sores on our skin which do not heal. I would kill the camels to eat, but they are old friends. We do not eat old friends to continue our own existence. It does not matter now. Food and water will not help. The illness is taking us along the course to death. There is nothing to be done. I do not want to crawl into the tent for fear they are gone, all of my family. I do not want to know I am alone. We have done so many things together, the pains and the joys we have shared . . . the working and being together, my woman and the young ones . . . no illness, no death can remove the bond that grew and blossomed among us . . .

CLICK!

I can still feel the echoes . . . it's a life I don't remember, if I lived it
. . . but the sharing of purpose, of unity required for simple survival . . .
nothing more than that can bring it out . . . the attachment beyond
husband-wife and parenthood . . . that, I remember . . .
*(Beyond physical manifestation, misinterpreted, misunderstood, and
often overlooked, this is a facet of the prime expression, it is part of the
learning process peculiar to the human experience.)*
. . . This is the goal in being human? To learn to do or be this?
*(Indirectly, that is correct. It is but part of a broad spectrum. One goal is
to become the generator and transformer of such radiation. It is important
that you perceive the scope and attunement of the recipient. The being on
the desert was attuned and therefore was only the recipient, but neither
transformer nor generator. The goal is generation and transformation only.
Do you desire this pattern of perception to continue?)*
If I have smoothed enough to do so . . .
(You have.)

CLICK!

We are lying around the protective defense circle of the encampment
. . . it is night. Our bellies are full and our feet hurt from the long march.
The fallen leaves are dry, and make a noise when we roll over. This would
be bad if we were the outer guards, but we need not concern ourselves.
The outer guards will sound the alarm if the enemy attacks by night. My
helmet is close to my left hand, as is my shield. Near my right is my kuri,
whose cold, sharp point and keen cutting edges have become as much a
part of me as the arm that wields it. On one side of me is my friend Cheti,
who snores so loudly in his sleep that he awakens the birds. On the other
is my friend Dorn, who sleeps like death itself, yet is instantly awake at the
whisper of his name . . . we are but a part of this great host who will, in
the morrow, meet and cut our enemy to pieces. We are three. I recall well
the day we met on the training ground, many seasons past. Cheti, tall and
stumbling, from the high mountains. Dorn, solid as stone, from the great
forest, and I, from the flat midlands. Not a word was spoken among us for

days as we learned the killing arts. How that changed with our first battle, that moment when we formed a triangle back to back, surrounded by twice our number of yellow-hairs! Cheti, calling out such stupid curses at the yellow-hairs that even Dorn was laughing, and laughing gave us fresh energy, so we fought our way out of the trap . . . then we were three. Through the battles, the wounds, many of both, too many from such as me to count . . . we are three. They are more to me than my brother, whose face and voice I cannot now bring to mind . . . more than any woman I have ever known, yet not the same . . . and the man in that village who asked me about my sons and daughters, and I replied I don't know my sons and daughters if I have any, they go with a woman and I have no woman, I am of the legion, so I have no woman or sons and daughters to whom I am bonded . . . just those women I can bed down when we capture a town . . . there was one, she was warm and did not scream but whispered in my ear and I was as gentle as I could be with her, I might have bonded with her . . . but we are three and it is different. I would lay down my life for Cheti or Dorn, that they would live instead of me, and I know without their speaking that it is the same with them . . . I do not understand why this is so, but they are me, I am them, and we are three . . .

CLICK!

. . . Yes, I have the percept three, three hundred, three thousand, three million, three billion, it is the same . . . common effort, willingly or not, long association, repeated shared experience . . . this special bonding beyond self can take place without awareness of what it is or its importance . . . often it can't be called love because local custom would then attach a physical sexual inference to it, male or female . . . thus it is covered over and sublimated . . .

(You are learning rapidly. Your human perspective serves you well. Do you wish to move to the next point in your survey?)

I understand what is happening, the human portion . . . if it is still of that value, I am fine . . .

(We will continue, then.)

CLICK!

I am standing in front of a stone building with a tall spire. Wide steps lead down to the cobbled square, and the square is filled with a flow of people, horse-drawn wagons and carts, and the dusty smell of human sweat, animals, cooking, and excrement from all manner of living things. I am a Priest, and although it is hot, I am wearing my brown-hooded robe that reaches to my ankles. It is cool inside the church, yet I am loath to enter. The Ritual is about to begin, and I must attend and participate as part of the duties of my calling. I am sick in heart at what I must do. It is so different from that which I dreamed those years ago, my life in the service of the Almighty. The glory of the tolling bell in the spire, the rich voices of the choir echoing throughout the arched roof in Holy Harmony, the majesty and mystery of the Processional, the bowed heads of the reverent, kneeling people, they are the same. These are the parts that brought open the rising need in me, and I answered. Now they are the same, but I am not. Where is the need? It has left, unfulfilled. Where is the mystery? It has vanished under the weight of the unfolding years and that which my eyes have seen and my ears have heard . . . the bell begins its tolling, and that is the signal that I must enter and join the others. I turn and pass through the smaller door to one side and into the Great Hall. I move slowly down the main aisle to the waiting group at the Altar. The High Priest stands in front of the Altar, wearing his white robe with the golden braided symbols across the front. On his head is the Holy Crescent Moon. Behind him are the Seven Keepers of the Realm, each holding a staff atop which is one of the Seven Sacred Stars lighted by a flaming taper. As I approach the Altar, I know what I will see upon it, and I am correct. A young girl attired in a flowing gown of bright red to hide the blood is lying upon its stone surface. Silken cords are attached to her ankles and wrists, then to large rings on the sides of the Altar. I know well the Ritual although I have never performed it. Once I have completed the Sacred Act in the name of the Almighty, I will transcend that status of a lowly Priest and become an Alternate Keeper of the Realm. When one of the Seven dies and departs for Chimmon, the Land of Eternal Joy and the Throne of the Almighty, I will become one of the Seven. When the High Priest departs, one of the Seven will take his place and assume his Power and Glory as the direct Communicant with the Almighty. Perhaps I may be that one . . . but now I am not sure. The dream of years past flickers within me and it is not this. If I do not perform the Ritual, I will be stripped of my robe, cast out into the street, where I will be stoned to death by the populace. I move next to the Altar, and the High Priest hands me the Ritual blade, a slender, sharply pointed knife with a carved silver handle. I have been instructed carefully where to insert the Ritual knife at various spots on her body so as to keep from causing her death immediately, but to engender exquisite ecstasy within her while the High Priest and the Seven give their Blessings . . . I raise the blade for the first swift insertion . . . and I stop, arm upraised. I am looking into the eyes of the girl. In them are fear, puzzlement, resignation . . . and beyond these, a knowing, a depth that carries me past the distortion of my dream and into what I was sure was always there . . . I lower my arm, turn, and drop the silver knife, only a knife, in front of the fat man who calls himself a High Priest . . . I cannot do it, no, I *will* not do it . . . and I am free! . . . and a bright white ray comes through the ceiling of the Great Hall and centers on me, flashes through my entire being, the silver knife melts to a mound of metal, the silk cords drop from the girl, and the Altar trembles and splits open as the girl rises from it and stands . . . the men in the robes kneel transfixed, their eyes staring into blindness at the brilliant white ray . . .

CLICK!

. . . Yes! . . . and somewhere in man's history, a legend is born . . . the event is only a dim memory to me, if even that . . . but the emotion I felt, I experienced . . . that is clear and strong . . .

(What you call emotion is essential to the basic learning process. It is a specific observable result of exposure to the loosh/love radiation. Therefore, it is the driving force, the creative energy which motivates human thought and action. Without it you would remain as animals.)

But animals show something, it is very close to what I know of as emotion . . .

(What you perceive is a reflection, a response to human radiation of such

*energy, which has been self-generated or transformed by the human. We
will demonstrate this for you if you wish.)*

That would be great, I would enjoy that very much . . .

(We shall see, as you put it.)

CLICK!

. . . Our little dog with the funny name, Steamboat, he is walking with
me along the road in early morning . . . he is such a friend . . . his
bright gladness at seeing me . . . he actually grins when he wants you to
know what a nice guy he is, just because that's what his human close-by
god does . . . his seeming need to be with you, enthusiastically do what
you want to do . . . just a word from me, and he comes running to me
joyfully . . . it's much more than the fact that I feed him, most of what
we do has no relationship to such . . . we have a bond that might be
called friendship, he's succeeded in making friends with his god, doing
things together, that's pretty good stuff, making friends with your god
. . . now he's been diverted into the wooded bank alongside the road,
eagerly seeking an ever-elusive rabbit, but after a short search, he will
return, bounding across the road to walk just in front of me again . . .
then I hear a vehicle, a car or truck, approaching behind the blind curve
and I call to Steamboat to come to me, stand and be where it is safe . . .
it is a truck, and it comes around the curve quickly, too quickly . . . just
ten feet away from passing me, Steamboat leaps down the bank from the
woods and directly under the wheel of the truck . . . there is a rending
scream as the wheel grinds over the lower half of his body, flattening it
completely . . . the truck moves away and stops, and the driver gets
down from his cab, sadly apologetic . . . I get to where Steamboat is still
trying to come to me, his front legs trying to drag the crushed half across
the road to where I am . . . I sit down on the road in front of him, and
he stops trying to move as I reach out and rub his head, tears forming in
my eyes as minuscule evidence of the deep sorrow within me . . .
through my hand, I feel the heavy tremors moving through his body from
the pain, and he licks my hand and looks up at me, asking, hoping his god
will take care of the pain . . . I look at his body, the damage so irrepara-
ble there is no hope . . . he licks my hand again . . . and I accept the

responsibility . . . I get up and move to the waiting truck driver, removing my pullover shirt as I go . . . a look passes between us and he knows that I do not blame him, that he should harbor no guilt . . . sadness shared, yes . . . but no guilt . . . I was responsible, not he . . . I move to the truck, remove the cap from the gas tank, and push the shirt into the tank, soaking it with fluid . . . then I remove the dripping cloth and move back to Steamboat, who has watched me expectantly, too weak to do more . . . I sit down, and his head drops into my lap, eyes looking up to me, asking, asking . . . gently, I move the cloth over his nose with one hand and place the other on his head . . . his eyes look at me deeply and the tremors in his neck subside slowly and are gone . . . I see and know the closeness we share is eternal, and he somehow knows this, too . . . the conscious awareness in his eyes dims and is gone . . . and they are only eyes with my tears in them . . .

CLICK!

. . . But that didn't happen! Steamboat is alive! He is back where I came from, somewhere near my physical body . . .

(That is correct. The event occurred earlier in this physical life, a different animal, dog as you call them. You identified it as your present attachment. In the earlier episode, uncontrolled emotion overwhelmed you and you were helpless. You did nothing to fulfill your responsibility. In your present state of awareness, you exercised the control that is so important, which displays your growing ability even in our synthesized demonstration. The paradox attached to such vital energy, emotion as you call it, is the opportunity for growth it provides and the simultaneous possibility of stasis and retrogression. Control and direction thereof thus becomes a prime purpose in the evolving human experience. Understanding and comprehension is the resultant and flows without effort. At no point is the goal to repress or suppress such energy. Instead, it is enhanced when directed and focused into the channels for which it was originally designed. What you call your curiosity is perhaps the most unrecognized and undistorted form of such energy. Yet it is the underlying force that produces what humans consider their most outstanding historical achievement.)

. . . This is coming too high and fast, I'll have to put this particular rote away and run it later . . .

(Do you wish to participate in your final demonstration?)

. . . As it is the last one, I assume it is the most stringent . . . if I could just remember it is only a demonstration, as THEY call it, seems more like a test . . . but if I could remember, it wouldn't be a test . . . there's something similar here to all of human physical experience, this not-remembering business and the importance of it . . . the final test, yes! . . .

CLICK!

. . . I am sitting alone in the house and it is quiet . . . even our furry friends seem subdued . . . both dog and cat lie half asleep in the front hall, facing the door, waiting . . . the sun has just set and twilight is moving in . . . soon it will be dark, and I can sit in the dark and see the house full of things, things she selected and liked so much, things she made do with until there was better, things her grandmother used, things she placed or hung in each room or put in closets and drawers where only she knew where they were . . . all an expression of her and bearing her reflection . . . but she is gone, she is not here as I expected . . . I don't need light to see the things to remind me she was here . . . the sight of them does not disturb me and I would not change or remove them because they have her strong imprint . . . I can find her in the dark or in the light, it makes no difference . . . she taught me so much without knowing she did . . . the very female human response to moments large and little, uncovered, uncolored except by her own perspective . . . all of these she shared with me . . . so that I lead not one but three lives, hers, mine, and our meld . . . and she helped me learn release from one of the most difficult of all, that physical sexual drive is not the fundamental of this energy I don't know what else to call but love, but one of the most common inducements to kindle the process . . . once the full flame is created, the inducement is not even the fuel that feeds it, but instead a multileveled minor physical note in an infinite chord . . . I now understand a mother and physical motherhood without being one . . . why a woman likes to be a wife and the admix of the idealistic and the realistic

that foments such liking . . . a lifetime of human gamut in a fraction
thereof . . . the whither thou goest, I go, is more than true, yet a release
from this part is needed and accepted . . . she goes with me and I go
with her . . . aloneness is an illusion . . . here or there, the flame is
eternal and we carry within us that which we have received and created
. . . she is returning now as I knew she would . . . and we will not
exchange goodbyes or forwarding addresses, our idents in one another are
indelible . . . just one final moment in this point of time . . .

CLICK!

*(Your perception was quite clear, Ashaneen. The demonstration was suc-
cessful.)*
   . . . It was very strange . . . one of us had released from the physical,
and I thought she was the one . . . then as it developed, I momentarily
became unsure, it could have been I . . . and I finally realized it didn't
make any difference which of us . . . the result was the same . . . now,
of course, I don't have to ask if it has happened, but I know it will one day
in our serial time . . .
   *(That is correct. The result is the same. We now believe you are prepared
to visit us, where we are as you call it, if that is still your desire. It will not
be a demonstration, but our reality. However, we will guide you and return
you to this point. It is important that you understand that such a visit,
momentary as it may seem, can produce within you changes that are irrevocable.)*
   . . . I do desire it, and I accept the responsibility for any changes that
may occur in me.
   (Open widely. Have fun, as you put it.)

CLICK!

*(I am in a bright white tunnel and moving rapidly. No, it is not a tunnel,
but a tube, a transparent, radiating tube. I am bathed in the radiation which
courses through all of me, and the intensity and recognition of it envelop
my consciousness and I laugh with great joy. Something has changed, because the last time, they had to shield me from the random vibration of it.*

Now, I can tolerate it easily, the actual energy itself. The radiation flow is two-directional in the tube. The flow moving past me in the direction from which I came is smooth, even, and undiluted. The flow that I am is moving in the opposite direction and appears much different. It is organized in a more complex form. It is the same as the wave moving past me, but it contains a multitude of small waves impressed upon the basic. I am both the basic and the small waveforms, moving back to the source. The movement is steady and unhurried, impelled by a desire I know but cannot express. I vibrate with joyous ecstasy just by the knowing.

(The tube seems to become larger as another joins it from one side, and another waveform melds into me and we become one. I recognize the other immediately, as it does me, and there is the great excitement of reunion, this other I and I. How could I have forgotten this! We move along together, happily exploring the adventures, experience, and knowledge of the other. The tube widens again, and another I joins us, and the process repeats itself. Our waveforms are remarkably identical and our pattern grows stronger as they move in phase. There are variegations in each which, when combined with another related anomaly, create a new and important modification of the total that we are.

(The tube expands again and I am no longer concerned with its walls as still another I enters the waveform flow. This is particularly exciting, as it is the first I perceive as returning from a completely nonhuman sojourn. Yet the intermesh was near-perfect and we became so much more. Now we know that, somewhere, a consciously controlled physical tail, much like a monkey's, is useful in ways far more than balance and acting as a third hand for holding things. It can be a very efficient means of communication far beyond a super sign language just as eloquent as the spoken word.

(Steadily and surely, one I after another joins us. With each, we become more aware and remember more of the total. How many does not seem important. Our knowledge and ability is so great that we do not bother to contemplate it. It is not important. We are one.

(With this, we divert from the underlying waveform and move away from it. We watch motionless in unified respect as the action of it continues away from us into an infinity. We also perceive easily the smooth originating wave coming from such infinity and dissolving into the pattern from whence we came.

(Flowing through all of us is a coherent energy that is our creation, that displays immensely the reality of the whole as far greater than the sum of the parts. Our ability and knowledge seem without limit, yet we know at this point such is valid only within the energy systems of our experience. We can create time as we wish or the need arises, reshaping and modifying within the percept itself. We can create matter from other energy patterns, or change the structure thereof to any degree desired, including reversion to original form. We can create, enhance, alter, modulate, or eradicate any percept within the energy fields of our experience. We can transform any such energy fields one into another or others except for that which we are. We cannot create or comprehend our prime energy until we are complete.

(We can create physical patterns such as your sun and solar system, yet we do not. It has been done. We can adjust the environs of your planet Earth, yet we do not. It is not our design. We can and do monitor, supplement, and enhance the flow of the human learning experience, as well as other learning experiences of similar content throughout time-space. This we perform continuously at all levels of human awareness so as to prepare properly those entraining units of our prime energy for the entry and meld into the totality that we are becoming. It is the essence of our growth to do so. Such assistance and preparation is forthcoming from us only by request from one or more levels of consciousness within the entraining unit. Thereafter, a bonding is in effect through which many forms of communication pass between us until the ultimate transformation occurs.

(We know who we are, and one I laughs and we all laugh at the name this I had given us. We are an INSPEC, *just one. There are many others around us.)*

(You are still incomplete. There are parts of you yet to be transformed, including that visiting portion so filled with curiosity. Each of us is incomplete. That is why we remain at this point, to reach back and gather additional and remaining parts of us until we are complete.)

(Our curiosity desires the effect of completion.)

(We move into the creative return flow again, the waveform that brought you here. When we do so, we leave this reality.)

(Can this be demonstrated?)

(It is not possible. It is not within our knowledge to do so. When you have transformed and melded totally into your whole, you will comprehend.

That is why this point came into being. It is not possible to continue until completion.)

(Continue to what destination?)

(We believe it to be the source of the radiation, the creative emission and return. Communication is closed with those who have continued. The desire to continue occurs upon completion. It is more than your curiosity, as you call it, and difficult to transmit in a form we can understand. There have been attempts by those completed who are to continue, without success.)

(The ultimate home?)

(A good beginning concept. A design which unfolds as perception grows. It is necessary now that you terminate your visit and return.)

(We will be with you, our curious I.) Return where! *(Your physical environs)* . . . Where is that! . . . *(In-human, your physical body)* . . . Oh, yes, I had forgotten . . . Do I have to go back? *(Reach for us and we will be with you in many ways. You have much to do. Go get them, tiger!)*

(And a rote, as you call it, to play with.)

CLICK!

The return to the physical was near-instantaneous, my face and eyes were wet. I sat up in the chair and remembered. I reached for the yellow pad and pen, to get the rote into words immediately. I knew I had changed. For the rest of my physical life, I would remember. But this would never change:

For those who would die, there is life.
For those who would dream, there is reality.
For those who would hope, there is knowledge.
For those who would grow, there is eternity.

10.
Newfound Friend

QUICK CUES

Blank: Don't understand
CLICK!: Change consciousness
Closed: Tune down or out
Curl: Organized energy
Dulled: Lost interest
Flickered: Uncertain
Ident: Name/address
Lighted: Idea, happy
M-Band: Thought spectrum
M-Band noise: Uncontrolled
  thought

Open: Receptive
Percept: Insight, intuition
Plied: The way it is
Rolled: Laughed
Rote: Thought bundle
Run the rote: Get details
Smooth: Get it together
TSI: Physical universe
Turn in: Consider
Vibrate: Show emotion

Real time: 3:05 A.M. . . . body rested, relaxed . . . sense of warmth
. . . gentle insistent signal, familiar . . . good enough, deep breath, ex-
hale, detach, unhook, down and out, then up . . . free of physical, up
slightly, roll, out of second body, leave it in parking orbit . . . now totally
free . . . begin to home on INSPEC ident . . . out of phase with physical, moving . . . usual easy process . . . rapidly through dense inner
rings . . . ought to be some way to wake all of them up at once, that
would be something . . . not even a good simulation of hell . . . if you
won't accept you're no longer physical, you're dead, dead, dead and still
alive . . . now more out of phase, into the center major ring, used to call
it Locale II . . . what an understatement, misnomer . . . at least
they've begun to understand and remember . . . dim forms, light up if
you focus on them . . . this is where my father was, Dr. Gordon, Agnew
. . . more out of phase in spiral, nearly past the last outer ring . . .
  Somebody grabbed me! Keep calm, cool, it can be worked out, hap-

pened before but not this far on the edge, no need to abort and go back to
physical . . . don't move, no movement . . . it's releasing me, easing
back . . . totally different energy pattern, but intelligent, yes, must operate on M Band . . . certainly not . . .

(Didn't intend to push you.) The form was open, vibrating. *(Your ident
almost exactly like somebody else, my percept was he was you.)*

I smoothed. *(That's O.K.)*

The form blanked. *(O.K.?)*

(There's no problem.)

The homing signal was still there, and I turned to move, when suddenly
the signal cut off. It was gone. This had rarely happened before, usually
there was a reason. Almost instantly I got the percept. I turned back to
the form. It was dulled and closed, receding.

(Hey, wait a minute.)

The form opened slightly, blanked, motionless.

(Can I help you?)

The form vibrated slightly. *(You're human, or used to be?)*

I smoothed. *(Well, yes, but not exactly the way you . . .)*

*(If you're human, you can't help, because you're addicted like all the
rest.)* The form vibrated heavily. *(Takes more smarts than any human or
anyone who's ever been human. They're contaminated.)*

I had a percept of great loneliness. *(Try me.)*

Small bits of rote drifted out of the form as it flickered half open. They
had a different pattern and I couldn't put them together, too strange. The
first response in me was wariness, then I remembered what I had learned.

I opened wide. *(Try me.)*

The form flickered, then lighted somewhat. *(Well, I have this friend,
and . . . there's a problem. Here—)*

A large bulky rote rolled out of the form and straight to me. I gathered
it in carefully, and certainly with caution. There are some rotes one would
just as soon do without. This one also had an alien ident. Slowly, I opened
it.

CLICK!

The Tour Guide checked to be sure all members of the group were present. It had been an extensive cruise and this was the last point of interest.

(May I have your attention, please? If you're ready, we will make one more entry into TSI. I'm sure you will find it most interesting.)

Ident AA dulled. *(I think I'll sit this one out.)*

Ident BB turned to his friend. *(Aw, come on, AA, it's only one more, then we'll be heading for home.)*

(One more, one more.) AA vibrated. *(The exciting and amazing time-space illusion! TSI! Experience it in person! I could have stayed home and got the same effect. See one, you've seen them all.)*

(This is supposed to be different.) BB lighted.

(Sure, sure.)

(. . . And I am instructed to caution you to be prepared for extreme discordant M Band radiation), the Tour Guide continued. *(So I suggest that you shield yourselves accordingly.)*

AA turned to BB, half closed. *(Same old buildup. Probably more rock, more dust, more craters.)*

(. . . Stay on the perimeter, keep a safe distance. You'll find enough to keep your attention at that point. Is everyone ready?)

(You coming, AA?) BB queried his friend unnecessarily. He knew him very well.

AA turned. *(Oh, all right. You'll never let me forget it if I don't.)*

CLICK!

The blue-green ball rushed closer until it blotted out all other perception. Then they were hovering just above tall rectangular masses set in orderly rows. In deep furrows between the masses, objects of various shapes were moving slowly. Noise level in the M Band was near unbearable.

BB focused down with disgust. *(What a mess!)*

The Tour Guide began his carefully prepared spiel. *(This is one of the major matter artifacts created by the dominant species, ident man or human if you remember your briefing. Local ident is New York.)*

BB dulled. *(Doesn't look very new to me.)*

(The human species are the ones that appear more vertical than horizontal,) the Tour Guide continued. *(The various colors you perceive are emanating from an artificially produced covering used principally for decorative reasons. The larger mobiles are in fact artificial physical bodies which are often temporarily inhabited by the dominant species, and use chemical reaction of an explosive force to provide operating energy.)*

(You were right, AA. It's not worth the effort and that M Band noise is turning me inside out.) BB scanned his friend. *(Getting to you, too, huh?)*

AA focused raptly at the activity around them. *(Fascinating, absolutely fascinating.)*

BB turned to him quickly. *(What?)*

(The incredible power. I've never felt anything like it.)

(What power?)

(Don't you feel it? So many different kinds, all randomly mixed together.)

(Where, what are you talking about?)

AA reached out, stretching. *(Coming from them. The M Band energy patterns, thousands upon thousands, some hard, some soft, and the texture, the texture!)*

BB blanked. *(You all right?)*

AA opened wide. *(I'm fine. In fact, I'm wonderful. I never knew anything like this existed.)*

BB suddenly lighted. *(It's the M Band noise! You've sopped up too much of . . .)*

(Not noise, BB,) AA cut in. *(Certainly not noise. It's an amazing mixture of resonance, beat frequencies, standing waves, incalculable patterns.)*

(Noise. That's what the prep briefing called it. That's what everybody calls it. Plain old M Band noise . . .)

AA turned inward. *(I wonder what it's really like.)*

(What do you mean, really like! It's all over the place. All primitive life sets have it. M Band noise is M Band noise. Come on, let's get out of here, the cruise group is leaving.)

AA still remained inward. *(To be there, to be in it must be spectacular.)*

(I wouldn't know and I don't want to know.) BB grunted.

(I've heard it can be done, BB.)

(Rumor, street talk.) BB vibrated impatiently. *(Come on, AA, we'll lose the group if we don't . . . AA! Where you going? AA!)*

CLICK!

AA entered the Intermediate Area, BB in his wake. He stopped in front of a tall burly form that seemed to resemble the humans he had just seen. *(I'm looking for the way to get to be human.)*

(This is ident Entry Station,) the form responded curiously.

(I want to do it.) AA vibrated. *(I mean, I want to be human.)*

The form blanked. *(You want to what?)*

(I want to find out what it's like to be human, the way they are over down there.) AA pointed. *(I don't mean permanently, just long enough to get the feel of it.)*

(Just long enough to get the feel of it.) The form turned inward, then out. *(Why would you want to do a thing like that!)*

(Well, uh . . .) AA tried to sort out the pattern in himself. *(We're on this TSI cruise, and when we went in over ident New York, I suddenly . . . it was very strange, I wanted, uh, wanted . . .)*

(The M Band noise,) BB put in. *(It got to him.)*

The form nodded. *(Yea, the M Band noise. It'll do it if you're not careful.)*

(I don't know how to express it.) AA flickered, attempting to coalesce. *(It seems very important that I try it.)*

(Just for kicks, a high, something new,) the form suggested.

(Well, yes.) AA lighted. *(At least at first. Now, something more than that, I've never felt an interest this strongly.)*

(Where you from?) The form smoothed politely.

(KT-95), BB came in quickly. *(I know it's a hefty skip from here, but we had got a lot of rote about time-space and the TSI. No one had ever visited it from KT-95, so when this cruise was offered . . . well, you know,)* he added, *(it can get kind of boring. You do something to break the monotony.)*

(I can do it?) There was slight anxiety in AA's query. *(Rumor rote back*

home had wild stories about it, but even in the cruise rote, there's no official mention, so . . .)

The form sighed. *(All you have to do is ask. That's all, ask.)*

AA lighted with unusual brilliance. *(That's just great! I certainly . . .)*

(AA, hold it, hold it,) BB cut in. *(You absolutely sure you know what you're doing? I remember some wild rote about parts of it that weren't quite so . . .)*

(I wouldn't miss it for the KT-95!) AA turned to the form. *(I ask. Now what do I do?)*

(Recorded: You asked.) The form turned and pointed. *(Just go that way and then turn right. Right, not left.)*

(Got it, down that way, turn right!)

(Not left.)

(Right.) AA leaned to BB. *(Stick around till I get back, old buddy. Will I have some stuff to feed you! Real rote!)*

(Yeah,) BB grunted sourly. *(The cruise group has already left. That means we'll have to pull skip all the way home. Just don't make it forever.)*

AA lighted brightly and faded into the haze. BB stirred uncomfortably.

(You can wait here if you wish,) the form offered.

(Thanks, I'd appreciate it.) BB dulled, then in passing, *(What's to the left?)*

The form spoke absently. *(Oh, left. That's another department. Don't want to get them mixed up.)*

(Oh, yeah.) Then perceiving the form more clearly: *(Hey, who are you?)*

(Ident Entry Director. ED. Just call me Ed.)

(Ed.) BB opened curiously. *(You ever been through this human stuff?)*

Ed was silent for a moment, pulling in old rote. *(Yeh. Coupla times.)*

BB drifted aimlessly about the station. The Entry Director hovered motionless, inward and closed.

BB ventured, *(Busy operation you got here.)*

Ed opened slightly. *(Yeh.)*

(Must be a lot more organization than appears on the surface, huh?)

(Yeh.)

(You must have picked up some pretty strong rote being here.)

(Yeh.)

BB reached out without much result. *(Haze is strange stuff. Cuts your percept back to near nothing.)*

(Yeh.)

(Effect of the TSI, huh?)

(Yeh.)

BB rotated slightly, then did a few quick spirals. *(We got a game back home where we do as many as a hundred of these one after the other. Pretty neat, huh?)*

(Yeh.)

(But you got to keep in practice if you're going to stay in the game.)

(Yeh.)

BB did several more tight spirals, then relaxed. *(My friend will come back to the Station when he's through, won't he? Back here?)*

(Yeh.)

(Good, I can't miss him.)

(Yeh.)

BB blanked. *(I can?)*

Ed popped open. *(What?)*

(My friend has to come back here to the Station, doesn't he?)

Ed closed. *(Hey.)*

(I don't want to . . .)

Ed opened, vibrated heavily. *(Hasn't your friend returned?)*

(No, not yet. My percept was . . .)

Ed accelerated. *(I should have seen he was the type. Come on, kid.)*

BB vibrated. *(What's up?)*

Ed faded. *(Your friend's got a problem. Come on.)*

He turned and receded rapidly. BB followed, flickering wildly. Ed turned left and waited for BB to join him. *(There. This is our big department. No rote. The real thing. Get your own rote.)*

BB blanked, flickered, wide open. Before him was the blue-green planet, indistinct. Around the planet were rings of haze, gigantic thick rings, of indeterminate number. Demarcation between them was vague as wisps and tendrils reached from one to the other. Except the ring nearly touching the planet itself. It appeared isolated. With this exception, the others were flowing rapidly through portals in the Entry Station. No, there was one more, on the outer edge. It came nowhere near the Station. Very thin.

BB focused intently. The M Band noise was horrendous, yet not nearly so bad as it had been down on the planet itself. Moreover, as he singled out each band, his percept showed that the noise was greatest in the bands close to the planet. The farther away from the planet, the less noise. Very little was present in the outermost band. Little, but still there. BB blanked further. M Band doesn't decline with "distance" or dimension; even the cruise TSI briefing rote had the whole story. If there was no M Band, no life. M Band with noise, still primitive, no percept, no communication worthwhile bothering with. M Band, no noise, great place to visit and gather rote, locals know where they are and what they are, easy but limited communication—but not a place to stay. Nothing. No decline of intensity, no mix, noise and M signals. It either was or was not. Must be an effect of the Intermediate Area.

BB focused tightly on a band in the center, nearly fell backward with shock, closed quickly and turned in. The band was composed of forms, living forms! He opened slightly, focused, one band after another. They were all the same. Thousands—no, millions, maybe billions of living forms. BB closed and blanked completely, totally dulled.

(Your friend's in there.) Ed came in both gentle and sad.

BB opened slightly, still dulled. *(What?)*

(When he hadn't appeared at the Station, that's the only answer.)

BB still blanked. *(He's in there?)*

(Yep.)

(What is it! There wasn't anything like that during the TSI cruise, when we stopped over . . .)

(You were focused totally on physical matter. Cruise groups pop through the Intermediate Area, like avoiding a bump in the road.)

BB blanked again. *(Road? Bump?)*

(Forget it, not important, human terms.)

(But all those living forms . . .)

(Repeaters.)

(Repeat, repeat what?)

(They want to go through another experience as human.)

BB closed tightly. Rote was coming so fast it was almost beyond control. Incredible that anyone would want to go the route a second time. The first looked bad enough. Yet the percept was obvious. Knowing AA, it was obvious. He opened. The shock wore off.

(Can we find him among all those others?)

Ed smoothed. *(Good possibility. Most First-Timers hitting the repeat route usually end up in the outer band. Can you spot him? I mean, could you get a percept on him easily?)*

BB lighted. *(AA? Got more rote on him than anyone in KT-95. No problem.)*

(Then you may well be able to turn him out of it.) Ed swung around. *(We better get over to the processing gate.)*

CLICK!

BB scanned intently the multitude of animate forms passing under him. AA and his impulses. Never did know when to stop if he got interested. But these thousands upon thousands . . . He turned to Ed. *(Must be big stuff to make all of these want to do it again.)*

(We warn them. It's all in the pre-brief rote.)

(Must not be too clear.)

(Here, run it yourself. I'll scan for your friend.) Ed tossed a bulky rote at BB. He ran it quickly. Halfway through, there it was: . . . remain fully established freedom of will and consciousness at the entry point. This is guaranteed and is required by the compressed learning system in use. . . . A final note of caution: Certain aspects of the human experience may produce specific and general effects which may be harmful and unless controlled bring about habituation, with undesirable consequences. Your imprint affirms your understanding of this section.

BB opened. *(That doesn't seem very clear to me.)*

Ed vibrated. *(That's as far as we can go. Otherwise it would ruin the learning process.)*

(What aspects, what effects?)

(It would ruin the . . .)

(Come on, Ed, it won't ruin me. I'm not going to be a human. I'll never touch the stuff.)

Ed dulled, then closed. *(Get your own rote.)*

BB vibrated. *(All right, I will!)*

Both remained half closed, focusing on the stream of forms passing through the portal. Each appeared different from the others, yet possessed some human trait, however small. In a few, BB's percept found a bright and intense radiation that made him confused and uncomfortable. It was his reaction to one of these that forced him open and smooth. *(Ed, you're just doing your job, and I'm pushed about my friend AA.)*

Ed opened. *(Yeh, I got the percept. Problem is, events like this don't happen often enough and I lose the rote.)*

BB blanked. *(Lose the rote! Impossible. Nobody does that.)*

Ed indicated the massive bands of living forms. *(They did, all of em.)* *(Lose what rote?)*

(Who they were. They forgot who they were.)

BB blanked and closed. No way anything like that could happen. It was vital to very existence. No one could be and do if you—how did Ed put it? —forgot who you were. Yet the percept from Ed was clear.

(Now, this outer ring,) Ed was continuing. *(They are made of three types. One is the First-Timer, such as your friend. He just started to forget. Then there's the Old-Timers, who mostly remember after going the route, uh, repeating being human a number of times. These hang around and do what they can to help. They don't remember quite enough to go home.)*

BB lighted with a great percept. (You're *an* Old-Timer, Ed.)

(Yeh. Anyway, you keep a scan for your friend. I'll run the rest of the rote for you, piece by piece.)

BB opened wide, sweeping focus on the stream of living forms. So many of them. Still, should be no problem finding AA. Wonder how Ed happened to get assigned to his job. Why him?

(Wasn't assigned to it. There was a hole where the ED used to be on my time around, so I just jumped into it.) Ed was smooth and warming. *(Then there's this third type, the Last-Timers. They make one more recycle, uh, one more physical life as a human, and then they're gone.)*

BB turned. *(Where do they go?)*

Ed rolled. *(I dunno. Home, I guess. They never show up back here. And, oh yeh. There's this other type we call the Seekers. Don't get many of them, slippery as eels. Unstable, flick in and out.)*

BB blanked. *(As what? Slippery?)*

(Never mind. Human stuff again.)

(Give me a rote and I'll run it.)

(Not worth it. Now, these Seekers, they're different. Near as I get it, they come poking around here and they still got a physical human body over there, alive and kicking.)

(I didn't have a percept you can do that. I thought everybody came back only after the physical body fell apart, wasn't operational.)

(That's what I had until I got here as ED. Then I began to spot them.)

BB was lighting strongly, *(There he is!)*

Ed was gentle, warm. *(Go get him, tiger!)*

BB blanked. *(Tiger?)*

(Go on!)

BB moved swiftly into the massive, flowing ring of vibrating forms. The M Band noise was nowhere near what he had expected, almost within tolerable levels. As he slipped through the edges of various radiation groups, he was quick to percept that many if not most had signal strength equal to if not greater than his own. But it was different. It was not just the noise, it was something different. Nothing like it in KT-95. Also, the forms obviously were aware of his passing . . . short flashes of curiosity, retracting to let him through, pleasant acknowledgment. Nothing like the pattern he expected from his earlier percept.

Then he was with AA. *(Some adventure, huh?)*

AA blanked, then lighted brightly. *(BB! What are you doing here!)*

(Came to get you, what else?)

(You didn't have to do that.)

(Well, you were supposed to return to the Station. What happened?)

AA flickered. *(I was?)*

(You sure were.)

AA flickered more deeply. *(I don't know. It seemed, uh, easier this way.)*

BB smoothed. *(How was it?)*

AA lighted. *(Astounding! I don't have anything to express it.)*

(Start at the beginning.)

AA rolled brightly, and hit BB with a solid rote before he could close.

CLICK!

AA moved among a large mass of beings of all shapes, sizes, and patterns. The crowd was so large that he could not easily perceive the other side, where it ended. None remotely resembled anyone he had known back home in KT-95. He dulled, disappointed. Were they *all* waiting to be human?

(All of 'em.)

AA spun his focus. A short, human-looking form leaned behind him.

(What?)

The form vibrated. *(Ident Routine Entry Dispatcher. RED. . . . Just call me Red.)*

(Red?)

(Not to be confused with . . . sorry, wrong department. You must have joined in when I was busy. Need to get a rote on you so I can try to place you properly. Roll it.)

AA opened and gave him the best rote he knew.

Red lightened. *(KT-95, hey? Well, that's a new one for me. Haven't had a KT-95 since I've been here.)*

(I don't believe there ever has been,) AA replied. *(No records, only side rote which doesn't mean anything.)*

(And you came in on a TSI cruise, and you want to get the feel of it, huh? M Band noise got to you, did it?)

(Well, no.) AA flickered. *(Not exactly, you see, I . . .)*

(Not important,) Red cut in. *(Just makes it easier to get you processed, as a matter of rote. Now, first, which is your preference, male or female? I can't guarantee your choice, but I like to match it up with the entry point when I can.)*

AA blanked.

Red vibrated. *(Oh, you don't know the difference. You are out of the woods.)*

AA blanked further.

(That's a human expression which . . . not important. I guess male or female doesn't make any difference in the long run, especially with you. So, any particular entry point desired?)

AA hesitated, then decided. *(New York?)*

(That's all? Just New York?)

AA lighted.

(New York it is, any available entry point. Either sex. Well, AA, that should make it fairly rapid for you. Of course, it would be immediate if you select Bombay, Calcutta, or a dozen or so other points. Lot of action there.)

AA dimmed and dulled. *(New York. At least I have rote. I've been there.)*

Red turned in and closed. *(Yeah, sure. Sure, you do.)* Then he lighted briskly. *(Take this pre-brief rote and focus through it all the way. You'll need to imprint your agreement and acceptance when you pass through the entry point. Ready?)*

Red lobbed the rote and AA fielded it easily. AA probed the outer edges, then opened. *(Hey, this is complicated! You mean I have to sort through all this stuff?)*

Red was closed. *(Yep.)*

(Why can't I simply go and be human? Why do I need all of this?)

Red went auto-rote. *(When in Rome . . .)*

(I'm not going to Rome, I'm going to New York.)

Red smoothed. *(Oh, uh, yes, well, it applies anywhere. It's the rules, kid. I don't make them. Now find yourself a quiet spot and run through it. I'll have you a general point, New York, in no time at all.)*

AA blanked. *(No time at all! I thought time was . . .)*

(Just run the rote, kid, run the rote.) Red unfocused and was gone.

AA leaned back and let the rote open:

Agreement and Understanding.

Human sojourn only.

First Entry Status (FES).

· Organized as a school for compressed learning. Successful graduates achieve tangent rating.

· For duration of human sojourn, firm agreement that time-space exists, has reality. Agreement of reality of particular entry point and its environs (matter, planet Earth, sun, solar system, galaxy, physical universe), of time indicated at entry point, of physical animate form designated as well as those of others, of past events recorded as human history, of complete biostructure as encountered.

· In order for learning system to function at maximum efficiency, temporary blanking of pre-entry activity is essential. Agreement to perform such blanking is hereby authorized.

· Anything to the contrary contained herein notwithstanding, all FES remain fully established in freedom of will and consciousness at the entry point. This is guaranteed and is required by the compressed learning system in use.

· A final note of caution: Certain aspects of the human experience may produce specific and general effects which may be harmful and un . . .

AA released the rote. Scare tactics. Need them to hold back the mobs that would swamp the place with applications. Well, it won't work this time. Can't get rid of old AA that easily.

He refocused on a nearby form. *(How's it going?)*

The form opened, then closed. *(Who wants to know?)*

(Ident AA from KT-95.) AA reached out, then withdrew quickly. *(Where you from?)*

(You don't want to know.)

(Sure, I do. Your first time, too, I guess. How, I mean what made up your mind to give it a try?)

The form dulled. *(I didn't.)*

AA blanked. *(Sure, you did.)*

(You don't understand. Here.) The form rolled a rote to AA, who picked it up gingerly.

The first layer was enough. Assigned HSTI–FES for retraining, don't come back until you're better. Details enclosed in . . . The rote grew too hot to handle. AA hurriedly rolled it back to the form, and the form reluctantly retrieved it. AA unfocused and turned away.

(A big event, isn't it!) A tall thin form emerged from the haze.

AA opened uncertainly. *(Yes, it is.)*

(After all the planning and preparation, I'm finally going to do it. Finally!)

AA blanked. *(Do what?)*

(Conduct my experiment!) The form lighted strongly. *(I've studied every aspect of the human system. Incredible how much effort it took. Only state of consciousness I can test it in. It could change everything!)*

(Really!) AA focused more carefully. *(What does it do?)*

The form closed. *(Sorry, might spoil the experiment if you had rote. Maybe we'll meet as humans. See you on earth!)*

The form faded, and as AA turned, he became aware of a tiny form huddled to one side. He focused. *(Hi.)*

The little one was wide open. *(Hi.)*

(Going to make the big leap, huh?)

(Yes . . . I hope so.)

AA blanked. *(You hope so! Don't you know?)*

The tiny form vibrated. *(I mean, it came so quickly, it was such a surprise. I'm still not used to it. It's really going to happen, after I tried so long.)*

(You mean they wouldn't accept you, wouldn't let you in before this?)

(I guess not. I wanted to, but it never happened . . . before now.)

AA opened more. *(I thought anyone could just walk up and get in, if there were entry points available.)*

(Oh, no. You have to qualify.)

AA stored and scanned. *(Ident?)*

The form flickered. *(What?)*

(Ident.)

(I don't know what you mean.)

AA blanked heavily, then focused softly. *(If you'll run me your rote, I'll try to help. I understand, the excitement and all the anticipation.)*

The form flickered more. *(What's a rote?)*

(Rote is information you have that . . .) AA cut off, then reset. *(Where did you come from?)*

The form lighted. *(Over there. It was easy.)*

AA followed the focus. *(You mean the planet where humans are?)*

(Yes, yes.)

AA vibrated. *(Then it's not your first time. You've been human? There must be some mix-up!)*

(No, no, there isn't.) The form grew brighter. *(I've never been a human, but I've studied them a long time. I've lived with them, they've fed and loved me . . . and now I . . . I'm going to be a human. They tell me I've earned, I mean learned it. And I'm going to be a good one. I know it!)*

AA gave warm support and swung away, then unfocused. He turned in deeply for some obscure rote that would explain it. Nothing.

The haze was gathering into clusters, some large, some small. Each had wispy spirals of rote that brushed through AA as he wandered among the clusters. In KT-95, that was usually a sign of poor discipline or at least leaky valves. Here, it didn't seem to matter. Further, there didn't appear to be any lessening of the crowd. If anything, there were more. This Intermediate Area was deceptive, AA decided. Has a tendency to distort. What he pulled rote as hundreds must be thousands—all jammed into the Entry Station. And that little mixed-up one. Couldn't rote anything, not even where she really came from. She? What's she?

Suddenly, an unusually large spiral reached out from a cluster and yanked AA inward. *(I need your help, I need your help!)*

AA disengaged just as he was about to fall into the opening cluster. *(What's the problem?)*

The form swept aside the last vestiges of haze. *(What are your plans after you enter?)*

AA opened slightly. *(Why, uh . . . to experience being human.)*

The form vibrated. *(No more than that?)*

AA rolled. *(I'm sure that'll be enough for me.)*

(Do you know what they're going through over there?)

(Well, I . . .)

(Untold suffering. Millions upon millions of them, lying and deceiving one another, violating every known law, including the ones they thought up themselves, illusion upon illusion, digging deeper and deeper patterns . . . It's horrible.)

AA began closing. *(I'm sure it's not as bad as you . . .)*

The form vibrated more heavily. *(It's worse. I've been studying and observing them for centuries. Worse!)*

AA blanked. *(Centuries?)*

(Now it's getting to a crisis situation, and somebody has to do something and nobody is, so I'm going to!)

AA smoothed. *(Do what?)*

(I'm going in there and change it all. I need your help to do it. I need yours and everyone else's I can get. Here, here's what we're going to do.)

The form threw a heavy rote at AA, who held on to it with some difficulty. The first layers not only shocked but astounded him. How could rote ever get so tangled and distorted? He turned in and closed. How to release gracefully? The solution came easily.

He tossed the rote back to the heavily vibrating form. *(Sorry, I can't help you. I would like to, but I can't.)*

The form vibrated. *(You can't! Why not?)*

AA smoothed even further. *(Didn't you go through your pre-briefing?)*

(Yes, of course I did.)

(The part about blanking all previous rote? If they do that, I won't have a rote of meeting you, anything about what happened here.)

The form dulled, then closed. The haze settled again in a cluster around him. AA unfocused and continued his float among the clusters. He became cautious and avoided all the larger exuding rote tendrils. The others he moved through, picking up fragments of events, patterns, states of awareness totally inconsistent with those of home, KT-95.

Suddenly, a quick sharp percept drove into him. *(Ident AA! Ident AA! Ready for you at entry portal!)*

AA spun quickly, focused on the signal, following it through the haze and clusters. Looming through the haze was a large vertical slot, vibrating with a vivid energy AA had never before perceived. Red and Ed were waiting beside it.

Red vibrated. *(All set and ready, ident AA.)*

AA flickered. *(What do I do?)*

Ed leaned in. *(Imprint here, acceptance and agreement terms contained in pre-briefing.)*

Two carefully controlled spirals emanated from Ed. AA sent his own spiral in between them, then activated. Ed pulled back the spirals and leaned back.

AA vibrated very highly. *(What do I do now!)*

Red hit it hard and high. *(Jump! Jump through the slot!)*

AA jumped.

CLICK!

Intense contraction, constricting . . . overwhelming signal input of unknown types . . . coming from parts of him he never knew existed . . . trapped, can't get out of here . . . nothing works . . . can't get

anything to work right . . . not what I expected . . . it hurts . . .
what's hurt? . . . what who expected? . . . turn down the signals, turn
them down, they're tearing me up . . . too many of them, too strong
. . . help, somebody help me! . . . trapped . . . please, please, somebody help me, get me out of this thing . . . this is the last of AA, screaming, screaming . . .

A new baby cried lustily in the bedroom of a New York tenement. Both
mother and midwife grinned happily, sweat running down their faces.

CLICK!

BB flickered. *(Is that all?)*
AA lighted. *(That's only the beginning.)*
BB turned in. *(Some beginning. You weren't very happy.)*
*(Oh, after a bit I learned, did I learn! There's so much I can't get it all
into one rote . . . What's wrong?)*
(I'm getting a wild percept.)
AA blanked. *(From where?)*
BB smoothed. *(Never mind, let's get on home. We're going to have to
pull at least four skips to get back to KT-95 on our own. So . . .)*
(Home! I can't go back yet.) AA vibrated rapidly.
(Sure, you can.)
(No!)
(Now, come on, AA . . .)
(I had only forty-five years. Then I got sick. I didn't get to finish!)
BB smoothed. *(Whatever forty-five years is, that's enough. Come on.)*
(I can't!) AA flickered violently. *(I have only half the experience!)*
BB blanked. *(Half?)*
(I was a male this last time! Now I'm going to be female!)
BB blanked completely. *(Male? Female?)*
*(That's right, old buddy, and they're as different as, as . . . That's what
I'm going to find out.)*
BB hardened. *(You're in trouble.)*
(Trouble? What trouble?)
(You got the pre-brief rote.)
AA flickered. *(Of course I got it.)*

(Then you know what's happening.)

AA blanked. *(No, what?)*

BB smoothed. *(AA, you're getting hooked, you're . . .)*

The huge portal loomed ahead, a myriad of vibrations. AA was fading into the massive portal along with the others.

BB vibrated as strongly as he could. *(AA, no . . . wait!)*

With a strange wave, AA disappeared. BB dulled and closed, and moved away from the stream.

(Sorry, kid.) Ed came in gently. *(I didn't think you had a chance of a snowball in hell, but I had to let you try.)*

BB dulled. *(What happens now?)*

(If he/she follows the pattern, he/she will get more and more and more involved in the human experience, dropping down a ring each time until he/she is at the bottom.)

BB flickered, still dulled. *(Then what?)*

Ed opened wide, carefully. *(They stay at the bottom and don't come back, or they begin to work their way back up. Most of 'em stay at the bottom.)*

BB dulled.

(Go on home, kid. Back to KT-95.)

BB dulled and closed completely.

He slowly drifted out of the Station, flickering dimly. The haze was less, filled with occasional clean signals which did not have his ident; thus they did not attract or penetrate and so were ignored.

Then a faint percept did penetrate. BB popped open. A form was moving past him. He vibrated, stretched.

(AA! You did it! You broke out. How . . .)

The form stopped, motionless. BB pulled back quickly. It was not AA.

CLICK!

BB opened wide. *(I got my idents crossed. That's why I hooked you.)*

I folded the rote back in slowly. *(You have a problem, all right.)*

Then there was a strong signal to return to the physical. I had a problem, too. I had the percept of BB in total blank and I must have receded almost instantaneously. I picked up the second, went back to physical, took a deep breath, and looked for the problem.

The dog was barking again to go outdoors.

11.
Rescue Mission

Time: 3:55 A.M. . . . full physical wakefulness, usual conditions plus the not so usual recognition of INSPEC homing signal presence in this consciousness . . . followed normal rollout . . . signal was strong . . . moved upward and out, through rings, past Intermediate Area—stopped. *Was* stopped. Feeling of tiredness, hadn't been aware of it before. No more homing signal, I was there. So were THEY. Great sense of warmth, companionship, more.

(Mister Monroe.)

When it came in that way, I was never sure it meant work or play, if I could possibly tell the difference—or something else. It was something else.

(Some alignment and balance are needed.)

I opened wide.

CLICK!

A huge white dog three times the size of our beloved Steamboat—what a name for such a nice little dog—has him by the neck, the massive jaws firmly shaking Steamboat back and forth in quick jerks, Steamboat's body already swinging limply.

(No, no!) I can't let it happen! Is it really Steamboat? It is! He's dead, Steamboat's dead! I'll kill that big son of a bitch, he'll never . . .

CLICK!

RESET.

A huge white dog three times the size of Steamboat has him by the neck in massive jaws that are swinging Steamboat from side to side, Steamboat hanging limply.

(Steamboat's dead! Dead! What a tragedy! I'll miss him, I'll miss him. Let go, big dog, so I can take what's left and . . .)

CLICK!

RESET.

A big white dog much larger than Steamboat has him by the neck and is swinging Steamboat back and forth, Steamboat hanging relaxed, eyes closed.

(Well, little fellow, if that's the way it is, thanks for staying around as long as you did. We had fun together. You gave me a lot of rote that always will be a part of me . . .)

Still in the jaws of the big white dog, Steamboat raises his head slightly, opens one eye, winks at me, and grins.

CLICK!

I was calm and relaxed. The tiredness was gone. More than that. My energy was strong and clear. *(Thank you.)*

(Happy to be of service.)

I rolled. *(Dogs will bark.)*

(Now you can move to your friend from the other system. He is lost. He will need your help.)

I flickered. *(I'm not sure I can help him.)*

(We will be with you. It is important that you help him.)

I blanked. *(Important?)*

(Important to you. We interrupted your signal so that you would perceive him. As you put it—time will tell.)

I smoothed. *(Shall I make him aware of you?)*

(Not yet. Take this—how do you say it?—rote with you and perhaps he can use it. We call it the BHP-1.)

I opened wide. *(Sure.)*

The rote came to me and I tucked it away. I turned and focused ident BB KT-95. There was some motion and there he was, still in the haze. And flickering.

BB vibrated. *(What happened! You faded out, then back. Somebody pull a skip on you?)*

I blanked. *(Pull a skip? What's that?)*

(Well, when we want to move from one pattern to another, we, uh, you know, pull a skip. If you catch somebody wide open, and you get in just right, you can pull their skip and they're off somewhere before they get a percept.)

I flickered. *(Why would you want to do that?)*

BB rolled. *(It's a game, fun!)*

I rolled with him. *(At least you're open now.)*

(So somebody did pull a skip on you!)

I smoothed. *(No, not exactly.)*

(Even a skip leaves a trace. No one I ever met could do what you just did. Neat. What was it?)

I flickered. *(Well, I, uh, I had to go take care of something.)*

BB blanked. *(Take care of what?)*

I smoothed. *(My body.)*

(What body?)

I rolled. *(My physical body, of course. My physical human body. I still got one and it still works.)*

BB closed tightly, then opened slowly. *(How, I mean, why, uh, what . . .)*

(I don't know. It simply happened. I'm trying to find out the why.)

BB turned inward, then opened. *(You're one of those slippery eels!)*

I blanked, turned in. Part of Ed's rote came up. I rolled strongly. *(I guess that's as good a percept as any.)*

BB rolled, then hardened. *(What about AA? Any more I can do?)*

(We'll try. You need a better percept of what's taking place.)

BB turned inward. *(I don't want any real rote of the stuff. I sure don't want to get addicted.)*

I smoothed. *(This rote won't do that. As a matter of fact, it'll begin an inoculation process.)*

BB blanked. *(Inoculation . . .)*

(You can close better. I'll push it slowly. Catch the edge. If you don't like it, don't take it in.)

BB opened slowly. I eased the BHP-1 rote THEY gave me at him and it spun slowly as he cautiously touched it. There was a long moment when everything stopped, no movement, no response. Then there was a click and the entire rote slipped into him.

BB turned inward and closed. I waited patiently. We were drifting slowly out where the haze was thinner. I had only two idents at this point. I either go back to where THEY were or back to the physical. I had nothing on AA, only part of BB's rote, which wasn't enough. It had to come from BB. I couldn't find AA for him.

BB turned inward, opened. *(It's all new to me. Real rote, huh?)*

(Yep.)

(And that's what AA got himself into?)

(Yep.)

BB blanked. *(This isn't your rote. Where'd you get it?)*

I smoothed. *(Coupla friends of mine. Most of the rote was new to me, too. At least I didn't have a percept like that.)*

BB hardened. *(Well now, I got a hook on what's going on. A little complicated, but once AA has a percept of this quality, he'll jump right out of the mess.)*

I flickered. *(Uh . . . there's a little more to it, you see.)*

(What do we do next?)

(I guess catch your friend when he comes out again. If you can find him.)

BB smoothed. *(I could find AA inside a black hole. Are you coming?)*

BB had the percept that I would follow and he was right. He dove into the haze and I was behind him, homing on his ident. We did a complete run through the ring where he had found AA previously. Not a flick. I was fairly sure that would be the case, which was bad news. Bad news for BB. There was always a chance that if AA was in the outer ring BB might convince him to pull out and let go. Bad news for AA? No one could make that percept, not even AA at this point.

In my few stopovers in the outer ring, it had always been utterly fascinating—the mix. Particularly the Last-Timers, those who knowingly were about to make their final recycle. They gave off a radiation that was unforgettable—tremendous vital power that seemed totally under control. Within that strength were all of the values and ideals that humans hold important—not in time-space context, not in external control systems that demanded performance in a specific manner, but something entirely apart, something learned from being human. Most important, all under control, all a cooperating, melding part of the whole. They were completely open. You could get a percept easily of the crucible of human experience that formulated such greatness—if you could handle it. I tried once and it was too much. I returned to the physical and was wistful for days thereafter. The key was that they got that way from being human. They were not that way at First Entry.

But now it was different. Their radiation had a familiar resonance, and I wondered why this was so. In the last time around, they evidently close it all down. Part of the vitality seeps through; it really all can't be closed off. Yet they don't select history-making roles in that final run—they've probably performed such previously. They are inconspicuous, the mail clerk, the plain dirt farmer, the sailor, the bookkeeper, not gathered as a group, but quietly spotted here and there in both time and place.

If you ask their destination upon completion, most simply respond with a gentle warmth: Home. The percept comes out that way, but there's an overtone, a flavor, a nuance that is only slightly familiar.

Yes, BB, there *is* much beyond the cold data. You pay the price and you get what you pay for. One way or another. How do you tell a fish what it's like on dry land? You don't try.

(Hey, I thought you were with me,) BB cut in.

I opened. *(I am, I am.)*

(He's not in this mob. Now what?)

I smoothed. *(Down another ring.)*

I turned, with BB close to me, and we moved quickly into the lower haze. It had a different texture. Actually, from this point, it was difficult to determine where one ring began and the other ended. A part of it was familiar to me. I had attended class here for a while.

I hadn't been closed enough. *(What kind of class?)* BB cut in.

(Where you learn how to help those who are still in a physical body.)

BB rolled. *(AA wouldn't be here. Nobody could teach him anything!)*

I turned inward. *(If you say so.)*

BB darted outward and down and I joined his descent. . . . We began to enter the familiar cleared areas in the haze. Houses, parks, fields of growing plants, woods, forests, large buildings, rows of churches, it went on endlessly. Humanoid forms were busily occupying themselves in numerous earth-type activities.

BB flickered. *(Haze is sure thick. What are they doing?)*

I smoothed. *(What they want to do.)*

(Just milling around like that?)

(Some are fixing up their houses. Some are working. Let's see. Others are playing golf. There is a poker game going on in that building over there . . .)

BB cut in. *(What building over where? I don't get a percept on anything!)*

I flickered. *(No building?)*

(Nope.)

(No houses, streets, trees, fields . . .)

(Just human-type forms moving around. And a lot of haze.)

I blanked and turned inward. The constructs—all of them were not physical matter, so BB ought to be able to get percept of them in some manner. The temporaries knew they were nonphysical; they built all of this to be in familiar surroundings while they thought over and prepared for their next human cycle, built it out of . . . I lighted. BB had no ident on such, thus he couldn't pull a percept. It was strictly humans only.

I smoothed. *(I don't think your friend is here. Let's move on.)*

BB flickered. *(Down?)*

(Yep.)

I swung over and did a flamboyant half-roll and dove through the border haze. You could spend thousands of years in the rings and never explore all aspects of them. Some parts are great, some not so great. I was told that whatever man can think of is somewhere in these rings; thus more is being added constantly as man thinks more. Also I was told some humans do spend thousands of years here, rotating in and out of physical earth life. Could be exciting stuff if you planned and thought it out carefully. But most of them . . .

(I got him, got him!) BB almost blew me away, he was vibrating so hard. *(Where?)*

BB was already spinning away and I was following closely. Curious to finally meet the notorious AA . . . then I nearly rammed BB, he pulled up so suddenly.

BB flickered. *(It's AA, but . . . there's something wrong.)*

I scanned to get a percept on his focus. There was a form, small, low energy base, female, old woman, no, not so old, just . . .

BB vibrated and moved in. *(AA! Hey, old boy, it's me!)*

The form flickered, half open. *(Leave me alone.)*

BB vibrated. *(It's me! BB!)*

The form opened more. *(What?)*

BB reached out. *(BB, that's who, old buddy, come to take you back!)*

The form opened wider, vibrated. *(BB! Where did you come from!)*

BB smoothed. *(Never mind, I'm going to take you back.)*

AA flickered. *(Back? Back where?)*

(Back where you belong.)

AA vibrated. *(Belong? I belong here! BB, I tell you, I'll never be a female again! I was all day hoeing in the fields, got up in that cold stone hut while it was still dark, made the cooking fire, then ground the grain into meal, then cooked food for the children, then he got up and I made his food, then the tax collector came and took three pigs, my three best, then my youngest baby died and I had to bury her longside the other eight, but I kept six of the fourteen alive till the plague got me, and all the time he just was lying around or hunting, or taking a club to me, then him and those other men came in sousing drunk on wine and laid it to me, all of them. That plague was God's will. It took me away from all of that!)*

BB blanked totally, flickering. I started to move in, and suddenly there was a barrier, a force pushing me back. I kept trying, but it wouldn't let me get close to AA. I had never felt anything like it. I finally stayed away.

BB opened carefully. *(AA, I came to help . . .)*

(I don't need help,) AA cut in. *(I know what I'm going to do. I'm going back and I'm going to be a warrior, a big powerful man, and I'm going to spread my seed from one corner of England to another. Old King Henry won't have nuthin' on me, he won't!)*

(AA!) BB vibrated heavily.

AA blanked, then flickered. *(What? Oh, it's you, BB. What do you want?)*

BB smoothed carefully. *(Let's go home.)*

AA flickered. *(Home?)*

(Back to KT-95. How about it?)

AA still flickered. *(KT-95? K-T-9-5. Yeah . . . yeah! What about it, BB?)*

BB smoothed softly. *(We need to leave and go back now. Be with our old friends and buddies, give them some new games, give the big rote you got here, big stuff in KT-95. Let's go.)*

AA flickered. *(Well, BB, you just might . . . you just might . . . No! I can't, I haven't finished here! I'm going to be a big strong warrior. Then I can kill men, kill, lie around, women will get food for me this time, hunt, souse when I want, no babies to carry around . . .)*

BB reached for him, but he faded quickly into the haze. BB started to follow, but I got in his way, and I stayed motionless as he slowly closed and dulled. Various forms moved past us, only one or two showing any curiosity. What small percept I had of AA indicated this would happen; he would drop faster than the typical First Entry. BB would have called it wild rote for sure if I had handed it to him before the fact.

(You're leaking.) BB opened slightly. *(You can't be closed and open at the same time. I got that percept as clear as if you'd thrown it at me.)*

I rolled. *(I'm still learning.)*

(I guess you're right,) BB went on. *(It would have been pure ragged-edged wild rote to me. Smooth, slick handle—anything, AA hitting a high one like that! What got into him?)*

(Being a female, a woman.) I plied carefully. *(Must have lived it three, four hundred years back, uh, past, uh, before now.)*

BB blanked. Serial time was too much for him. I had a percept that was new to me, too. I had always assumed repeaters lived sequential lives relative to time. Either this is not the case or AA is the rare exception.

BB opened slightly. *(That's the way it is being female?)*

I flickered. *(Well, uh . . . that's the way most females lived back then. It's different now . . . I mean, different for some of them.)*

(And how many of you humans are female?)

I flickered again. *(About half, I guess. Ought to be half.)*

BB vibrated. *(Why would anybody want to be a woman!)*

I smoothed. *(There are compensations, balances. Some males suspect women secretly rule the earth.)*

BB focused intently. *(Do they?)*

I turned inward, then rolled. *(I'm male at this point, and I suspect they do.)*

BB turned inward and closed. I was indeed learning from him in an inverted form. Evidently his KT-95 was nothing remotely like being physical and human. Explaining the process even with a cloud of rotes seemed too big to me. Still, there was a sense of warmth, friendliness, even familiarity with BB that didn't fit. I liked him. Nice fellow. Very human in his responses. Maybe the energy base *is* common through all systems, physical or otherwise. Only the experience, the rote is different.

BB popped open. *(So what about AA?)*

(We can try again.)

(But you're not on it.)

I blanked. *(On it?)*

(Your percept has it as wasted effort.)

I lighted. *(I leaked again?)*

BB rolled. *(A little.)*

(AA is in a pattern. I'm not very smart, but my percept is, you can't change it but you have to try.)

BB smoothed. *(Once more, only once more.)*

(Where have I heard that before!)

(I owe it to him, is that the way you put it?)

I plied. *(One more. But it gets kind of rough from here on.)*

I turned and gathered up courage, closed tightly. The haze ahead was much thicker, dull gray, with only occasional flares of light moving through it. I understood the lights; they were those from the outer rings coming in, trying to help or meeting loved ones at their physical death. I had tried this several times, although I don't seem particularly suited for that kind of action. Usually, I pass through these rings as rapidly and unobtrusively as possible.

We entered slowly. Almost immediately, I began to feel uncomfortable and my percept indicated BB was more so. Any prospect of locating AA was totally up to him. I threaded our way among the countless forms hanging motionless. Actually, their movement was so slow as to be almost imperceptible. These were the ones who had just been released from their physical body via death and vaguely knew they had but didn't have the rote to do much, if anything, about it. Occasionally as we passed, one would lean in our direction, which I had learned indicated the beginning of remembering—or the last vestiges of the forgetting process. My usual reaction was: Had I been like that? Had I *ever* been so unaware? It depressed me to accept the fact that I probably was. I don't remember or I don't want to.

For the first time, I realized the M Band noise was lower in this muck. Almost immediately came the percept, naturally: stupid. Nobody is doing much thinking at all. They're in a state of shock from dying, having nothing to hang on to, so scared they can't handle it, so they put their heads in the sand and try to hide. The typical wave of compassion went through me, and I cut it off. Others are working on the effect, this end of the blockage. I'm supposed to be with those who try to help cut back the cause. I don't know which is more difficult.

(He's not here.) BB came in grimly. He was barely open.

I turned inward. I had long ago defused the rote of my painful early climb—no, blundering is more apt—through these close-in patterns. My subsequent training experience was minimal at the most. But I knew the next ring inward. It wasn't nice. Beyond that was physical life. The two were tightly interwoven, the thick ring just slightly out of phase with physical matter. It was the interface between one reality system and another. Even from this perspective, it was difficult for a novice to distinguish instantly the differences in the two. But I could.

That was the problem. The inhabitants of this ring couldn't. They didn't or couldn't or wouldn't realize they were no longer physical. They were physically dead, no more physical body. Thus they kept trying to be physical, to do and be what they had been, to continue physical one way or another. Bewildered, some spent all of their activity in attempting to communicate with friends and loved ones still in bodies or with anyone else who might come along, all to no avail. Others were held attracted to physical sites in which they had instilled great meaning or importance during their previous human lifetime. All had long forgotten or blocked deeply the technique that once was so basic: the M Band.

Still others interpreted their change in status as simply a bad dream or nightmare, and were waiting and hoping to wake up soon.

I moved in cautiously, with BB tight behind me. He was almost completely closed, just scanning for ident AA, no more. I don't blame him. I would have turned and spun away fast if it had been my first run through the place. The M Band noise was thunderous, a cacophony of fear, anger, and about every other human emotion, every desire, every need connected with human physical existence. All open, naked, uncovered, up front. As we entered more deeply, I kept expecting BB to signal me, but he didn't. Physical earth and those aboard for the ride were intermixed now as I speeded up the search, moving faster and faster. But you could tell the difference. Those still physical seemed less distinct, not quite but almost transparent. Suddenly, I got a pull from BB and stopped immediately.

(I got him!) BB vibrated strongly. *(Not much, all covered over, but it's him!)*

I flickered. *(Where?)*

BB leaned. *(That way!)*

I turned inward. That way, that way, that way . . . was out of time, no, another time. Moving to another time ident was not exactly something I performed often, not willfully. Then I had the percept from our last contact with AA. It was a different time frame, too. Get lost, left brain. Then, very clearly, there was that soft vibration in me. *(It is important for you to go. He will help.)*

I lighted brightly.

CLICK!

BB vibrated. *(I thought you couldn't pull a skip!)*

I flickered. *(Well, I . . .)*

(And both of us in the same pull!) BB rolled. *(You don't accept your own strength.)*

I smoothed. *(That's a skip?)*

(Just like we do it in KT-95.) Then BB cut off as he scanned the action below us.

We were hovering over a rugged countryside, rocks, sand, very little vegetation. Sunlit cloudless sky overhead. Directly below us was a dusty road. Marching along the road three abreast was a column of men, eighty or ninety in number. Each was dressed in some kind of knee-length coat, no sleeves, wide leather belt just above the hips, heavy vest over the chest. A short double-edged sword hung through a loop in the belt. Metal plates were strapped to the arms. A round, pointed shield was in each left hand, a long wooden spear in the right. They were marching very rapidly. This was out of the ring. This was real physical life rote.

The M Band noise was much less. I opened more. *(You ident your friend?)*

BB flickered. *(It's very solid, but . . . that's him! There's the human out in front alone, then AA is the one just behind him . . . but he's different. So much other rote on top of him. AA is weak. Can't get any strong percept. The other stuff is too strong. What's going on!)*

I smoothed. *(He's still in a physical body at this point. He's a warrior.)*

BB blanked. *(What's a warrior?)*

(He kills other humans.)

I turned away from a totally blanked BB, reached out, and focused for a percept on AA. Almost immediately, I hit a wall of resistance that pushed me back violently. Try as I might, I couldn't force through it. It was the same as I encountered before when I reached for AA.

The column of troops moved along the road and deep into a ravine, and I saw the enemy troops hidden above on each side of the ravine. A great sense of knowing came through me, and I reached out frantically to the warrior AA, but the barrier threw me back. I knew what was going to happen and it did. When AA's column was deep in the ravine, the hidden soldiers stood and unfolded the ambush, and a shower of spears rained down. AA was one of the first to fall. He writhed in the dusty road, face down, trying to get up to join the battle, but the spear in his back had driven through him and into the road, pinning him down. Blood poured into the dust, and after a moment his body relaxed and went completely limp.

I vibrated strongly at BB. *(Get down there, get to him. I can't, so you've got to! Bring him back up here.)*

BB moved quickly, and I focused as he went down to the battle scene. I give him credit, all the action and killing didn't flicker him in the least. He tugged a struggling AA out of the warrior body, and brought him up toward me. As he did, I was astounded. As he came closer with AA, a barrier kept pushing me back. Finally I signaled BB to stay where he was. AA, still in the shape of the warrior, struggled and vibrated heavily. *(Gotta kill the enemy. Kill them, kill them. Gotta get up and kill them . . .*

Where's my spear, my shield? Gotta get up and kill them. I'm missing all the battle. Leggo of me. You're makin me miss the fightin, it'll be all over and I'll have missed out . . . Gimme my spear. Where is it? . . . Gotta go and fight, go and fight and kill!)

BB vibrated. *(He doesn't know me! I can't hold him much longer!)*

I flickered. *(Let him go.)*

BB blanked. *(What?)*

I smoothed. *(Let him go. There's nothing you can do for him at this point.)*

BB released the struggling form, and the AA warrior slipped quickly down into the battle, trying fruitlessly to pick up a shield and spear and join the battle. Unable to do so, he stared at his hands, bewildered, then began to beat at the enemy troops with his fists, which passed through them as if they didn't exist. But he kept on trying.

I turn to BB. He was dulled and completely closed. *(Come on, let's go back.)*

BB opened slightly. *(Back where?)*

CLICK!

We were in the Intermediate Area near the Station. BB was dull, motionless, half closed.

I lighted. *(How did you like that skip! Right on target!)*

BB opened slightly. *(Yeah, fine.)*

I suddenly became uncomfortable. There was something I had forgotten. It was important. I became more uncomfortable. Something demanded me, my attention. There was an urgency. Yes! My body! Got to get back.

I vibrated. *(Gotta leave! I'll be back!)*

BB opened wide. *(Hey!)*

He faded to a pinpoint, then out as I dropped away quickly. I barely noticed passing through the rings . . . then there was my second in orbit around the physical . . . I slipped in easily and slid for the physical, and in. I sat up, feeling tired, unusual. The problem that called me back was strongly evident. My body was too cold. The blanket had slipped off.

12.
Hearsay Evidence

Time: Indeterminate, night . . . Went through usual unhook pattern, no signal present . . . with many options open . . . decided to return to BB on my own if I could . . . ident BB KT-95 . . . then ran stretch-out method . . . through the rings without incident, then to edge of thin haze of Intermediate Area . . . went motionless to get percept of BB close in, as he didn't seem evident . . . percept brought surprise . . . he was directly under me. Closed and dulled so tightly, no wonder he was hard to find.

I opened and vibrated. *(Hey, BB, I'm back.)*

BB opened slightly, then lighted. *(Well! I had about given up on you. Had you stuck in your human body.)*

I rolled slightly. *(Sometimes I am.)*

There was no percept from him regarding AA, and I wasn't going to bring up the subject if he didn't. It was a tender rote at this point and I knew I didn't have the answer he wanted. If there was one at all. Just to keep the action going, I stretched, did about three snap rolls, and returned with a flourish.

BB plied. *(What was that?)*

(Just getting some exercise.)

BB opened. *(We got a game back in KT-95 where we use that kind of stuff. Want to try it?)*

I lighted. *(Sure!)*

BB rolled slightly. *(You just try to do what I do. That's all there is to it.)*

He turned, spun off, and I stretched behind him. Focused tightly on his ident. It was like holding on to a greased pig on a sheet of ice, only the ice was three-dimensional—no, worse than that, it had many dimensions. It was whirling, stopping, starting, moving slow then fast, passing through strange flashes of percepts, into a brilliant sun and out the other side, dodging around clusters of forms who seemed startled at their percept of us. All the time I hung on to BB's ident much as the last skater in a crack-the-whip, in and out of clouds, bands of energy that were like gusts of hot and cold air, electrical shocks, straight through the walls of a magnificently spired city. I was afraid I couldn't hang on to his ident much longer, afraid if I let go I'd be thoroughly lost. He stopped suddenly and we were back again in the thin haze of outer earth environ. I was shaking.

BB vibrated brightly. *(Good fun, huh?)*

I flickered deeply. *(Yeah, good fun. Who invented that one?)*

BB blanked. *(Invented?)*

(How did it get started?)

BB plied. *(Oh, I don't know. Always been around. You can begin a complete new one if you want. The fun of the game is to add to the old something new inside, in the middle, or on the end, sort of a surprise. Get it?)*

(Yeah. We humans have something like it called follow-the-leader.)

BB lighted. *(That's right, follow-the-leader! You did real well at it. You must play the game a lot.)*

I flickered. *(Not, uh, not recently. But I did fly airplanes and that helped.)*

BB blanked, and I went on. *(Incidentally, what happens if you miss a turn, or lose the ident?)*

BB rolled strongly. *(You lose!)*

(What happens to the losers?)

BB flickered. *(I don't have any rote on that. They never come around to play again. My percept is, they get lost.)*

(And stay lost?)

(Well, they never come around to play again, as I indicated, so I don't have a rote on it. Often we have as many as a hundred playing in a group. Nice game, huh?)

(Yeah.) I then had one final query. *(What is all that stuff we went through?)*

BB plied. *(Don't have a rote on that either. Nobody bothers with that junk, it's just a game.)*

Some game. I had a clear percept on my dropping BB's ident anyplace along the track. I would have lost and have been lost. I probably would have stayed lost, too, I'm sure. But it didn't happen, and I got a strong percept to know the game before you get into it, certainly if it was played in KT-95.

There was the other part, where and when the game took us. What was the effect of such energy as the two of us expended upon the areas we pushed through so indiscriminately and without purpose. How many ants did we destroy because we didn't look or care where we stepped on the golf course fairway. What happened when a hundred played the game? The locals would consider such things natural disasters or God's will, whether ants or archetypes. Either way, it's a strange percept, possibly being such an instrument. One illustration of ultimate impersonality, perhaps.

BB cut in. *(Hey, you all right?)*

I opened. *(Yeah, sure.)*

(You were closed and flickering. Had a percept you were going to skip back to that physical body again.)

I opened and rolled. *(No, no. Not yet, anyway.)*

(Why bother with it? Why go back at all? Leave it where it is.)

I turned inward. The percept had come up more than once, to say the least, and so far I had rejected it. The first question always present was: What would I do or be if I did? There was still a missing element. I knew I could pass through the rings easily and I might hang around in one of the upper segments and participate. Plenty of interesting action there. Most if not all of it was focused on helping the human process work better. That seems a good and essential part of the training system, but it's still preparation. Preparation for what? That was where the missing element came in. Those Last-Timers in the outer ring were going Home, but my percept Home had seemed to grow dimmer rather than clearer and cleaner as it was supposed to. I hadn't visited There in a long, long time.

I opened carefully. *(Well, it's, uh . . . I haven't quite finished school, learning yet . . . and I need a physical body to do it.)*

BB had blanked completely.

(It's sort of a game,) I went on, *(and I've agreed to play it.)*

BB lighted. *(Oh, a game! Yeah, I can get that one.)*

(I'll give you a short rote on it if you think you can take it.)

BB rolled. *(After that last skip with AA, I can handle anything human.)*

I turned inward. He had mentioned AA without flickering, and that was great. He was smoothing. I put together an edited rote, short form, of my nonphysical action since 1958, leaving out the THEY sections, and tossed it to him. He took it in, closed, was still, completely motionless. Then he opened wide, rolled, and flickered.

I vibrated. *(It's not that funny!)*

BB finally smoothed. *(I got an ident I can use for you! RAM the Bam!)* He was off again, flickering and rolling hard.

(Just RAM will do.)

He finally quieted down. *(Well, Ram, I get the percept that you were just a locked-in, hooked-on human until this thing came up. You had some strong action after that! You didn't have much smarts.)*

I plied. *(I still don't have much.)*

(And you sure do things the hard way.)

I rolled a little. *(Percept you can do any better?)*

BB flickered. *(Why, any dumb curl with only half his ident could . . .)*

I cut in. *(How about with no ident?)*

BB blanked, then vibrated. *(No, you don't. You're not going to get me in that game! I'm staying the way I am!)*

I rolled and turned inward. I guess, from an external perspective, much of my response in my early OOBE states would seem ludicrous. Now I can laugh at much of it myself. At least I know the human school game *can* work. But there are many unknowns. What do you do after you graduate? Where and how do I practice what I've learned?

BB broke in. *(Say, uh, RAM.)*

I opened. *(Yes?)*

BB flickered. *(I take it back. You're not really a dumb curl.)*

I rolled. *(Thanks. I needed that.)*

BB blanked. *(You did?)*

(That's a joke. Human fun.)

He turned inward, then went on, opening. *(How did you get a percept and start running this leaving-your-body game?)*

I flickered. *(I don't know. It just happened.)*

(Other humans do it, too?)

(I know at least some do. I've met them. Problem is, most go OOB during sleep and they don't remember it when they wake up back in the physical.)

BB turned inward, and I knew he was sorting out and scanning the rote I had given him. Things like sleep and wake-up needed new percepts on his part. Also I knew what he was leading up to. But he put it off.

He opened, flickering. *(These three curls that came down the . . . uh, beam, you call it. Who were they?)*

I plied. *(I don't know.)*

(They seemed to know you.)

(Maybe they were from KT-95.)

BB rolled. *(That is wild rote . . . oh, joke fun. But you seemed to know them. You wanted them to take you with them. Why?)*

I flickered. *(I don't know.)*

(Ever meet them again?)

(Not that I have a percept of.)

BB turned inward again, then out. *(What about these curls that helped you when you needed it, or percepted you did. Who were they?)*

I smoothed. *(Probably from the upper rings. There's plenty of that going on. Again, most humans don't have any percept on it except what they call dreams, uh, wild rote.)*

BB turned inward again, then opened, flickering. *(Well, I get the percept that there's too much wild rote floating around here.)*

I blanked. *(Which in particular?)*

(That rote on human compressed learning, human structure, the one you tossed me.)

I flickered. *(Yes?)*

BB went on. *(That's not wild?)*

(My percept is that it fits.)

(I got another rote, and when I overlay the two, one of them is certainly wild.)

I blanked. *(What rote is that?)*

(The one we got in the TSI brochure, about all the places and things we would be visiting. All about earth and humans, how it got started, what it's for . . . all of that stuff.)

I closed, then opened slowly. *(They don't match up?)*

(Here, get your own percept.) BB tossed a rote at me, and I took it curiously. And unfolded it.

CLICK!

Someone, Somewhere (or both, in millions, or uncountable) requires, likes, needs, values, collects, drinks, eats, or uses as a drug *(sic)* a substance ident Loosh. (Electricity, oil, oxygen, gold, wheat, water, land, old coins, uranium.) This is a rare substance in Somewhere, and those who possess Loosh find it vital for whatever it is used for.

Faced with this question of Supply and Demand (a universal law of Somewhere), Someone decided to produce it artificially, so to speak, rather than search for it in its "natural" form. He decided to build a Garden and grow Loosh.

In the natural state, Loosh was found to originate from a series of vibrational actions in the carbon-oxygen cycle and the residue was Loosh in varying degrees of purity. It occurred only during such action, and secondarily during the reactive process. Prospectors from Somewhere ranged far and wide in search of Loosh sources and new discoveries were hailed with much enthusiasm and reward.

So it was that Someone and his Garden changed all this. Far off, in a remote area, he set to work on his experiment. First, he created a proper environment for the carbon-oxygen cycle, where it would flourish. He created a Balance with much care, so that proper radiation and other nourishment would be in continuous supply.

He then tried his First Crop, which actually did produce Loosh, but only in small quantities and of comparatively low grade, not significant enough to take back to the heart of Somewhere. The problem was twofold. The life period was too short and the crop units themselves were too minute. This brought about limits in quality and quantity, as the crop had no time to generate Loosh in such close tolerances. Moreover, the Loosh could be harvested only at the moment of termination of the life span, not one moment before.

His Second Crop was no better, if as good. He changed the environment to another part of the Garden, where the density was gaseous rather than liquid and the higher-density chemicals formed a solid base and thus were still available. He planted numberless units in many varieties in a new form, with a great increase in size, some many thousands of times larger and more complex than the simple unicellular First Crop. He reversed the carbon-oxygen cycle. Yet all had a basic uniformity. Like the First Crop, they would reseed at regular intervals and terminate their life spans automatically. To avoid the uneven distribution of chemicals and radiation which had been prevalent in the First Crop, he immobilized the Second Crop. Each was designed to stay principally in its own section of the Garden. To this end, each was given firm tendrils which burrowed deep in the more dense chemical matter. Attached to this was a stem or trunk which helped elevate the upper portion upward for its share of needed radiation. The upper portion, broad, thin, and somewhat fragile, was designed as a transducer of carbon-oxygen compounds to and from the crop unit. As an added thought, brilliant color radiators accompanied by small particle generators were mounted on each unit, usually near the top and symmetrically centered.

He set up circulating patterns in the gaseous envelope around the crop, principally to aid in the reseeding process. Later, he discovered that the same turbulent effect served as a means of harvesting the Loosh. If the turbulence were violent enough, the Crop would be blown down, the life span terminated, and the Loosh would discharge. This was especially useful when an immediate Loosh supply was desired at a particular point rather than at Harvest Time.

Despite all of this, the Second Crop was most unsatisfactory. While it was true that a much greater quantity was attained, the unrefined Loosh produced was of such low grade that it was scarcely worth the effort. In addition, the growth period was now too long and no increase in quality resulted. Some vital element was missing.

Someone hovered over his Garden for a long period in study before he attempted the Third Crop. It was indeed a challenge. True, he was partially successful. He had grown Loosh. Yet the product of his efforts fell far short of the wild, uncultivated variety.

It was inevitable that he perceived the answer. The Third Crop was living proof of this Truth. The original carbon-oxygen cycle must be included. Mobility must be restored. Both factors had shown great promise in high-grade Loosh production. If size could be added to this, much could be accomplished.

With this plan in the forefront, Someone removed various sample units from the First Crop, which was still thriving in the liquid portion of the

Garden. He modified them to exist and grow in the gaseous area. He adapted them first to take nourishment from the Second Crop, which he permitted to abound for this very purpose. Thus it was that the first of the Mobiles, the Third Crop, came into being. The Mobiles took nourishment from the Second Crop, thus ending its life span and producing low-grade Loosh. When each huge Mobile terminated its own life span, additional Loosh was produced. The quantity was massive, but the frequency pattern of the Loosh residue still left much to be desired.

It was by accident that Someone came upon the Prime Catalyst as regards Loosh production. The monstrous and slow-moving Mobiles had a life span far out of proportion to their nourishment input. The growth and life-termination process was of such length that soon the Mobiles would all but decimate the Second Crop. The entire Garden would be out of balance, and there would be no Loosh production whatsoever. Both the Second and Third Crop faced extinction.

As the Second Crop grew scarce, energy needs of the Mobiles became acute. Often two Mobiles would seek to ingest the identical Second Crop unit. This created Conflict, which resulted in physical struggle among two or more of the ungainly Mobiles.

Someone observed these struggles, at first bemused with the problem, then with great interest. As the struggles ensued, the Mobiles were emanating Loosh! Not in fractional amounts, but in sizable, usable quantities and of a much higher purity.

He quickly put the theory to the test. He removed another unit of First Crop from the liquid Garden area, redesigned it for the gaseous environment—but with one significant change. The new Mobile would be somewhat smaller, but would require the ingestion of other Mobiles for nourishment. This would solve the problem of overpopulation of Mobiles, and at the same time would create good quantities of usable Loosh during each conflict-struggle, plus a bonus if the new class of Mobile terminated the life span of the other. Someone would be able to transmit to Somewhere practical amounts of reasonably pure Loosh.

Thus it was that the Rule of the Prime Catalyst came into being. Conflict among carbon-oxygen cycle units brings forth consistent emanations of Loosh. It was as simple as that.

Satisfied that he had found the formula, Someone prepared the Fourth

Crop. He knew now that the Third Crop Mobiles were too large and too long in life span to be ultimately practical. If grown in large numbers, the entire Garden would have to be expanded and enlarged. There was not space enough to grow such massive single units and the proportionate leafy Second Crops to support them. Also, he reasoned correctly that more rapid and increased mobility would expand the Conflict factor, with a resultant higher Loosh output.

In one single motion, Someone terminated the life spans of all the lumbering Third Crop Mobiles. Going back to the First Crop in the liquid area, he modified and expanded them into a multitude of shapes and sizes, gave them complex multicellular structures of high mobility. He designed into them a pattern of balance. There were those that ingested a Second Crop type of carbon-cycle unit (basically immobile) as an energy source. There were others, very highly mobile, who required for energy the ingestion of other mobile Modified First Crop units.

The completed circuit operated quite satisfactorily. The stationary Second Crop modification in the liquid environment flourished. Small, highly active liquid-breathing Mobiles took nourishment, "ate" the Second Crop modification. Larger and/or other active Mobiles consumed for energy the smaller "plant eaters." When any Mobile grew too large and slow, it became an easy target for the smaller Mobiles, who attacked in voracious numbers. The chemical residue from these ingestive actions settled to the bottom of the liquid medium and so provided new nourishment for the Stationaries (Modified Second Crop), completing the circuit. The result was a steady flow of Loosh—from the life-span termination of the Stationaries, from the intense conflict among the Mobiles to avoid ingestion, and finally from the sudden termination of the life spans of such Mobiles as the inevitable product of such conflicts.

Turning to another portion of his Garden—the gaseous area with a dense-compound base—Someone applied the same techniques with even more advanced improvements. He added many varieties of Stationaries (original Second Crop) to provide sufficient and diverse nourishment for the new Mobiles he was to create. As in the other Garden area, he made such Mobiles into a balance of two species, those who ingested and drew energy from the Second Crop Stationaries, and those who required other Mobiles for sustenance. He created them in literally thousands of original types, small, large—yet none so large as the Third Crop Mobiles—and ingeniously gave each some appurtenance for conflict. These took the form of mass, elusive speed, deceptive and/or protective coating and color radiation, wave-action and particle perceptors and detectors, and unique higher-density protuberances for gouging, grasping, and rending during conflict. All of the latter served neatly to add to and prolong the conflict periods, with the resultant increase in Loosh emanation.

As a side experiment, Someone designed and created one form of Mobile that was weak and ineffective by the standards of the other Mobiles in the Fourth Crop. Yet this experimental Mobile had two distinct advantages. It had the ability to ingest and take energy from both the Stationaries and other Mobiles. Second, Someone pulled forth a Piece of Himself —no other source of such Substance being known or available—to act as an intensive, ultimate trigger to mobility. Following the Rule of Attraction, Someone knew that such infusion would create in this particular Mobile species an unceasing mobility. Always, it would seek to satisfy the attraction this tiny mote of Himself engendered as it sought reunion with the infinite Whole. Thus the drive for satisfaction of energy requirements through ingestion would not be the only motivating force. More important, the needs and compulsions created by the Piece of Someone could not be satiated throughout the Garden. Thus the need for mobility would be ever-present and the conflict between this need and that of energy replacement would be constant—possibly a continuous high-order Loosh emanator if it survived.

The Fourth Crop exceeded all of Someone's expectations. It became apparent that a consistent, useful flow of Loosh was being produced in the Garden. The balance of "life" operated perfectly, with the Conflict Factor producing immense amounts of Loosh and a steady supplement brought into being by the constant life-span terminations from all types of Mobiles and Stationaries. To handle the output, Someone set up Special Collectors to aid in the harvest. He set up Channels to convey the raw Loosh from his Garden to Somewhere. No longer did Somewhere depend principally upon the "wild state" as the principal source of Loosh. The Garden of Someone had ended that.

With the success of the Garden and the production of Loosh by cultivated means, Others began to design and build their Gardens. This was in accordance with the Law of Supply and Demand (Vacuum is an unstable condition), as the amounts of Loosh from Someone's Garden only partially met the requirements of Somewhere. Collectors on behalf of the Others actually entered the Garden of Someone to take advantage of those small emanations of Loosh overlooked or ignored by the Collectors of Someone.

Someone, his work completed, returned to Somewhere and occupied himself with other matters. Loosh production stayed at a constant level under the supervision of the Collectors. The only alterations were ordered by Someone himself. Under instructions from Someone, the Collectors periodically harvested segments of the Fourth Crop. This was done to ensure adequate chemicals, radiation, and other nourishment for the younger, oncoming units. A secondary purpose was to provide occasional extra amounts of Loosh created by such harvesting.

To reap such harvest, the Collectors generated storms of turbulence and turmoil in both the gaseous envelope and the more solid chemical formations that were the base of the Garden itself. Such upheavals had the effect of terminating life spans of multitudes of the Fourth Crop as they were crushed under the rolling base formation or smothered under waves from the agitated liquid area of the Garden. (By peculiarity of design, Fourth Crop units could not maintain their carbon-oxygen cycle surrounded by the liquid medium.)

The Garden pattern of "Life" might have gone on thus throughout eternity had it not been for the perception and inquisitiveness of Someone. On occasion, he would study samples of Loosh from his Garden. There was no motive in doing so, other than the fact that Someone may have held a remote continuing interest in his project.

On a particular analysis of a Loosh sample, Someone had casually examined the emanations and was about to return it to the Reservoir—when he became aware of a Difference. It was very slight, but there it was.

His interest centered immediately, he looked again. Woven delicately in with the more common Loosh emanations was a slender fragment of purified and distilled Loosh. This was an impossibility. Purified and distilled Loosh resulted only after the "wild state" Loosh had been processed many times. The Loosh from the Garden of Someone required the same treatment before it could be used.

Yet here it was—so finely graded in its refined radiations that it could or would not return into compound with the raw substance. Someone reaffirmed his tests, and the result still was positive. There was a factor in his Garden of which he was unaware.

Quickly, Someone left Somewhere and returned to his Garden. Outwardly, all seemed the same. The solid-base gaseous areas of the Garden were an endless carpet of green reflection from the thriving Second Crop. The Modified First Crop in the liquid area was in perfect accord with the Action-Reaction Law (a Division of Cause and Effect). Someone perceived without delay that the Difference—the source of distilled Loosh—lay neither with the First nor with the Second Crop.

He found his first momentary touch of distilled Loosh emanation in one of the units of the Fourth Crop (which by then had filtered throughout the plantings of the Second Crop). The flash came during the unusual action of this unit as it entered into a life-terminating struggle with another Fourth Crop unit. This alone would not create distilled Loosh, Someone knew, and he probed deeper for the source.

It was at that moment he discovered the Difference. The Fourth Crop unit was not struggling in Conflict over an ingestible remnant of a weaker Fourth Crop unit or a tasty frond from a nearby Second Crop stem—or to avoid termination of life and ingestion by the other conflicting Fourth Crop unit.

It was in Conflict to protect and save from life termination three of its own newly generated species huddled under a large Second Crop unit waiting for the outcome. There was no doubt about it. This was the action that produced the flashes of distilled Loosh.

With this clue, Someone examined the actions of other Fourth Crop units in the Garden. He found similar flashes when other Fourth Crop units took the same action in defense of their "young." Still, there was an inconsistency. The sum of all such flashes of distilled Loosh emanation from all such actions by the current Fourth Crop units would not amount to half of the total he had found in the sample from the Reservoir. It was obvious that another factor was present.

Systematically, he hovered over the Garden, extending his perception to all areas. Almost immediately, he found the source. High-order distilled

Loosh radiation was originating from one particular section of the Garden. Quickly, he hurried to the spot.

There it was—an experimental Modified Fourth Crop unit, one of those that contained a Piece of Himself in its functional pattern. It was standing alone under the leafy upper portion of a large Second Crop unit. It was not "hungry." It was not in Conflict with another Fourth Crop unit. It was not acting in defense of its "young." Then why did it emanate distilled Loosh in such great quantity?

Someone moved closer. His perception entered into the Modified Fourth Crop unit and then he knew. The unit was lonely! It was this effect that produced distilled Loosh.

As Someone drew back, he noted another unusual inconsistency. The Modified Fourth Crop unit suddenly had become aware of His Presence. It had collapsed and was jerking in strange convulsions on the solid-base formation. Clear liquid was being expelled from the two radiation-perceiving orifices. With this, the distilled Loosh emitted became even more pronounced.

It was from this that Someone propounded his now famous DLP Formula, which is in effect in the Garden at this time.

The balance of the story is well known. Someone included the fundamental in his formula: ". . . The creation of pure, distilled Loosh is brought forth in Type 4M units by the action of unfulfillment, but only if such pattern is enacted at a vibratory level above the sensory bounds of the environment. The greater the intensity of said pattern, the greater the output of Loosh distillate. . . ."

To put the formula into effect, Someone designed subtle changes in his Garden, all of them familiar to every historian. The splitting of all Crop units into Halves (to engender loneliness as they sought to reunite) and the encouragement of dominance of the Type 4M unit are but two of the most noteworthy innovations.

As it appears now, the Garden is a fascinating spectacle of efficiency. The Collectors have long since become Masters at the Art of the DLP Formula. Type 4M units dominate and have spread through the entire Garden, with the exception of the deeper portions of the liquid medium. These are the principal producers of Loosh distillate.

From experience, the Collectors have evolved an entire technology with complementary tools for the harvesting of Loosh from the Type 4M units. The most common have been named love, friendship, family, greed, hate, pain, guilt, disease, pride, ambition, ownership, possession, sacrifice—and on a larger scale, nations, provincialism, wars, famine, religion, machines, freedom, industry, trade, to list a few. Loosh production is higher than ever before . . .

CLICK!

I was closed tightly, turned inward, stunned. My first reaction was, there had to be some mistake, this was not the story-history of earth, BB had it mixed up with some other port of call on their cruise schedule. Yet as I ran the rote again, the overlay of what little I knew of earth's zoological and human history was uncomfortably accurate, albeit from another perspective. The food chain of earth's ecobiologic system had been well established. Knowing this about Mother Nature, some of the hard-core philosophic speculators had often pondered where the human animal fit in the process. The downside was obvious, who ate *us!* Before, it had been just that, speculation. Now . . .

BB opened, plied. *(You get the percept, RAM?)*

I dulled. *(Yeah, I get it.)*

(Well, then,) BB went on, *(what's Loosh got to do with learning?)*

I opened slightly. *(And you got the rote before you came to Earth?)*

BB smoothed. *(Like I gave you, it was in the TSI cruise brochure. It was in with hundreds of other rotes we got before we left.)*

I opened more, but tightly. *(Where did the brochure come from?)*

(Why, uh . . . yeah, from the Cruise Director.)

(Where did he get it?)

BB flickered. *(I don't have a rote on that. He just dumped them on us and rolled, "Here's the exciting and interesting stops we'll make on the cruise." I got a good percept because it was the last one we'd visit, so it was the last rote we got. That's why it's so clear. Some of the others are dim because they were in the middle. Not the earth rote, or humans. It's all clean, not wild at all.)*

I hardened. *(And where did the Cruise Director come from?)*

BB lighted. *(Oh, he and the rest are a bunch of curls from the system next to us.)*

(Why did they offer the cruise to you in KT-95?)

BB smoothed. *(Well, it was sort of a, uh . . . trade. We do it all the time with systems near us.)*

(What did they get in trade?)

BB lighted. *(Games, games! We got more games than any system four skips in any direction!)*

I turned inward and closed. It was getting too hot to handle. If the rote was real . . . a huge if. I began to drop off. Anger, the feeling of being on the receiving end of a huge deception. The resentment at being manipulated, wanting to strike out at those who were conning me . . . us . . . all humans . . . who were taking something from us without our consent or permission. What happened to the freedom idea? Was *every* thought and action we took guided—no, *directed and controlled* just to produce more Loosh, whatever that was, for a breakfast table or a fuel tank in a Somewhere? And what could I do about it, even knowing? I dulled deeply and dropped off more and more . . .

(Hey RAM!) BB was fading rapidly. *(Where you going!)*

Return to the physical was near-instantaneous, exactly as if I had pushed the panic button, which I had not done for so long. Strong sense of tiredness, both mental and physical, neglected to check time of return. Low energy, no desire to do anything. Unable to get to sleep. Got up, went to the kitchen, and made a cup of coffee. Sat and stared at the cup.

With no energy or desire for exploration during the two weeks following, in a depressed state, the only production that surfaced was:

It is sunset. The Guernsey has walked many miles around the pasture in her forage for food. The grass had been more lush today here, though she did not bother to consider why. She had come through the gate calmly when He directed her to do so, instead of the gate across the road. He knew she would find better grass here, and that was why He moved her here, though she did not realize it. She only did what He directed.

But now, at sunset, it is time again. She must go to His place. There is a goading pain on her underside that tells her this. At His place up on the hill, it is cool and there is more food. And He will take the pain away.

The Guernsey moves up the hill and waits beside His place. Soon, the gate will open and she will walk into her position in His place, and eat the grass He places before her. While she eats, He will relieve the pain until morning.

After that, the Man will walk away with white water in a round container. The Guernsey does not know where he got the white water nor why He desires it.

Not knowing, she doesn't care.

13.
Shock Treatment

It took me several months to adjust to the loosh rote. "Adjust" is a very broad word to describe a complete cycle of shock, rejection, anger, depression, resignation, acceptance. My sequence paralleled remarkably the pattern others have discovered and studies as to human response when notified of approaching death from illness or injury.

Something *was* dying in me. I had long realized that the God of my childhood did not exist, at least not in the form and substance envisioned by my enculturation. However, I had deeply accepted the concept of creator and created—I had but to look around me at the elaborate and intricate order of design, of the symbiosis that made the whole process operate, the trees that grew plumb-line straight up if given the chance, that provided me and other oxygen breathers with what we needed while we fed to them unknowingly for a long period our waste products, which they needed to exist . . . the balance of the entire planet, whose outer filtering bands of energy permitted just the proper quantity and quality of sunlight so critical to biologic growth . . . and of course the food chain.

The loosh rote explained everything very neatly. Most important, it explained the purpose, the reason for it all, the why of it. This factor had long eluded me. The loosh answer was simple and obvious. The reason was there, in very prosaic fashion. We were indeed producing Something of Value. Loosh. If one finally was able to get past the emotional barriers involved, it became hard even then to find holes in the general concept. An explanation of total human behavior and history.

That left the INSPECS.

Were they the gardeners, the loosh collectors, or the overseers? The question tantalized and tortured me for many weeks before I finally decided I must find out one way or another.

On a particular night, after great difficulty in getting two cycles of sleep, I awoke with a start and lay quietly in bed. Evidently my fear of

what I might find was greater than I thought, as I unhooked with diffi-
culty from the physical, then slipped out of the second body as it hovered.
I scanned for the INSPEC homing signal, but there was none. This discon-
certed me at first, but I was determined and foolhardy. I used the ident
INSPEC—the total rote I had on them—stretched out, focused, and let go.
There was a quick, short sense of spinning movement, no impression of
passing through the rings, then deep blackness, and I was motionless.
Nothing more.

The percept was forming that the ident I had used wasn't enough. I
might be at the gate to INSPEC territory, but I didn't have the passport to
enter. I had never tried to go to them, they had always met me. I had no
percept of their reality/state; therefore I had arrived only at the site of our
meetings. If I focused on . . .

A warm vibration washed through me. *(Very good, Mister Monroe. You
are quite correct.)*

I began to relax somewhat. At least I had gotten this far, and at least
THEY didn't call me RAM.

*(Perhaps you would like it better if we used the ident by which we know
you best. We believe you are ready for it now.)*

Ready for it, a name, they know me best . . . What could that be?

(Ashaneen)

Ashaneen. It was both familiar and strange. Again, that feeling of trying
to recover from severe amnesia, and the gentle patience of those trying to
help me remember. But the loosh . . .

*(We are aware of the disturbance you have undergone. It was necessary
that you experience this. It goes with the territory, as you put it.)*

Then the loosh rote *was* real! I began to flicker . . .

*(It is the translation that is not real. The difficulty of placing earth and
human values properly into perspectives and energies that are not of time
and space is a factor very familiar to you.)*

I turned inward, picking up the loosh rote. Loosh, an energy generated
by all organic life in varying degrees of purity, the clearest and most
potent coming from humans—engendered by human activity which triggers emotion, the highest of such emotions being—love? Is love loosh?

(Continue, Ashaneen.)

But according to the rote, loosh is thrown off when life ends its physical existence, when pain occurs, anger, hate . . . these can't be the same as love.

(How would you define love in your terms?)

I knew that would be next in the order of things, and I couldn't come up with an answer. Throughout history, great minds and greater philosophers had given it a try, with only partial success, and I was none of these. I wouldn't even consider trying.

(But you know it exists. Love is not an illusion.)

I released the loosh rote and turned deeply inward, scanning. It was easier from this perspective, or perhaps it was the presence of the INSPEC energy. It presented itself much as a simultaneous mixture and sequence of musical chords and short melodies, only it wasn't sound, it was patterns in colors of light. Scattered among the clutter of harmony, dissonance, discord, excitement, fun, fear, and emotion, and beginning shortly after birth, I had the percept of occasional surges of white . . . first from my mother and father, then smaller flashes I was unable to identify as to source. I kept scanning through my early years for any slight glimmer of white originating in me, that *I* put forth. To my dismay, all I could find was one small white glow for an Airedale dog named Pete. I was certain that the girl in high school, what was her name? . . . not even a flicker, either way.

(Most common misconception, early-manifested survival drive.)

I agreed. Yet I could understand why. The bright red and pink chords and urgent melody were impressive even from this viewpoint; no wonder an ignorant curl such as I was would come up with the wrong percept. I went on through the mess that was I in a fast-forward mode, and I could spot sure and solid white surges here and there of which I had then been unaware, and their reality depressed and saddened me—because I found no significant emission from me that was remotely similar. It was all coming in, and I took it and didn't respond. I finally cut it off, would go into it no further. I wasn't much of a loosh producer. Too many other color chord patterns and melodies. Except for now. I knew some strong emissions in a few points were coming out of me. Did it take *that* long!

(You understand waveforms. All come from the same baseline, the colors and the white. The difference is frequency and amplitude.)

I knew what THEY were doing, and I appreciated it. My focus was being diverted from what I thought was unpleasant back into an abstract yet trunk-and-roots position. Using the same stuff—interactive experience—one began to learn to express anger, pain, fear, and all the rest, and finally —hopefully, if you passed the course—a special energy waveform labeled love. Yet we don't really know what it is and, with my suspicion growing, how to really use it.

(A carefully designed school of compressed learning.)

To learn to be high-quality loosh/love producers. The fact that human physical consciousness was for the most part totally unaware of being involved in the process may be an important ingredient itself. Precious few are cognizant of the nonphysical agenda, at least overtly. It was getting pretty heavy for *my* cognizance. Yet I began to get a very faint percept, elusive but it was there. What would happen if the Guernsey cow did discover that her milk had value? What could she herself do with it if she didn't have a calf to feed it to? Could she save it? Could she spend it on more hay or protein-vitamin blocks to lick? What if she then discovered man was taking the milk she produced? Rebel, refuse to deliver any more milk? Then she would no longer have a pasture in which to graze, protection from wild dogs, a bull when she needed it, and most of all, no barn to go to where she could get relief from the pain. Without a sense of serial time, she forgets that the pain eases eventually. Perhaps even knowing, she wouldn't care. She wouldn't want to mess up a good thing. Therefore: Who cares? Who *would* care!

(To use your term, you can't beat the machine.)

The percept was still there, faint, still to be explained or satisfied. What about those who *do* beat the machine? There always have to be exceptions, no machine is perfect, only one anomaly is needed to prove a statistic or create one. Are they carted off to be ground up into hamburger meat? If so, is hamburger a sort of super loosh or something entirely different? Is this also a part of the machine product, or is it rust that is scraped away and discarded?

And the bull calves, what is their role? Never will be loosh producers; it takes only one bull for every fifty cows, so there's a surplus. In nature—the machine?—left alone, there's a way that is automatically taken care of . . . the impersonality of that prospect of dominance and predation is certainly not in the winning column. Hold it there, the percept is getting stronger. There *would* be no loosh production without at least one, uh, one bull. So he is an *indirect* loosh producer, vital to the method. That would infer, so are grass, hay, water, minerals, and the rest.

(Remember your waveforms, beat frequencies you like so much.)

Let's see, here. If a smart transmitter propagates certain waves, they can resonate with other related vibrations of like kind to form a multiple pattern which if thought of as light—would be: white! So in and of itself, you don't have to be the end-product antenna or transducer, just one of the oscillators. You may never display actual loosh radiation, but you have a vital part in its production. Remembering the scan of my early years, I felt much better.

(Then why are you disturbed?)

The percept still itched inside me, THEY were right. What would I do with loosh/love if I had a large warehouse full of it? Hand it out? It would only come back with interest and I would have to build another warehouse to hold the compounding, growing volume. The percept surged brightly. It was so obvious . . . Someone, Somewhere. If I could . . .

(You are not ready at this point.)

Ready to go to Somewhere? To meet Someone? And in all of this, how do you fit in, my friend? If I had the courage to ask these . . .

(We are not Someone, as you put it, nor are we from the Somewhere you indicate. Also, we are not the keepers of the Garden of Earth, nor the gardeners. Nor do we collect and transfer human-developed loosh/energy elsewhere or when. We do not fit into any portion of the human compressed learning process. However, we have observed its generation and growth from its inception. We do participate when needed without interrupting the learning sequence. Such need is expressed when there is blockage in the flow. Such participation ultimately serves a vital need for us.)

I had a need to ask the question. Is . . .

(Somewhere is not the heaven of your history. It was created, as were all other systems.)

Then Someone . . .

(Is a creator who was created. You are a creator who was created. Each of you does carry a small rote, as you call it, of Someone, who created you. Through that rote of Someone, your creator, you carry a percept of the creator who created Someone.)

I turned inward. Even with this viewpoint, it was hard to set aside serial logic. The easy percept was how the multitude of distortions, misconceptions, misdirections came about. A little knowledge *can* be dangerous, and human creative imagination took over from there. If there had not been a Someone . . .

(Humans would not exist.)

I went over the idea of loosh/love. It must be quite a place to handle that much loosh, this Somewhere. It would fall neatly into many concepts of heaven. I grew wistful. Maybe we could go just to the edge of Somewhere, so I could get a feel of the place/state where there was so much love, surely near it, but not *in* it, just to observe from a distance. It would answer so much . . .

(That is not too much to ask, Mister Monroe. We can arrange it. Close tightly . . .)

CLICK!

. . . Even closed tightly, the radiation was so strong that it was nearly unbearable . . . I felt as if sweat were pouring off me, I was melting . . . but it wasn't heat . . . and I began to heave with great racking sobs and I couldn't understand why . . . then the radiation eased, and I opened a little. There was a form between me and the radiation, shielding me, and I could perceive a corona effect all around the form from the radiation beyond. It reminded me deeply of religious paintings I had seen, only this was live and in something far different from pigmented color . . .

(This is as close as you can tolerate. We are diverting most of the effective energy patterns, which are in themselves only the random residue, the leakage as you might call it, from the fundamental. Focus through us rather than the outer rim. It will help.)

With great difficulty, I narrowed and held on the center of the form . . . and I began to cool and calm down . . . slowly my rational and observing self began to emerge again, dominating the overwhelming emotional surge that had enveloped me . . . it was as if I perceived through a darkly tinted window and I had to work continually to keep the emotion below the threshold level, the wondrous and brilliant joy, awe, reverence, melded into one yet with flashes of each sparking momentarily . . . all coursing through me as I responded to the radiation, unable to prevent it and barely keeping it under control. This would most emphatically be the ultimate heaven, the final home . . .

(Observe more carefully. You are capable of doing so.)

I looked through the smoked-glass shield that was my INSPEC friend . . . and I was grateful, for I knew if I responded to this degree from just the reflection, the leakage, the full force of the radiation would have shattered me, I was *not* ready for it, if this was the percept from the distant edge . . . there, in the long view, was a radiant living form of incredible size, my first percept that of a tall standing humanoid, arms outstretched in front, palms upward . . . but just as quickly, it was not . . . instead, a shining globe, edges indistinct, behind it another, identical in appearance, behind it another, a continuous cascade moving away into infinity, beyond my percept ability . . . from each came numberless beams or rays, some huge in their diameter, others no wider than a pinpoint, all uniform in size throughout their length and beyond my percept as to their destination, some of them moving past me so close that I felt I could reach out and touch one . . .

(Would you like to do so? We will help you if needed.)

I hesitated, then with the warm assurance from the shielding INSPEC form, I stretched a part of me out, cautiously, and touched the smallest ray nearest me . . . in an instant, the shock spread throughout all what I thought I was, and I *knew*, and in knowing, knew that I would forget if I tried to remember, because what I was could not yet handle the reality of it . . . yet I never again would be the same even without remembering, except that it occurred and the indescribable joy of knowing only that it did take place and the echoes would reverberate in me throughout eternity, whatever my eternity was . . . gently, I felt myself being detached from the ray, and I collapsed behind the shielding form of my INSPEC friend. . . . Friend? INSPEC? I realized then how provincial my percepts were. I also realized how limited they were . . . the radiating globes, the rays emitted . . .

(You responded very well for the initial exposure. Your human loosh/love energy is transmuted into the center of what you perceive. From there it is redirected into what you call the rays, to the points where it is needed most.

When you have progressed, we can guide you to one of the destinations so you can observe the results.)

My percept was not strong enough to bring any flicker whatsoever as to what exposure to the full force of such rays might be. But my human curiosity wouldn't let the basic question go unanswered, now that I had smoothed somewhat.

(It was created. It was always there, we have no percept of a beginning. Are you ready to return now?)

I turned inward and closed tightly.

CLICK!

. . . We were back again in familiar blackness, only now it seemed empty and sterile, but the INSPEC energy was still beside me . . . now I would have to put together a new ident for them, if they could hold up so calmly under . . .

(INSPEC will serve as well as any other.)

But I couldn't let it alone. As shaken as I was, I knew I had to ask, because I had known they were greater, but how much greater now might be a depth . . .

(We are created, just as you are created. More than that, it is important that you obtain from your own percept. In your own—how do you put it?—time, you will find the reason for this.)

Suddenly, I felt a strong, urgent signal pulling at the back of me. I resisted at first, not wanting to leave, but the signal was persistent. With the warm pattern of understanding from my INSPEC friend, I turned and followed the signal. Instantly, I was hovering over my physical body. There below me was my second body. I slid into it easily, then into the physical. My right arm was tingling due to lack of circulation. I evidently had been lying on it at an angle. I flexed the arm several times, musing as I had so many times before: Suppose there were no signal to return, how long would I stay away, would I never return? It was then, lying there in the darkness, listening to the whippoorwill and the night crickets outside, the soft earth-scented breeze flowing in through the open window, feeling the hot warmth of our little dog Steamboat sleeping contentedly against the soles of my feet, the even breathing of Nancy sleeping beside me—that I felt the wetness of my cheeks and a few remaining tears in my eyes.

And I remembered. Not much, but I remembered! I sat up in bed, wanting to jump up and shout in incomprehensible joy. Steamboat raised his head and looked at me curiously, then dropped back. My wife shifted position as I sat up, then gradually resumed her even breathing rhythm. I would not wake her, she needed her rest and recharge.

I lay back and remembered. Sometime before dawn, I, too, fell asleep.

14.
One Easy Lesson

Time: 3:40 A.M. . . . awake, alert, rested, relaxed . . . unhooked easily from the physical, slid out of the second immediately, and waited for a signal. There was none, so I let go and let the total self take over. There was the usual blur of movement, not too extensive, and I had the ident of BB close by me. My percept of him was totally different. He was tightly closed. And dulled. The thin outer haze of the Intermediate Area made him even less distinguishable.

I tried to smooth casually. *(Hey, old buddy, what's up?)*

BB opened slightly. *(Oh, hello, RAM.)*

(I had it you would be pulling skips back to KT-95.)

He dulled. *(Sure.)*

I smoothed very gently. *(Anything I can do for you?)*

(No . . . no.) He started to close. *(I'm just hanging around.)*

He had the set of someone who had lost his best friend, which was exactly the case from his perspective, and partially so from another—partially in that the same AA, when he finally emerged, would be the fundamental, with the unique variegation learned from the in-human experience permanently interwoven and overlaid throughout the being that he had become. It could be construed as a loss if BB did not accept the change or expected only the stasis of KT-95 that had been AA.

I tried another approach. *(Well, you just can't stand here forever.)*

BB blanked. *(Forever? What's that?)*

I flickered. *(It's, uh . . . human expression.)*

He vibrated. *(I want nothing to do with that human action!)*

I put it to him hard and straight. *(You're going to have to get some kind of rote about human. If you don't, you won't know your friend AA when he comes out. You won't have any ident on him whatsoever.)*

BB vibrated. *(Sure, I will! You don't lose things like that!)*

(It won't be the same. Pick up your rote when you tried to pull him out.

Even then, you had trouble with his ident. I guarantee you that's just the small part of it, he was only on his way in, he was just getting started.)

He turned inward and closed. I suddenly got the percept that I had done it again. What would I do with him? He wasn't a stray cat or dog I could take back, feed, and find a home for. It was ludicrous. Fix him up with a human body? How would I do *that?* And he certainly wasn't going to join the line and go human via the Entry Station. Can you learn to swim without getting in the water and getting wet?

I tried to ease out of it gracefully. *(Maybe it's best that you pull a skip and go back to KT-95, let it go at that.)*

BB opened slightly. *(I did. Went and came back.)*

I waited. I wasn't going to get in deeper if I could help it. I knew he would go on and he did.

(There was a hole and the hole was empty. You ever been like that?)

I plied. *(Yeah, I've been there. It'll stay empty because it's designed for one curl. No other will fit in.)*

(AA was one smart curl, you can believe it. Too smart for his own good. Look what it got him.)

I plied again. *(It happens.)*

I was about to turn and disengage as carefully as I could, but I was too late. I had the strong percept that he would come to some solution and it would involve me. I was too right.

He had lighted very brightly. *(You can do it!)*

(Do what?)

(Feed me rotes about humans. Then I'd be ready for him.)

I flickered. *(I wouldn't know where to start.)*

(Then show me how it works.)

(How am I going to do that? You'd have to be in-human . . .)

(No, no, I wouldn't,) BB cut in quickly. *(You move around without a physical body.)*

(Well, yes, but . . .)

(You and me, we had a hook right from the start, RAM. Like old friends. I got a solid ident on you. So you be my Tour Guide, quick and short. How about it?)

I smoothed. *(What's it like being human in one easy lesson?)*

He lighted more. *(That's it, that's it!)*

That was it all right. Not quite the blind leading the blind, but close. All I could do was give him a skim over what I did have as the basics, show him . . . yes! Show! That ought to make it clear.

I opened. (*All right. The main thing about being in-human is survival. That's the biggest percept of all. It drowns out about everything else for most humans.*)

He blanked. (*What's survival.*)

(*Staying alive.*)

(*What kind of problem is that? You're alive, you stay alive.*)

I smoothed. (*Not if you're in a physical body. The imprint comes up for most to mean stay alive in a physical body, no more. They use most of their energy trying to survive, one way or another. That's the cause of virtually all human problems. The drive for survival is so strong it messes up everything. End of lesson.*)

BB rolled. (*Come on, that's the wildest rote I ever had thrown at me!*)

(*It's not so funny if you're in it. You believe it as real and nothing else.*)

He continued to roll, and I realized there was only one way he just might get the idea. Show him. Take him down on the beach and watch the swimmers . . . (*Come on, follow my ident.*)

BB lighted. (*Sure, RAM!*)

I turned, did a half-roll, and dove down through the rings with my new KT-95 friend close behind me. Never mind the big centers, get down to the basics . . . that would be back from civilization, outlying physical areas . . . middle of Asia, yes . . . that would do it . . . I pulled to a stop just over a bleak hill with a ragged forest down one side. A man was crouched in the edge of the forest. BB was beside me and I turned his focus on the man. What looked to be a small deer was grazing in the grasses not far from the man. The man raised a gun, took aim, and fired. The deer fell, twitching its legs, and the man ran forward, pulled the deer's head back, and slashed its throat with a knife. Blood gushed out from the deer's throat, and it finally went limp. The man hoisted the deer over his shoulder and moved along the edge of the woods in the direction of a stone hut. We followed as BB pushed at me.

(*That human, he killed that other being.*)

I plied. (*Yep.*)

(*Why did he do that? Not much survival going on there!*)

(Not for the deer, that's the other one, the animal . . . uh, the other being. The human needs the body of the deer.)

BB blanked. *(What would he want with that? He's already got a body.)*

I smoothed, here it comes. *(To survive. He needs it to eat.)*

(Eat! What's eat?)

(He puts it in his own physical body to give it energy to survive, so he can stay alive. That's what we ident eating.)

(The other being, the uh, deer, it didn't survive, stay alive . . . uh, physically. I got a good percept of the energy leaving it.)

One easy lesson! *(Well, humans are what we ident as the dominant species, uh, beings alive here. They are at the top of what we call the food chain. Food is what we call the stuff we eat. Little species get eaten by bigger species which in turn get eaten by bigger species until you get up to human. He isn't the biggest but he's the smartest, that's why he's the dominant species. He eats about everything that grows.)*

BB was turned inward and flickering as we followed the man to the stone hut. The man shifted the deer carcass off his shoulder and hung it head down on a rack outside the hide-draped doorway. Then he went inside.

BB flickered. *(Isn't he going to, uh, eat it?)*

(He will later. Has to cure it a little first, let the blood drain out of it. Want to go inside?)

He didn't really have a choice, as I led him through the stone wall. Inside, there was a small fire burning in the center of an earthen floor. Around the fire were three persons, a woman and two small children. The woman was stirring a pot hung over the fire, the two children watching hungrily. The man sat down and joined them, took off his heavy coat, and accepted the bowl the woman handed him. He started to eat, using his fingers to pull pieces of food from the bowl and sipping from its rim. BB pushed at me urgently.

(What was that he did!)

(Right now he's eating, he's taking pieces of food and putting them into his body, and the little stuff, he just pours it in.)

(Yeh, yeh, I got that percept, it was before! He slipped off part of his body!)

I blanked, then lighted. *(That was his coat. It's not his body, it's a piece*

*of stuff he puts on to keep warm. That's the next thing in the survival need
—to keep your physical body so it's warm enough or cool enough and to
protect it from getting hurt. That's the reason for the cabin, the, uh, hut
we're in now. It helps protect the physical body. The fire . . . the, uh,
radiation in the middle, that helps them keep warm.)*

I had the percept that BB was focused as one would be fascinated by a
cobra weaving its hooded head directly in front of your face. I focused on
him, trying to determine exactly what and how much of the scene was
penetrating him as a real rote. How do you explain warm and cold or such
a simple thing as a cooking fire, or the constant attention and servicing a
physical body requires, to one who has never been in one? Then BB was
pushing at me again.

(RAM, RAM!) He was vibrating strongly. *(He's killing the other one!)*

I turned. The man had moved the woman back from the fire and
pushed her to the ground. He was on top of her, his body holding her
down, arms around her tightly, hers around him. Her long rough dress was
thrown up over her hips and they were writhing violently, her open legs
locked around his waist. The two children were eating from the bowl,
totally unconcerned. Not being the voyeur type, I could be quite clinical.

I smoothed. *(He's not killing her. They're, uh, reproducing.)*

(What's . . .)

*(They're putting their two energies together to form a third. They're
making copies of themselves, like the smaller two there eating by the fire.
I'm sure they made those two.)*

(Why would they do that?)

*(It's the biggest part of the survival stuff. Make a copy of yourself and
keep on living in your copy. It's basic in all living species, not just humans.
The rote is that you reproduce first, before you get around to eating, cold or
warm, whatever.)*

(But they already made two.)

*(That's a sort of guarantee that at least one will survive to make more
copies. If those two young new ones die or get killed before they make
copies, then the third they're making right now might live long enough to
get copies made.)*

BB flickered. *(Why would they die, or how would they get killed?)*

(That's one of the problems of physical life. It's easier to die or get killed

than it is to live. The strong survival drive is needed to achieve balance. That produces other problems.)

(What problems?)

(We'll get to them along the way.)

He focused on the couple below, who by now had completed their sexual act and were back eating before the fire. *(The two big ones are not the same.)*

(Humans, but different. Run the rote when you caught up with AA—he wanted to go back and be a female. Then the next time around, he had been a female. Humans are either male or female. It takes a male and a female to reproduce, to make a copy.)

BB turned inward, then opened. *(Which are you?)*

(Male.)

(You ever been female?)

(I don't have any rote on it, so I guess not.)

He opened more. *(Nothing like this in KT-95. Never had a percept like it, to make a copy of yourself. Fascinating!)*

I cut in. *(Well, it's not exactly a copy of yourself, it's a physical mix of the two, and you hope it might be a copy of you, but it never really turns out that way. It's just a physical vehicle. The curl who enters it might be a total stranger.)*

BB rolled. *(Don't get concerned, RAM. I'm not that fascinated.)*

(I get a percept that stronger curls than you have been caught into being human.)

He smoothed. *(At this point, I don't get any part of this survival stuff. That would be too much for me. The eating, I can adjust to, the warm and cool. If they can do it, I can do it. The reproducing, copy making, that would be fun, make a big game out of it.)*

I couldn't hold it back. *(Famous last words. Come on.)*

He blanked. *(No percept on that one. Last words?)*

I turned, went through the wall, sure that BB was following. I homed in on the one place that I knew would give him a strong rote on how distortion could accumulate. Ident New York, center of Manhattan, start with West Forty-second Street. The movement was quite short, and we came in at sidewalk level. The usual evening human composites were crowding one another, jostling, strolling, hurrying, and loitering. The eateries, the old movie houses overplugging underdone X-rated pornos on their marquees, the gimmick and gut shops, record stores blasting it out, the car and truck traffic filling the street—it hadn't really changed in thirty years, only more of the same. Yes, this would show it. BB was in the middle of the passing parade, unnecessarily ducking and trying to avoid bumping into people. I steered him over to the curb, out of the rush and crush.

He flickered. *(Where'd they all come from?)*

(Crossroads of the world, they used to call it. Come from everywhere, lot of them live nearby.)

(Why do they come here, this place!)

I smoothed. *(The percept is, you can find anything you want here in New York.)*

BB vibrated. *(Still doesn't come out new to me, even down in it.)*

(It's just the ident, that's all. But they're doing the same thing as the man back there by the woods, every one of them. Trying to survive. Doing anything to keep alive.)

BB flickered. *(I don't get the same percept. And the M Band noise is shaking me up too much. The scratchy stuff in the band, it's the worst! Never got that before anywhere! Where's it all coming from?)*

I smoothed. *(Close a little, that'll make it easier. The noise is coming from us humans. The scratchy stuff that screeches so much I finally figured out. It's their emotions.)*

(Emotions?)

(I won't try to give you a percept on it, you have to be human to experience it. It's the next-biggest problem after the survival drive. Makes humans do things they really don't want to do.)

He flickered, half open. *(Why do they make all the noise?)*

I plied. *(They don't know they're doing it.)*

He turned inward, closed. Then he opened slightly. *(You're human. How come you don't make M Band noise like that?)*

(I do. I just have it under control for the moment. Back in the physical, I blow it all over the place, I'm sure.)

BB opened and smoothed. *(All right. If you can take it, so can I. Now, what about this survival stuff?)*

I spun a slow 360. *(Within a short time-distance from this spot, you can get all of your survival needs taken care of and more. As much as you want, any kind you want, whenever you want. You ident it and you got it.)*

BB flickered. *(All the, uh, food to, uh, eat?)*

(From the hamburger joint over there to the top of that tower over in the distance. Go in and they will supply you.)

(The warm and the cool, the, uh, hut to stay in, the stuff you put on your body?)

(All here.)

(How about making copies, the, uh . . . yeh, reproducing?)

I rolled. *(I suppose you could get that, too, if you looked hard enough. Most of it here is, uh, doing the action without making any copies.)*

BB blanked. *(Why would you want to do it if you're not making copies!)*

I flickered. *(My percept has it that the survival imprint was so strong it wanted to make sure each species took the trouble to reproduce. So the act of doing it was made to be, uh . . . fun.)*

He blanked again. *(Fun! Those back there didn't act like they were having fun!)*

I plied. *(You have to be human to get that percept. It can't be handed out in a rote either. Anyway, you can satisfy that part of the survival drive, too, as much as you want.)*

BB lighted brightly. *(Then what's all the mix-up about! It's all under control! Humans get what they want, there's plenty of it, each curl soaks it up and goes back where he came from.)*

I turned inward and closed. This was turning into a hard lesson for me, not him. I was pretty sure it wouldn't work and it wasn't. How do I convey to him the fact that all humans have to spend most of their waking hours working one way or another just to survive, that humans want the same thing and kill each other to get it, that they get so involved in surviving they don't know when to stop when they have enough, that humans form big clubs they call nations and try to destroy other nations who they think threaten their survival, that the whole thing occupies their thoughts and actions so deeply they forget completely any other existence but physical human . . .

(You're leaking again, RAM,) BB cut in. *(You got it right. I wouldn't get a percept on any of it. What's this work stuff? You mean humans kill and eat each other? What do you mean, they forget?)*

I did the best I could. *(Work is what humans do to get money, uh, energy to pay, uh, give to other humans so those humans will give them what they want to satisfy their survival needs.)*

(Money energy, huh? Must be pretty strong stuff. I have no ident on it.)

(You wouldn't. Only humans have it, and it's strictly physical. Won't work anywhere except on physical earth and with other humans. Worse than that, each group of humans, uh, nations . . .)

(The big clubs . . . we have game clubs in KT-95.)

(Yes, the big clubs of humans. Each has its own type of money energy and they trade money.)

BB smoothed. *(So if I want a deer to eat, or a hut to be in, a cover for my body to be in, I got to give money energy to get it.)*

(You work, you pay, and you get.)

He focused on the cars moving by. *(How about those covers? Can you get them for money energy, too?)*

(That's all it takes.)

(It's too messed up for me.) BB smoothed completely. *(If I had to be human, I would stay away from all the rest of it and just hang around making copies and let it go at that. . . . What's so funny?)*

I was rolling hard and couldn't keep closed.

He blanked. *(That takes money energy, too?)*

I plied. *(One way or another.)*

Suddenly, I felt an urgent signal to return to the physical, loud and clear. I tried to resist it, and worked to get BB's attention at the same time. I had to go back, but I couldn't leave him where he was, he wouldn't know how to get out . . . but the signal was too strong and I couldn't help myself. I began to move away, slowly as I resisted, then accelerating quickly as I decided to go back and see what the problem was and return as fast as I could. I reached the second, slipped in fast, and pulled up into the physical. I sat up in the bed and looked around. Everything seemed normal, no full bladder, no tingle in an arm or leg from poor circulation, no aches or pains. Must have been external, phone ringing, jet aircraft overhead, whatever, it wasn't important. I immediately remembered BB, and I had the thought of him standing bewildered on the curb at Forty-second and Broadway. I went through a quick relaxation to try to get down and OOB, but I was too keyed up, I couldn't hold it together. On about the sixth try, I fell asleep.

When I awakened, it was morning. I thought of trying to get out and help BB, but it was the wrong time for me. I spent the day in my typical pattern, with BB flashing in and out of my consciousness. This was a case where I was 100 percent responsible and I knew it. Finally, late in the afternoon, I felt tired enough to relax, and went up to the lab, entered, and locked the door. I set up some sound signals and went into the booth. I lay back on the water bed, put on the headphones, and almost immediately started to relax. The rest was easy. I detached from the physical, rolled out of the second, started to reach, and stopped. There was a form directly in front of me.

(Hey, RAM, where you going?)

I vibrated. *(How did you get here!)*

BB was very smooth. *(When you started to pull that short skip, I just followed your ident. I wasn't going to stay in all that M Band noise if you didn't. Much better here.)*

(I should hope so.)

(Your survival must be going strong. You got more than one hut.)

I flickered. *(This is not a hut, it's where we work.)*

(I got a solid percept of you coming out of the physical body there. That yours?)

I vibrated. *(Certainly it's mine! I don't go into other people's bodies.)*

(Why not?)

I flickered. *(Well, uh, it's against the rules.)*

(What rules?)

(I don't know, it doesn't, uh, the percept is, you don't do it. I don't think I could if I wanted to.)

(You do a lot of turning and twisting when you come out, you know.)

I plied. *(I don't have a percept from outside watching me in action.)*

(We do much the same back in KT-95 in a game we play. Gets us in and out of the system over us. Hey, what are all those curls doing in that big hut over there?)

I vibrated. *(You didn't go over there, did you?)*

BB smoothed. *(Just hung around a little. Couldn't get your attention, so*

I had to do something. Tossed a couple of rotes to one or two. They were glad to get them. What they doing?)

(They are trying to break the survival habit . . . and to relearn what they forgot. It's a school.)

(I don't get any percept you need a school to do that.)

I turned. *(You need the rest of your one easy lesson.)*

I reached and stretched, headed for the lowest of the cycling rings, staying just out of phase with the physical. This was the part that was the rough stuff but I was sure we would be ignored and unmolested if we stayed just on the upper fringes. I didn't look forward to it. For purposes of comparison, I used the same Forty-second Street ident in New York. It was a short run and we came out fifty feet over the street. BB was beside me.

He smoothed. *(Back here again. No difference, except a big mass more of humans.)*

(Focus on the ones that you perceive best.)

BB opened, and evidently the change in the superimposed mass was apparent to him. The man rushing out from the curb to flag a taxi and running through it, and stopping bewildered as car after car passed through the space he seemed to occupy. The thin young male in long hair, who looked to be no more than eighteen, trying to get the attention of the young group leaning against a parked car, asking for a hit from the joint being passed around but unable to get their attention because they can't see or hear him. The burly policeman in full uniform swinging his night-stick, strolling along the storefronts totally unaware that he is unobserved. The smartly dressed woman of indeterminate age trying to find a coin for a newspaper in her purse as she unknowingly walks through the side of a nearby building. The older man trying to buy the offerings of two young hookers standing by a doorway leading upstairs, angry because they don't know he exists, watches as a physical man steps up, waves a double saw-buck in one girl's face as she turns and leads him up the stairs; the first man following. The old woman walking slowly along the street, oblivious to everything around her, reaching down occasionally to the sidewalk and attempting to pick up a half-smoked cigarette snipe, but her hand passes through it. The dark-skinned man standing defiantly in the middle of the passing crowds, intense hate on his face and knife in hand, slashing through each passerby without realizing he is damaging or hurting no one. The unshaven old man at the open bar across the street, trying to pick up and toss down every drink set in front of a customer, then climbing on a customer's back to try and get the taste and effect of the drink as the customer feels it, unnoticed and to no avail.

I turned to BB. *(Had enough?)*

He flickered strongly. *(What's the matter with them?)*

(They've died physically and they don't know it. All they remember is human physical existence and they're trying to hang on. That's all they got, they think.)

(Can't you give them a different percept?)

I smoothed. *(If you mean me, I have to have help when I get into that run. There are others who make a career of it.)*

BB blanked. *(Career?)*

(That's all they do, try to get the attention of such humans. Would you like to get a percept of an extreme distortion of the survival drive?)

He flickered. *(Sure, lead on.)*

I knew he was shaken, but I had to push him all the way. Then I could be positive he would appreciate the outer rings. I reached, homed on ident sexual pile, and stretched. After a short movement, we stopped. We were less than ten feet away. Beside me, BB focused, blanked, and closed. I waited, and he finally opened again slightly. I focused away from the pile of writhing human forms and half-closed. It was about all I could take.

BB vibrated weakly. *(What happened to them!)*

(They've died physically and they at least know they're different, not responsible, they think, so they're letting it all hang out.)

(But, uh, what are they doing, like that?)

(They have no interest but reproducing, not to make copies, but just the act of reproducing. That's all they know and all they care about. They keep trying but get no satisfaction because it takes a physical body the way they know it—and they don't have any.)

BB attempted to focus again, and turned away. *(Let's get out of here.)*

I wanted his rote to be absolutely real. *(Convinced?)*

(Yeh, yeh, let's go.)

I reached and stretched outward, positive he was close behind me, moved slowly outward. We passed through the density of still gray forms who were neither here nor there, barely conscious and waiting for something to happen—and it would, all positive. Very little M Band noise there. I eased us to a stop in the center of the next-innermost ring. There were forms all around us, very human. Each was aware and active in a tight circle that included only their own rote.

BB nudged me. *(Why you stopping here? Noise is still heavy.)*

I opened. *(There's a big difference. These know they no longer have physical bodies, but not much more. Focus in on a couple, and you'll get a percept.)*

BB turned and faced a woman who seemed to be walking in slow motion, in one place. She appeared middle-aged, overweight, tears running down her face . . . *(I'm sorry, I'm sorry, Mommy didn't mean to leave you, baby doll, but she just couldn't help it, but I'm coming back, I'm coming back to help you just as soon as I can . . . I'm coming back somehow . . .)*

I indicated a man who looked to be in his sixties, pacing back and forth rapidly, pounding his fist in the palm of his other hand . . . BB refocused . . . *(Damn, damn, damn! Just when I had it all set up to go out and enjoy myself. Damn! Now she'll spend it all on clothes and trips everywhere and I'm left out. Got to get back somehow, got to get what's coming to me. Damn! Damn! . . .)*

We turned in the direction of a man who appeared to be sitting down, indeterminate age, slowly shaking his head from side to side, staring blindly . . . *(Never got a chance to tell her I didn't mean to beat her up. I was drunk, I was drunk, that's all. What a hell of a note. What am I going to do now? I knew that turn in the road was coming . . . There's got to be something I can do . . .)*

A thin young girl in blue jeans attracted our attention. Hands on her hips, she was looking around defiantly . . . *(Shit! Is that all there is to dying! I don't see any God or angels . . . I knew it, knew it! Shit!)*

We moved carefully around the various animate human forms, singled out another, a man of middle age, gray-haired, standing and looking at the haze, arms folded . . . *(Well, I did the best I could. Left them money in the bank, house in good shape, insurance will take care of the mortgage. Right front tire on the station wagon needs replacing. Hope Ben will take care of the contract on the Holmes deal. Company is going to miss me.*

Would have enjoyed one more dinner at Luigi's, never get seafood like that again . . .)

BB swung to me. *(He's closed up tight. We can't reach him?)*

I plied. *(Go ahead and try.)*

He moved directly in front of the man, tossing small rotes at the man's face. Each time, the man waved his hand as if he were brushing a persistent fly off his nose. Other than that, there was no response. BB finally gave up and followed as I turned and moved outward through the haze of the ring. It was hard for me to accept now that I had once been as deeply focused in HTSI, but I was sure it was so. If my rote of it was there, it was deeply covered over. I like to think I released it, of course.

One more stop before we reached the null point should do it. When the haze began to lessen somewhat, I came to a stop. A woman was standing amid what seemed to be jagged rock outcrop. She was aware of us immediately and began to scream. BB started to back away.

The woman came at us, waving her arms. *(You stay away from me, you spawn of the devil! I was a sinner, but I didn't sin any more than everyone else, I tell you! You can't take me to hell, because I'm a good woman! You go after those harlots down on Front Street!)*

She stopped abruptly, sank to her knees, head bowed, sobbing. *(Please don't take me to hell . . . Please! I just want to be with my daughter. She's around here somewhere, she was so good. She couldn't help dying before me. I know she didn't go to hell . . . Please, please!)*

I did what I could. *(Your daughter was good. If you just rest quietly, she will come and find you. Think of her, sit quietly and think of her, and she will find you. What was her name?)*

The woman's sobbing eased, but her head remained bowed and she was unable to think clearly. I did get a percept. *(Claire will find you very soon.)*

The woman slowly raised her head, eyes open in wonder as I turned and led BB further outward through the haze.

BB came beside me. *(You sure swung that one, RAM.)*

I plied. *(Beginner's luck.)*

He blanked. *(What's . . .)*

(More human stuff. Come on.)

Sometimes my navigation wasn't as good as I would like it to be. We finally broke through the haze into a cleared area. This was my intended stopping point. To the right, the surf of a white-capped blue ocean crashed regularly against a rocky shore. Overhead, the sky was a lighter blue with no clouds. In front of us was a simple log cabin, and behind the cabin rose a forested mountain. It could be either Maine or California, but it wasn't. It wasn't anything.

(Hey, why we stopping?) BB cut in.

(Ident Charlie. A friend of mine. Try it.)

He did, and I knew what was happening. All I was perceiving suddenly came into BB, the ocean, the shore, cabin, sky, and mountain. He flickered. *(We back on your earth?)*

I smoothed. *(No, Charlie made it.)*

BB blanked. *(Charlie made it!)*

(He likes to be reminded of his favorite physical place, so he made a copy.)

(He can do that?)

(It's like a rote, almost.)

The door of the cabin opened, and Charlie came out. He was his usual short, round-bodied, round-faced self and wearing his usual plaid shirt. His hair was dark and straight this time instead of his usual tight blond curls.

He approached and we shook hands. *(Well, Robert, I see you got out again.)*

(Hi, Charlie. What happened to your hair?)

Charlie flickered. *(I, uh, got a new friend. She likes it straight and brown, so I changed it. She's in the cabin. Want to meet her?)*

(We just stopped by for a minute. Next time maybe.)

He looked in BB's direction. *(You got somebody with you?)*

I smoothed. *(Yeah, a friend.)*

He stared intently. *(I can just barely see the edges of something.)*

(Say hello to BB.)

Charlie looked dubious. *(I can't see you, but hello, BB. Welcome to Fantasy Land.)*

BB flickered. *(Uh, hello, Charlie.)*

Surprise crossed Charlie's face. *(I heard him! I heard him but I can't see him!)*

BB rolled a little. *(I get you fine, Charlie!)*

Charlie turned to me. *(You taught him the OOB routine. Now you have a traveling companion. That's great!)*

I smoothed. *(Not exactly, Charlie. You see . . .)*

(You will have to teach him to fine-tune a little better, Robert. I can't get even a clear outline, just something like heat distortion on the desert. You still hear me, uh, BB?)

BB must have pulled a percept from Charlie, who was wide open. *(Loud and clear, Charlie. Zero level, plus or minus three DB.)*

Charlie looked pleased. *(That's my language, BB! At least I hear you. Say, how do you like what I've done here? Took some doing to get the ocean waves to hit the rocks accurately, I tell you. Hey, Robert, you like sunsets. Watch this one.)*

We turned and looked out over the ocean. Slowly, the light blue sky darkened, and flares of red, orange, and yellow melded together on the horizon. Layers of clouds appeared which added perspective and texture to the scene. The edges of the clouds took on rose and mauve hues. It reminded me of Oahu in Hawaii.

Charlie turned to me. *(How's that for a first draft?)*

I explained to BB. *(Charlie was an electronics engineer in his last physical life.)*

(I thought I was pretty good,) Charlie added. *(That was nothing compared to what you can do here. What's your field, BB? You work with Robert?)*

BB flickered. *(I'm from KT-95.)*

Charlie looked puzzled. *(KT-95? New one on me. Where's the company located?)*

I decided to give it to him straight. *(He's not from earth, Charlie. He isn't even human.)*

He looked taken aback, but only for a moment. *(Now, come on, you're not going to start that kind of talk again!)*

I laughed. *(He's for real, Charlie.)*

He turned to where he perceived BB stood. *(Robert has been feeding me all these wild ideas about other worlds, energy fields we know nothing about, that type of thing. I can go along with him as to possible intelligent life on other planets somewhere beyond our solar system, but that's not what he means. Human life, even operating the way I am now, I can handle that, too. So he got you to help him pull a fast one on Charlie. You put yourself a little out of sync to make yourself look hazy, and whammo. Robert has himself a super being.)*

BB flickered. *(Now, Charlie, I didn't . . .)*

(O.K., I can go along with a gag as good as the next one.) He chuckled. *(Where did you say you're from?)*

(KT-95, Charlie.) BB smoothed. *(It's different from here.)*

(Sure, I bet it is.) He laughed. *(What do you do there? I mean you, personally.)*

(I, uh . . . play games.)

(What kind of games?)

(They're hard to explain, but I can show you one.)

Charlie smiled. *(O.K., show me. I'm a Missouri boy.)*

I cut in. *(I don't think you should . . . BB. We, uh, we don't have enough time.)*

Charlie laughed hard. *(Had to bail him out, huh, Robert? You should have coached him more. I suppose, BB, you've come to earth to save us humans from ourselves, stop the nukes from going off or some such thing.)*

BB blanked. *(No, no. We were on this tour of TSI and . . .)*

(Just visiting, that it?)

(That's all. Then . . .)

(Just where is this KT-95 you say you came from?)

BB flickered. *(Uh, just pull a couple of long skips that way.)*

Charlie turned to me, grinning. *(Nice try, Robert. I appreciate all the trouble you and BB took to dream it up. Bring me a little hard data and I'll believe you.)*

I smiled. *(I'll keep trying. We have to leave now. Thanks for your hospitality. I liked your sunset.)*

Charlie and I shook hands, and he turned to BB. *(Come back and visit, BB. You don't have to wait for Robert to bring you.)*

BB vibrated. *(I don't?)*

(Come whenever you feel like it. Next time you won't have to detune. Then I can see you better.)

(By the way,) I put in, *(you decided yet about your next physical life?)*

He shrugged. *(I'm still thinking about it. I'm in no hurry.)*

(That's good. Be selective next time.)

(That I will.)

I smoothed. *(Take care, Charlie.)*

We lifted outward, and soon we were back in the haze, and I could tell from the change in texture when we passed the null point. From here on out, things would change rapidly. The question was, where to drop in next? BB was tight beside me, and I knew he was trying to sort out the solid shots of rote he was receiving. I tried to get a percept of the impact on him, but he was closed too tightly. But I didn't really need a percept. Charlie had impressed him. Here was another human being—albeit without a physical body for the moment—that he could relate to easily. After the mess in the lower rings, here was a Charlie who seemed perfectly normal, who knew how to do things—play?—in ways that were new and exciting to BB, and a being who had a sense of humor much as *he* did. Only one small problem. Charlie wouldn't believe BB existed if he had the real rote.

I decided we were deep enough into the outer ring, so without an ident I pulled to an easy stop. The haze was less dense, and the shape of buildings, irregularly spaced, began to take form—each a suitable distance from another, each different in design either extremely or slightly. Many seemed to be constructed of stone, most were equipped with spires, steeples, domes, or towers in various configurations, some had elaborate stained-glass circular windows. We moved down near the front of the nearest building. As we did, a woman emerged from the front door and descended the wide steps. When she reached the last step, she looked up and stopped short. There was no fear in her eyes, just uncertainty.

I decided to set her straight. *(We don't bite.)*

She responded immediately. *(I didn't expect you to. I was trying to decide where to refer you. We have so many committees. You don't act like a newcomer.)*

I smiled. *(We're just visiting.)*

(Our minister says there is no such person as a visitor here,) she replied confidently. *(You wouldn't have found us if you didn't have our faith. It's really all right to be a newcomer. I'll take you to Thelma. She's in charge of the welcoming committee.)*

I smiled. *(No, thanks just the same, we're only passing through.)*

She looked puzzled. *(You keep using "we." Do you think you're more*

*than one person? We have a class on multiple personalities that you can
attend. Dr. Frankel conducts it.)*

BB cut in. *(Why can't she perceive me, RAM? Charlie did.)*

She smiled at me. *(What did you . . . Oh. Your name is Percy RAM
Charles?)*

(Not exactly,) I answered. It was interesting. She was mixing BB's radiation with mine to fit her percept.

(Isn't it wonderful to know, really know you have everlasting life?) She
stretched her arms outward from her side. *(Oh, I remember so well how I
felt when I died and they brought me here. How I harbored little secret
doubts, and I do understand how you feel. Sunday school and the reindoc-
trination classes will clear those up for you. Don't worry. It's just unusual
that you arrived here on your own.)*

I had to ask it for BB's sake. He was focused very intently on what was
taking place. *(Then this isn't heaven? This isn't where God is?)*

She laughed lightly. *(That's exactly what I asked when I was a newcomer. Don't be disappointed. We're only at the gates of heaven. Our
minister, Dr. Fortune, preaches sermons about it every Sunday. I must
confess they're quite different from the ones Reverend Wilson used to
preach back when I was living physically, in Lexington.)*

(Are you going back?)

She frowned. *(You mean back into a physical life?)*

I smoothed. *(I guess that's what I mean.)*

She was thoughtful for a moment. *(I don't know. Dr. Fortune has sermons about it. He says when you leave here, you can go back again or you
can go somewhere else.)*

BB cut in. *(You get that, RAM? This, uh, Fortune curl found himself a
solid percept!)*

I turned to BB. *(That's right.)*

The woman was staring at me. *(You mumble your words, don't you? Yes,
I think Dr. Fortune's perception is right. But he's a man, not a girl.)*

I persisted. *(Then people do leave here?)*

She smiled. *(Oh yes. We lose several of our congregation every Sunday.
Dr. Fortune says it's all right.)*

(What happens to them, do you know?)

(They get up after services and walk out the front door ahead of everyone

else. After that, we don't see them again. They're gone when the rest of us leave. It's a, uh, ritual our church conducts here.)

I took it as far as I could. *(Do they finally go to heaven?)*

She was very open and clear. *(Most of our congregation think so. Dr. Fortune is ambivalent about it. At the close of each service, he issues something like the call that the Reverend Wilson did back in physical life. People get up, walk down to the front of the church, and there he says something to them the rest of us can't hear. Then we sing a hymn, and they march out.)*

(What do you yourself think? Where are they going?)

She hesitated. *(I don't know. Things are so different here from what I expected and I've learned so much . . . I just haven't made up my mind.)* Then she laughed. *(But you're asking me questions. The welcoming committee are the people you need. I'll take you over to . . . Wait a minute, where are you going?)*

(We, uh, I have to leave now.) I called out to her as we moved upward, *(See you in heaven, I hope!)*

She stood and gazed in wonderment as we moved out, and I finally lost her in the haze. I've often been curious as to her reporting of our visit—if she did. We moved slowly as I tried to plan a suitable stop for the last part of the lesson. I was glossing and skipping over so much that I was unsure as to the value of the entire trip. This was no job for a neophyte, and I certainly was just that when it came to quick, easy lessons. I was still too human myself. BB gave me the answer when he pushed at me.

(Hey, RAM, we going to heaven now?)

I rolled a little, then smoothed. *(Not yet. I have the percept I couldn't if I wanted to.)*

(Then how about where there are humans who will toss a few rotes with me, not you? This is supposed to be my lesson and all I do is hang around, you know what I mean? Let's go back to Charlie.)

I didn't reply, but the percept flared brightly, and I began moving rapidly. I was positive where our last visit should take place. I led us to the very outer fringes of the outermost ring, where the haze was quite thin. The rim had a glow to it as we approached, and as we entered, the glow broke down into soft individual light sources, those who resided here. These were the teachers, the helpers, the so-called guides of the inner rings—all on temporary but dedicated duty. I had one ident in particular and I homed in on it, with BB following. It was only moments later that we eased to a stop. One form broke away from a group and approached us. It was only slightly humanoid in shape, glowing softly.

I opened. *(I took you at your word, Bill. We've come visiting.)*

The form smoothed. *(We were expecting you, Bob, and this is your friend from KT-95. Welcome, BB.)*

BB flickered. *(Uh, hello.)*

It was no surprise that Bill was aware of BB and the whole sequence of events. I sometimes get the dim percept that my entire adventure, including this one, had been neatly planned from the beginning. Thus, I let Bill and BB get it together and they did.

BB began it. *(You're human like RAM here?)*

Bill rolled a little. *(I have a solid mass of human rote, BB. I've been through the mill, as it were. But at this point, I don't have a physical body as Bob does.)*

(You want a rote from me? What I am and that stuff?)

(That's not necessary. I have a fine percept of you, your friend, uh, AA, and KT-95. What I would like is your percept of the human experience with your one easy lesson.)

BB flickered. *(It's uh, not too solid. You sure you want it?)*

Bill smoothed. *(Just as it is.)*

(Yeh. Well, uh . . . it's the wildest bunch of games inside of games . . . With, uh, rules on top of rules that get so mixed up you don't have any percept at all of which game you're playing. Then they get so busy playing so many games they forget it is a game, the whole thing. Even why they're playing it and how they got in it to start.)

(That is very well put, BB.)

(Why, I could take the rote I got, just what I got, the real rote, go back to KT-95, and feed it out one after another, each part as a game, and keep those curls back there skipping so fast they would spin out.)

(I'm sure you could.)

BB flickered. *(But there's some missing parts . . . and, uh, the game isn't any game without it.)*

Bill was very smooth. *(Such as . . .)*

(How do they keep score! Who does the keeping!)

(Good questions.)

BB vibrated. *(Where's the fun! Why play a game if you don't have fun playing it! All those humans in there, I didn't get a percept of just one having fun.)*

Bill plied. *(They do part of the time, and some but not many most of the time, and very few all of the time, but they're hard to find. Your broad percept missed these fine edges.)*

BB flickered. *(There's one other thing.)*

(Yes?)

(This other part that messes up the M Band so badly . . . the scratchy stuff. RAM called it emotion. I don't have the least percept of that. He puts it I have to be human.)

(Emotion is the points, the score.)

BB blanked, and I waited for Bill to lay this one out. I would like to know, too.

Bill went on. *(Emotion is what makes the game seem so wild, but it is the game, the one game in which all other games are played. The others feed score to the big game in the form of emotional energy. The big game is to control and develop this emotional energy to its most effective condition, which is vaguely set by us humans as love, until we graduate. The more we score, the more fun it becomes. Most of us here—where you are now—we spend our energy going in to help other humans, however and wherever we can, to improve their score—and so have more fun.)*

BB turned inward and closed. Finally he opened again. *(Uh, Bill?)*

(Yes, BB?)

BB flickered. *(I don't have any percept of this emotion and love energy stuff. Not a single skim.)*

Bill vibrated gently. *(Of course you do.)*

BB blanked. *(I do?)*

(Why are you here now? Why did you take the trouble to come back from KT-95? Why have you been . . . hanging around? Why did you want to go through this one easy lesson with Bob? Why not just go back to KT-95 and play some games?)

BB blanked completely, then slowly turned inward and closed tightly. There wasn't the slightest radiation or movement in him that I could perceive. Bill reached out gently, but BB gave no response. I had never been present when anything remotely like this had happened to anyone nonphysical, except those in the stunned-out ring right after physical death—and I hadn't ever watched the start of the condition in that case. I began to vibrate.

Bill opened gently. *(You'd better go back now. We'll take care of him.)*
I vibrated more. *(Will he be all right?)*

(It's a big rote he's absorbing. The fact that he's never been human makes it . . . different. He'll be fine.)

I began to think that I never should have taken BB on the tour, when Bill cut in. *(Bob, I was the one who gave him the rote that put him down. He's in the equivalent of what we used to call shock. Head back now, your energy is weakening. We will take good care of BB. He will recover.)*

I turned reluctantly, did a half-roll, and dove down, following the ident of my physical body. I was relaxed and sure because there was no better help for BB than Bill and his friends, except perhaps the INSPECS—and the line between the two was very, very thin. I picked up the second and reentered the physical without incident. Everything was calm and normal, except that I forgot to check the clock.

I kept thinking about the thin line in the weeks and months that followed.

15.
Promised Plan

Time: 2:32 A.M. . . . . awakened with full physical awareness, felt the familiar INSPEC signal, soft, not insistent, but there . . . feeling of relaxed confidence . . . went into short focusing routine, then unhooked from the physical, then the second . . . much like doing two slow half-rolls in an airplane . . . homed in on the ident, and with very little sense of movement, I was with them at our usual point of meeting. I knew now that I would never go beyond this point again, into where they are, until I had fully released my physical body. Even with the compelling attraction that the knowledge of it evoked, I believed I could handle it, at least for now.

(We enjoy your human terms. Handle, as you use it, does not imply a point of grasp for your physical appendage, but capability to act properly. Therefore we do learn from you.)

I still found it hard to imagine their learning anything of significant value from me, but if THEY felt that way, fine.

(We learn much of importance from and through you, Ashaneen.)

I still remember the first time I became aware that I didn't have to form questions, how disconcerting it was that THEY perceived every thought that I had, including questions before I got a chance to ask. It all smoothed out when I accepted the fact that whatever I thought, believed, responded to emotionally, was just being human and no judgment was passed therefrom. What a joyous freedom!

(Yet you would not know of it as a freedom if you had not experienced the repression.)

Yes, the comparative factor seems always to apply. Without it, perhaps there can be no change or at least the awareness.

(At this point, we believe you are ready for another awareness. You may now appreciate the prospect of what you are attempting to perform in your present time. It is not to state that you alone may bring into earth reality

such prospect. Yours is but a small part of a whole that may come into being, aided and supported by many, many others who contribute their small parts, just as you are doing. However, with your effort in your present time, you can complete your portion and you can return home, only to return and share in the fruits of what you are propounding when they have matured. These fruits are what we are about to show you.)

Their use of the term "home" brought a surge of nostalgic yearning, and I turned inward and closed. Echoing through me came the fragments of the rote I could never totally express—the serenity, complete feeling of belonging, to recall the vitality I had forgotten, the crisp, warming clarity of . . . and yet it was not quite right. Something was missing, too deeply hidden, or had I . . . I opened.

(We thought it might be important to you. We can show you this as an observer, not as a participant.)

Even as I vibrated, I blanked. If THEY planned it, it must be something big, but I couldn't read them as THEY did me. What . . .

(We can escort you to a physical earth possibility at a point in your time measurement beyond the year 3000. The principal inhabitants are what we call H-plus, humans-plus, to indicate modification from those in your present time. As you are now, you will be a visitor.)

Well! So that was it! I had made only a few visits into future time. I would never have the guts to try such a jump by myself, but with them . . .

(Close tightly. It will be better that way.)

My excitement was great and my vibrating reflected it, so I turned inward, folded it all back in a loop, and closed. This would be the real rote, not the projections and imaginings of those looking at the small trends which always . . .

CLICK!

We were high above the earth, much as one would perceive it from halfway to the moon, which was still there, behind us. The earth was the same blue-green color, with white covers of clouds partially obscuring the land below. We moved in steadily, and I was happy to see that the deep gray and brown rings were no longer there—which meant the blockage got cleaned up. Good! No more repeaters. But it was the new feature that pulled my focus and wouldn't let it go. Around the earth was a single flat ring, much like the ones around Saturn, and it was radiating and sparkling, not from the reflection of the sun, but from its own internal source.

(You will understand fully the meaning of the ring as we progress.)

As we moved around, not through, the sparkling ring and headed inward, I became aware of another change. The M Band was full of communication, but no noise. No noise! That could mean only one thing—man had finally got it together. Further evidence was the lack of the haze M Band noise creates. No more random thought-clutter. This at least gave me a beginning percept of what I might expect.

We came into a low altitude, at about eight thousand feet, and began circling the earth over the northern hemisphere, east to west near a 28-degree latitude just a few miles off the coast of what appeared to be Japan. The seas were soft light green, and gentle swells some ten feet from trough to crest moved majestically over the surface. Deeper, I could perceive schools of fish leisurely weaving along, not too fast, their track matching neatly the contour of the distant coastline—thousands of them, silver sides flashing as they made their quick changes in direction. There had indeed been changes if they schooled so closely to the shore, so many of them. It was familiar, yet there was a missing element. I scanned the ocean surface and knew immediately what it was.

No ships. I reached out along the horizon and far beyond. Not even a rowboat or dinghy. I scanned overhead across the sky with its streets of white cumulus clouds. No aircraft, just gulls and terns sweeping and searching among the heavy swells, and higher than that, beyond cloud base—nothing. No jet contrails, no jets.

Then we had crossed the coastline and were over Japan. Off to the north was Fujiyama, a white cone glistening in the sun. Below us was a neat carpet of tidy fields in large checkerboard squares, each a subtle shade of green—correction: much more than greens. Spotted among the green like a gigantic bouquet were clusters of fields each of a different color, one a mass of bright orange, another deep blue, whites, reds—fields of blooming flowers, bushes, and evidently hybrids of the two, because no flower could be *that* large. It was a pattern that could be seen only from high overhead, yet there were no aircraft—and that began to give me another faint percept.

As we moved west, I became aware of other missing signs. There were no roads, not so much as a lane to service the fields. Also, no buildings, no houses, no barns, no sheds—I scanned in all directions and there were none. No cities, no towns, no villages, no power lines, no cars and trucks, no bicycles—all gone. The air was clear and clean, no smoke or smog.

Then I had a flashing percept. There were no people. That was what I actually was looking for—men, women, children. What terrible catastrophe took them all away!

(They are there. They are fewer in number, but it was not an event that made it so. What you perceive is by design.)

We began to move more rapidly, westward, across the unending array of colored bouquets set in green, some so large they appeared to be many miles in width, and soon we were again over water, the Sea of Japan, as I remembered it, and still no ships on what once was such an important transportation route. Back over land again—the Korean peninsula?—and the pattern was different. In every direction were tall and stately trees with close upward-turned branches, of a species unfamiliar to me . . . but again no sign of human artifact to indicate Kilroy had been anywhere near the place.

(Your percept is—how do you call it?—obsolete.)

Before I had a chance to turn inward on that one, we were over water again, moving even faster, and back over land. This would have to be China. Surely with its teeming millions, some had to be visible. Evidently they didn't have to be at all. We swept over mile after mile of deep green forests broken only by occasional grassy clearings and wide rivers and streams. Where are the rice paddies so vital to human sustenance?

(There are a few, but for a different purpose. Bird sanctuaries.)

The land below became more rugged, and soon we were skimming between the ranges and peaks of very mountainous terrain. Vegetation was sparse, and snowcaps flashed by as we passed at what seemed Mach 2 speed, or greater. I would be more comfortable with a little safer altitude; my old half-bold pilot experience was coming out. Being half-bold had let me grow old but not gracefully. The sheer snow-laden rocky side of a high ridge came rushing at us.

(You can move through it and out the other side. It is no different now.)

The ridge was almost upon us. I closed tightly just as we were about to crash. There was a slight change in the texture around me momentarily, and it was gone. I opened, and scanned behind us. The high range was fading in the distance. Passing through physical matter is not yet my habit! Quickly, the earth below was beginning to level out again, the color of the forest changed into lighter greens, and the cleared areas became larger. I tried to remember my geography—we were over the Middle East, I thought . . . yes, there they were coming up, still the rolling, sandy, near-desert areas, where the oil came from. I scanned in all directions, and saw very symmetrical clusters of trees, but no tanks, no pipelines, no pumping wellheads, nothing to indicate man had ever set foot in the area. Either the oil fields were pumped dry or there was no longer a need for oil.

(Both percepts are accurate.)

We moved out over water again—Mediterranean Sea?—and higher, faster, a scrap of land blinked by underneath which I could not identify and more water, heavy waves, this must be the Atlantic . . . land again, a sudden slowing and we landed gently in a field of grass amid rolling hills. I looked around me, wondering why we had stopped at this particular place. It was very faintly familiar. I was standing on a knoll, in a field of rich green grass whose blades were so even they must have been recently mowed . . . no, not cut, they were growing evenly. The edge of a woods of oak trees, limbs spreading broadly, rose behind me. In the far distance, a series of ascending green-blue ridges formed giant stair steps upward . . . Why stop here, why at this place?

(It is their wish. They are expecting you.)

The INSPEC energy faded and I was alone. I seemed very physical as I stood there. I could feel the sun on my face. Light, cool breezes ruffled my hair. Hair? I wasn't supposed to have . . . They were expecting me? I scanned in all directions, but with no ident, no, no, there *is* one, and it's very, very familiar . . . over in the woods. I turned and walked . . . walked? . . . that inferred legs. I looked down and I did indeed have legs, very normal and very human, bare legs and bare feet, and I could feel the grass in my toes as I walked. I touched the rest of me as I headed for the large oaks, my body was physically real and warm under my fingers. I glanced down, and it was my body as a bean pole twenty-two years old

. . . hah! No clothes! That's some kind of progress. Now I could feel the soft wind against my body, the air in my lungs as I breathed. It was the first time that I could remember that I experienced a fully operational physical body in this state of consciousness. But I don't see why I had to go all the way back to a skinny six-foot, one-thirty-seven-pounder . . . I reached the edge of the woods and started to enter, when I ran into a barrier, something that threw me back into the field. I stopped and looked, but my percept showed nothing. The familiar ident I couldn't associate with anything was behind the barrier, so I tried again. It gave a little, but no more—and the invisible force itself was familiar yet I couldn't connect the ident and the barrier. Something was missing.

(You can stay in the grass and we will join you there.)

No sound, it was NVC! We made it! Humans did it! We made the quantum jump from monkey chatter and all it implied! I was eager to meet the welcoming committee, whoever they were. I didn't have to wait but a moment. A man and a woman came out from under the trees and stood in front of me. At least that nice polarity hadn't changed. Both appeared to be in their late twenties, attractive, well formed, skin a suntan color, the man's hair light brown, the woman's dark. They smiled as I inspected them.

I opened. *(Well, I guess we haven't changed as much as I thought we would. Not physically, anyway.)*

(Sorry about the mix-up, RAM.) The man rolled. *(Your host forgot about the barrier, so we're taking his place.)*

I blanked. *(You must know me with that RAM stuff.)*

The man warmed. *(Yeh!)*

(And you're sure a familiar one to me. The ident is fuzzy. The way it comes out I know it's not right.)

The man vibrated and rolled. *(Not in a thousand years would you believe it! It's more than a thousand, so now you* better *believe it!)*

I had a bright flashing percept, and I *didn't* believe it. *(BB!)*

BB rolled. *(Who else!)*

I turned inward and found the rotes that had percepts on the barrier, where it had repelled me before, and I knew who my host was to have been. *(That's AA back in the trees.)*

BB opened wide. *(He was sure eager to meet you in person. He was so eager he forgot about the barrier. But he's getting percepts.)*

(Does he know what the barrier is?)

BB smoothed. *(Yeh, he knows. But he told me you have to find out for yourself.)*

I turned to the woman, no longer able to resist the enormous pull she knowingly or unknowingly was exerting upon me . . . her smile told me it was the former, but she was closed tightly and I respected the signal. Like BB's, her ident was strong, far stronger . . . but it was fuzzy. How could I forget such a vital, important . . .

Her smile was mischievous. *(You don't.)*

(Well, what do you want to know first?) BB cut in. *(I could run you my rote but it might not be what you want.)*

I turned to BB. *(Exactly what year is it?)*

(Year? Oh . . . time. They gave up that kind of measuring somewhere after they reached the 3000 mark. Didn't need it anymore. What next?)

I flickered. *(Where are we? I know from the way we traveled on our approach that we're just inside the United States near the coastline.)*

BB smoothed. *(AA thought this would be where you would like to come first. Not the United States any longer. No states or countries anywhere. Don't need them. But you ought to get a percept on this particular place.)*

I turned and scanned around me. It *was* familiar. The knoll where we were standing, the rising tiers of blue-tinted ridges to the west . . . Blue ridges! The percept was total. How many times before had I stood on this very knoll and looked to the west, had made the stairway of rounded hills my launching chute, the flood of living human experience I had attached to this spot, this site . . . the houses, fences, buildings, roads, all were gone. The lake. The lake was still there. And trees, so many more trees and of varieties I had never seen before, and to the east, there was . . . water. Water where once was a four-lane highway, water stretching off into the horizon.

(We call it Virginia Bay for old times' sake. Part of the ocean.) BB was very smooth. *(You always yelled about the law of change. Some of us hibe here also for old times' sake.)*

I blanked. *(Hibe?)*

The woman opened ever so slightly. *(We store our favorite human bodies here under the oak trees until we need them.)*

(Which is not too often,) BB added.

I turned inward. Hibe . . . hibernation. Sure, why not? Simply a vast improvement on the old OOBE pattern. But to leave it lying around under an oak tree . . .

(We put a super Reball around it,) the woman responded, smiling. *(It's so tight not even a virus can get through, so certainly it won't be bothered by ticks, mosquitoes, or anything larger.)*

The rote was building fast. "Reball," short for resonant energy balloon, which we were clumsily trying to generate, with mixed success, an energy field around the body to shield and protect, back when. And there are still ticks, mosquitoes, viruses, and bears no doubt.

BB grinned. *(No doubt at all.)*

I looked at him. *(What did you mean, not too often?)*

BB swung to the woman. *(You tell him.)*

The woman opened somewhat wider, and I could feel the attractive radiation diminish, and I knew it was deliberate. I also was sure she knew I would not attempt any further percept of her, if that was the way she wanted it. At least *that* hadn't changed either. Women still like to be mysterious.

(Not too often is about twice a week, more or less.) She smoothed, watching my reaction.

She got one. I blanked.

(All three of us here in human physical on the same day is quite unusual,) she went on, enjoying every moment. *(We did it just to meet you.)*

I smiled. *(I appreciate it, believe me.)*

(Remember how you used to say . . .) She laughed, then started again. *(You were always saying we are more than our physical bodies. Now it's the other way around. You, I mean we keep telling the new ones they are more than their energy selves.)*

I turned inward. This was more than I had ever contemplated, but one thing hadn't changed. One answer led to a hundred other questions. I needed to start at . . .

(You want your usual baseline. Well, we are still human beings, or beings being human. I guess?) She looked at BB, who simply shrugged. That was

unusual. AA must have instructed him to let the woman do the talking—correction: communicating.

I tried another direction. *(On the way in, I didn't see a single house or building, no roads, nothing to show that man was here or ever had been, no cities, factories, aircraft, cars. How come?)*

BB laughed. *(You didn't look very hard.)*

The woman glowed. *(Isn't it beautiful?)*

I was smoothing more. *(I can understand how you can sleep under the trees in weather like this, but how about winter? You still have to keep warm.)*

(The Reball takes care of that,) she answered. *(It keeps an air temperature layer all around the physical, just whatever you want it to be.)*

(How about food? You have to eat.)

She held out her arms in front of her body, level with her shoulders, palms upward. She closed her eyes and stood quietly. After a few moments, she lowered her arms, opened her eyes again.

(That gives this body enough energy for at least a week.) She sighed contentedly.

I flickered. *(You mean you don't get to taste food anymore, real food?)*

(Oh, that. Sure.) BB got into the act again. He reached down, scooped up a handful of red loam from between the grass roots. *(What'll you have? Wild rice? That's my favorite.)*

I watched, fascinated . . . decided to go with the game. *(No, uh . . . Silver Queen.)*

BB blanked. *(Silver Queen? What kind of . . .)*

(Here, I'll do it.) The woman took the dirt from BB, cupped it in her right hand, and stared at it intently. The dirt began to bubble and boil, changing color, re-formed into a small full-kerneled mature ear of white corn.

She handed it to me and I took it. It was hot to the touch. I carefully put it up to my mouth, took a bite. It *was* Silver Queen, the sweetest corn I ever tasted, with the freshness of just being picked. It even had melted butter, no, oleo dripping from it. I looked at the woman as I chewed avidly. She smiled knowingly. If she kept leaking percepts, I'd have her ident whether I wanted to or not and she wouldn't have her secret. I handed her the corn, and she bit into it. We both chewed and tasted.

I swallowed, wondering where the corn went when I did so. It didn't matter, so I smoothed. *(All right, you've convinced me. What about no roads, no transportation? Suppose we wanted to go to Japan. That's not within walking distance.)*

BB grinned. *(Why, we just pull a skip, that's all. Short version, of course. Why Japan?)*

(I noticed some very unusual patterns of growing things there when we came in.)

The woman smiled. *(It's very lovely, isn't it?)*

(First stop, Japan.) BB turned toward the woods, and the woman followed. *(We'll be right back.)*

I watched as they disappeared into the grove of oaks. I stood there waiting, mulling over the strange mixture of physical and other energies that was now earth life. I found I was unable to determine where one began and the other left off. There was no longer a sharp dividing line. Was it all like this?

(All ready?) I turned and there was BB and the woman standing beside me. They seemed different, lighter. *(We had to drop off the bodies.)*

I suddenly remembered. *(No tricks, BB.)*

BB rolled. *(No chance. She's handling the ident. You and I just play follow-the-leader after her.)*

I focused intently on BB, and stretched.

CLICK!

We were hovering over a rolling landscape, at about ten thousand feet. Directly below us was what seemed to be the center of a lotus blossom, the outermost petals in magnificent glowing colors spreading out in all directions for five or six miles. Beyond these were descending tones of green, from the very light of a fresh new leaf to the rich dark of the lower tropical rain forest. She and BB were beside me.

The woman vibrated. *(This is one of the nicest.)*

I could see why. I opened. *(Who did this?)*

(A group who wanted the area to give a percept of the beauty that began here. It was in existence when I came. Now others just take care of it.)

I got a clean, clear percept. *(The rest of the world, the earth, is it all like this?)*

(It has been restored to its original ecological balance, the way it was before humans upset it so severely. It's all back together again, every tree, every plant, every animal . . . all of it.)

(Plus a few improvements,) BB put in.

(But it's not all laid out in huge gardens such as this.) I focused on the woman.

(Only a small part,) she came back. *(The rest is made up of forests, woodlands, pastures, and prairies. Even the desert areas have been restored.)*

My percept had been quite clear. Humans had taken over Mother Nature's work—with a few improvements. I didn't need to ask the hows of it. The rote of the woman converting dirt into an ear of fresh sweet corn said it all. If a human could do that . . . I had to complete it. I was sure of the answer before I asked.

(Suppose we wanted to walk around down there. I mean in a physical body.) I smoothed carefully. *(How could we do it?)*

The woman vibrated. *(I'm sure there are any number of bodies under those beautiful cherry blossoms.)*

I pressed. *(We each could take over one, just like that?)*

(Yes, of course.)

I had to know. *(Suppose they all were already occupied . . . so to speak.)*

BB couldn't stay out of it. *(We'd make some new ones. Doesn't take long. You want to go down?)*

I flickered. *(No, no, not yet anyway. But what about the physical bodies you left under the oak trees? Can just anyone occupy those if they want to?)*

BB rolled. *(Sure, why not?)*

Why not? That took some fast adjustment. Then I pulled out the rote from back when, where others *had* occupied the physical bodies of our volunteers in the laboratory, communicated verbally, activated other portions of said body, including playing the piano . . . all without any wear and tear, or concern . . . why not!

The woman was smoothed at BB. *(I don't get the percept he's ready.)*

(Sure he is,) BB came back. *(He's a big boy now. It would give him the whole rote in one gulp. Have so much fun it would blow him away!)*

(Let's go back to the dorm first, as AA planned,) she came back easily. *(Then maybe go from there.)*

I opened. *(Do I have a choice in this?)*

She rolled. *(Of course you do.)*

I smoothed, holding back the vibration. *(Let's do what she indicates. I've had too much experience with your fun, BB. No offense.)*

BB rolled. *(Sure, sure.)*

The woman turned to me. *(Close tightly.)*

I did.

CLICK!

We were floating amid thousands upon thousands of white sparkling forms, each animated and vibrating. At first, the brightness and radiation was so overwhelming I was sure I would have to push the panic button or scream for my INSPEC friend. Then it lessened, and I felt the warm sense of understanding entering from all external points of me. I knew the forms had deliberately diverted their radiation, whatever it was, away from me so it conformed to my level of tolerance. I wondered how I must ident to them . . . probably a dull gray piece of fog.

(Welcome to the dorm of the renovated super-human school of compressed learning!) The ident was BB, no mistaking that. *(AA decided "dorm" was the best term to use. I have no percept what a dorm is.)*

I caught the smooth yet vague ident of the woman on the other side of me. She was bright and sparkling exactly as all the others. I knew she was human—or did I?—so must be all of the other sparkling forms.

I opened as much as I could. *(What's this place?)*

(You passed it when you entered earth.) As she sent it to me, I immediately got the flash of the sparkling ring. *(This is our reference point until we decide to . . .)*

She trailed off and closed. I tried to smooth. *(Decide to do what?)*

She opened slightly. *(I, uh . . . graduate.)*

I let that one rest for the moment. *(What do you do in the meantime?)*

She rolled lightly. *(Well, for one, we make and gather . . . what did you call it? . . . loosh. Like honeybees. Or Guernsey cows. Only now we know what we're doing and why, and we're happy to do it.)*

I turned inward and closed. This one I did understand, but the vastness of the change was near-unbelievable. But I was here, and the evidence was all around me. The interstate to freedom.

I opened again. *(What else do you do?)*

She lighted smoothly. *(Experience Earth Consciousness. Not just in physical human form—remember we could only feel part of it, just a part? Now we go through it completely, from the smallest unicellular life up, millions of different life cycles, most of which we were unaware of as only physical humans. Even the physical earth itself has an active consciousness.)*

I let that one go by, too, because I couldn't resist the follow-up. *(The natural food chain process, it still exists and you experience it? From beginning to end?)*

She came back gently. *(It's an important part of the learning process. We couldn't make loosh without it.)*

(Hey, RAM!) BB could stay out of it no longer. *(Some change, huh? No more haze, no more M Band noise, no more locked-in rings! Want me to show you around?)*

I turned to the woman, but she didn't respond, so I took that to mean it was all right. Also, she had closed. Evidently she wanted to keep her secret, and with a little more of her ident leaking, she wouldn't have any secret.

I followed BB. *(Lead on, old buddy.)*

We moved easily through the sparkling forms, and I hooked on to BB's ident to keep from getting lost. I could feel the radiation ease back in front of me, providing a pathway, so to speak, of low-level energy that I could tolerate. I was surprised when, passing various forms, a spark would fly out and touch me. In the sparks were spoken words that I heard very clearly . . . Hello, Bob. Hi, Robert . . . But I couldn't get an ident on any of them. Finally, BB stopped. In front of us was the First Entry Station. It appeared much the same. There was a large cluster of gray forms hovering around it.

(Lot of changes.) BB smoothed. *(But you wouldn't notice them if you didn't know better.)*

I ventured, *(Such as?)*

(Heavy cutback on the survival imprint, for one.) BB rolled. *(You remember that lecture you gave me, complete with living illustrations in the old rings? You'd be amazed at the difference that one change made.)*

I opened. *(I am.)*

BB blanked, then went on. *(Yeh, well, another thing is a solid pre-briefing and training before entry, especially as to continuing contact during physical sleep cycles.)*

I blanked. *(But you don't even sleep here, do you?)*

(No, don't need to.) Then he lighted. *(Oh, yeh, that's the other point. These first-timers go back before the changes as their first entry point, some of them almost back when humans first began being human. They take one human physical life cycle and one only, and come back here and join in. No repeaters, just one-timers.)*

I turned inward, then opened. *(Is this one-timer pattern going on back where I came from?)*

BB lighted. *(Oh, sure.)*

I flickered. *(I haven't had a percept on that taking place.)*

BB smoothed. *(Sure, you have.)*

I blanked. *(How?)*

(That last outer ring, remember? Didn't come near the repeater department? Just went up and faded out?)

I flickered again. *(But they were the ones going home.)*

BB vibrated triumphantly. *(Well?)*

I turned inward and closed. The whole thing was getting out of hand, or better, out of my mind-set, beyond my ability to absorb and understand instantly. And BB was pulling at me.

(Come on, RAM.) He vibrated. *(Let's live it up, let's have some fun.)*

I flickered. *(Fun? Well, I don't know, your idea of fun . . .)*

(Just usual stuff, I guarantee it. Things we do every day down there. Also, I got a hard rote from, uh, AA as to what to show you and what not to.)

I scanned beyond the gray forms around the Entry Station and into the sparkling lights beyond. *(Where is AA now? I never get a good ident on him.)*

BB indicated behind us. *(He's back there. That barrier thing won't let him come closer. But I'll bet he's going to follow us. You ready? Just short skips, that's all.)*

I felt much more confident, with that small percept. I reached out and stretched, holding on his ident.

CLICK!

I'm floating over a wide brown field, just about three thousand feet up . . . I'm flat on the bottom and strong life energy is pouring up at me from below . . . I'm getting larger and larger and I eagerly convert the energy into being me . . . I'm a whirling vortex and my action takes water out of the energy and helps me get bigger, and I become more conscious, more aware . . . as I get bigger, I'm able to know more . . . I'm like a round puffball on top, and I feel myself growing upward more than outward . . . now there's much of my life energy flowing in me, building up . . . *(Wait, that's . . . electricity!)* . . . if I can keep growing enough before the water leaks out, if the energy from below lasts long enough, I'll get strong, really strong . . . but I'm drifting away from the energy shaft and I can't stop the drift, so I'm not getting enough to, enough to . . .

CLICK!

We were floating over the earth, over a heavy forest. The brown field in the near distance was familiar. BB hovered in front of me.

He vibrated. *(Fun, huh?)*

I flickered. *(What was that!)*

He indicated behind me. I turned. It was a medium-sized cumulus cloud, white on the side where the rays of the sun touched it, gray on the back, with a dark flat bottom. Clouds have consciousness? The basis for life? Waters, minute bits of chemicals . . . and electricity! All the ingredients. What would a thunderhead be? Or a tornado, a hurricane, weather lows and highs!

BB cut in. *(Ready to go again?)*

I reached out and stretched, following.

CLICK!

I am in green water . . . it is lighter above me and darker below . . . my mouth is opening and closing automatically, taking in water, which flows through my head and out my ears . . . no, not ears. Gills . . . I'm a fish, a very big fish! . . . I can feel my stabilizing fins waving gently to keep me in place, my vision is split, I can't see exactly straight in front of me . . . behind me is almost a blind spot, but my peripheral seeing is tremendous, detail is exquisite, but not many colors, only one or two . . . I try moving, just thinking about it, and I speed forward very rapidly, turn right, left, roll, steep climb, then dive . . . wait, something on the surface when I climbed, gotta go back, grab it, hungry, hungry . . . I shoot uncontrolled through the surface, mouth open, gulping in something as I do . . . then out of the air and back into the water, diving with a great sense of satisfaction and something wiggling and crunching in the back of my mouth . . . a bug? . . . deeper, but it's not dark as I thought, I can still see wonderfully . . . I am aware of another fish diving with me, tail and back of the body sculling, sculling strongly . . . am I doing that, too? . . . I am! . . . it just takes care of itself . . . I just think and it works, like walking or running in a physical human body . . . I stop. Ahead of me is another fish, it is coming at me . . . no, it's gigantic, the water is deceptive, it's incredibly bigger than I am . . . it has hunger signals radiating . . . go, go, it's after *me*, swim, swim fast, it's coming after me . . . up to the top, up, up faster . . . signal in from my sides, another fish swimming violently beside me . . . signal from the stripes on my sides . . .

(RAM, when you're in the air, skip! Skip!)

I broke through the surface into the air, reached out, and stretched.

CLICK!

I was just above the water, and I saw the body of my fish, with a second one alongside it, arch through the air and reenter the water with the smallest of splashes . . . but immediately there was a rushing, a swirling under the surface.

(Fun, huh?) It was BB beside me. I couldn't reply, I was shaking so

hard, so he went on. *(I guaranteed AA I wouldn't let you go through the end of it. He had a percept you weren't ready and he was right. But you asked her about the food chain . . .)*

I vibrated. *(All right, all right!)*

BB smoothed. *(You always want it the way it is, don't you?)*

I smoothed also! *(Caught me by surprise, that's all.)*

(Well, this next adventure is quiet, nice and quiet. Ready?)

Everything is relative, including BB's idea of quiet. I reached and stretched . . .

CLICK!

I am waving gently up and down and bending, flexing . . . coursing into me from the smallest part of me, which is long and narrow with many tubes running through it, comes my share of the glorious life force, coming from the Whole, the family of which I am a part . . . and I know how much the Whole needs me and I gladly, joyously serve . . . as the energy that makes me waver and flex flows past my flat sides . . . *(Wait, that's just air, wind!)* . . . I take from it the parts needed by the Whole and send it back through the narrow tubes because it is needed . . . I do this so easily I don't think of it as work, it's breathing . . . it's what I'm for, to breathe for the Whole as I take ashes from the Whole and spread it out into the energy . . . my happy exchange . . . and the other, oh so important, my special shape . . . my profile, configuration . . . receives a special signal that the Whole understands, needs, and uses . . . all I do is receive it and send it on . . . and I'm happy, supremely happy . . . with a total knowledge of belonging, performing as I was designed to do . . . beautiful balance, giving . . . receiving . . . security and strength of the Whole . . .

CLICK!

BB was beside me. *(Gets to you, doesn't it?)*

I flickered. *(Where was that!)*

He indicated, and I turned. Very close to me was a leaf, an oak leaf. It was attached by a long stem to a branch. Beyond the branch was the

massive tree trunk, solidly dug into the earth. To have passed such knowing without awareness . . . I understood more this new Human school.

(Ready to go again? This is my favorite.)

I flickered. *(Well, uh, I'm not so sure. Maybe we ought to . . .)*

(This one we designed ourselves,) BB cut in. *(If you don't like it, give me
a signal and we'll pull a quick skip.)*

Reluctantly, I reached and stretched, followed.

CLICK!

I am lying down in soft thick grasses, lying on my side . . . I open my
eyes . . . tall trees surround me on all sides, their leaf-laden branches
form a canopy far overhead, sunlight filters through to provide good but
not overbearing luminescence . . . a large tan-colored panther is standing over me, staring at me intently.

(Come on, RAM . . . let's play!)

I roll over and stand up . . . stand up! . . . I have four legs! How
sure and stable it feels! . . . my head is out in front of my body, now I
have to turn to look at my back and hips . . . fur-covered, sleek . . .
what's that waving behind me? . . . it's a tail, I have a tail . . . I think
about moving it, and it jerks . . . back and forth, back and forth, how
about that! . . . but it goes up and down just a little bit, more down than
up . . . a scent gets my attention . . . smells, smells, I didn't know so
many different smells existed . . . know instantly if they're near or far
. . . the signal input is as good as or better than my seeing . . . and
hearing, I could know everything just from listening . . . I flex my legs,
pull in my claws . . . yes! I have claws! I feel great! Watch out, world,
here I come . . . such a glorious sense of being alive . . . totally alive, I
want to run, jump, climb . . .

(Well, come on, then!)

The tan panther lopes off through the trees, and I follow . . . faster,
now into a gallop . . . now running all out, dodging through the trees,
easily avoiding low branches . . . the exhilarating flow of smells passing
my nose and I sample them all . . . my eyes and ears picking up, identi-
fying and sorting a myriad of signals, all familiar . . . a large tree is dead
ahead and the tan panther runs right up the side of it and I follow, digging

in claws, pulling up, and digging in claws. It is waiting for me, sitting casually on a thick branch . . . I pull up beside it, sit back . . . he waves his tail . . . and I wave mine in reply.

(Pretty good for a beginner, RAM.)

I am too stimulated to reply. I am remembering the great sense of power in my muscles, sorting out the massive input that had come through my senses . . . how could humans have ignored and distorted such profound perceptions . . . have picked up so little of it when a lower animal . . . lower? . . . picked up so much.

(Have to go down now.)

The tan panther stands up, turns, and walks down the tree to the ground . . . walks *down!* I didn't know cats could do that, they always back down . . . I stand up, and slowly back down, jumping the last eight feet easily.

(Just lie down under the tree, near the trunk. Then pull a short skip, very short.)

I lie down in the tall grass, and very reluctantly reach and stretch.

CLICK!

We were hovering just above the ground, and I looked down. Below us, breathing shallowly and slowly, lying in the grass, was the body of the tan panther . . . and another panther body, a darker brown one, which I had occupied.

Beside me, BB rolled. *(Liked it, huh?)*

I vibrated. *(Wonderful!)*

(Well, we got one more for you to sample. This one, NA, uh, she picked out. She was sure it was your kind of stuff. You'll be alone, but she said you would know what to do. I'll just guide you there. Ready?)

Wondering what *she* would pick, I reached and stretched.

CLICK!

I am floating high over a rugged, snowcapped mountain range, and I can see for hundreds of miles in every direction . . . and I can see down, down on the ground . . . beautiful focus, in the most minute detail . . .

the leaves on trees, small animals as they move over the rocks . . . and I
am moving slowly, making a wide easy turn, the standing wave from the
mountain ridge offering solid and steady lift under my wings . . . wings!
I turn my head. Extending out from my shoulder is a broad arching wing
tapering to a round point, feathers ruffling in the slight turbulence. I roll
my head to the left, there is one to match from the other shoulder . . .
I'm not floating, I'm soaring . . . as a bird, *am* a bird! . . . a super
sailplane that does exactly what I think! I break the turn, and the feathers
on the trailing edge bend down on one side, up on the other, instant
ailerons . . . let's reach for maximum lift . . . there it is, more under
the left wing than the right, turn into the lift . . . feel the lift getting
stronger and stronger . . . it's peaking out, turn and circle . . . tighten
the turn, highest point of lift . . . must have a fifty-to-one glide ratio
. . . spiral up, tighter and faster . . . perfect control . . . air is thinner
. . . keep higher airspeed . . . wonder where the stall point is . . .
nose, no, head up more, higher angle of attack, more, hey, that's pretty
good! . . . would never think a bird body could . . . oops! it does stall
. . . easy to pick up speed again . . . Yeah! Just fold the wings and
doooooown we go!

(Hey, uh, RAM.)

And I bet these wings can take a big G load coming out of a dive if you
open them slowly . . . let's see . . . we'll just dive a little faster . . .

(RAM, you know what you're doing?)

That's about fast enough . . . now to open the wings a little at a time
. . . slowly . . . now back on the stick . . . uh, tail feathers up a little
at a time . . . there! All back to normal, back to cruising speed . . .
what a . . . hah! What a bird! Must be a condor . . . wonder what a
quick sparrow would . . .

(RAM, just pull a short skip. Now!)

I sigh . . . reach and stretch . . .

CLICK!

I was back in among the sparkling forms, and I closed tightly. The
radiation was making me break out in waves exquisitely familiar. After a

moment, the radiation lessened and I opened. I had ident immediately on BB, and the vague ident of the woman.

BB rolled. *(That big old bird must be wondering how his wings got bent.)*

I rolled with him. *(Oh no. There wasn't one strained tendon or muscle, not one feather out of line when I left. I guarantee it.)*

BB turned to the woman, a sparkling form I already had ident as her. *(He's your problem. I'll check with, uh, AA, and see you at the site.)*

I turned to the woman. *(The site?)*

(That's where we first greeted you.)

I turned inward. There were so many points left unanswered, and I had a percept that my visit was growing short. Get to the key items, those first.

I focused, completely open so nothing would be distorted. *(The first-timers, when they come back . . .)*

(One-timers,) she corrected.

I went on. *(If you have that constant input, you must have an output to keep the flow, the movement active.)*

She waited quietly . . . politely? . . . or had she percept of both questions and answers. I went on. *(So humans do graduate from here, the dorm. Question: What happens to the graduates?)*

She flickered. *(I . . . I don't have a percept of that. They just click out.)* *(One at a time or as a group?)*

She smoothed. *(Usually several at once. Every so often, one goes alone.)*

(And they never return?)

(No. They don't.)

(Any communication with them? After they leave?)

She flickered. *(Not in a way that we can understand.)*

I wanted to follow up on that one, but I was sure it would come out. *(Any indications or symptoms they are about to graduate?)*

She smoothed again. *(Oh yes. They no longer need to experience earth, so they begin to go physical less and less. Finally, they stop completely.)*

(Is that all?)

(No, their . . . uh, radiation begins to change. And they begin to close. After that, they click out.)

I had the percept she was beginning to vibrate. *(I don't want to act like an inquisitor, but . . .)*

She opened more. *(Go on. We expected you to ask just what you are.)*

I took another direction. *(I need as much of a rote as I can get. I may not get another chance.)*

She smoothed neatly, but there was a little roll in her response. *(Oh, I'm sure you will.)*

(In time-space,) I went on, *(are there many other growth patterns in consciousness similar to humans and earth?)*

She rolled. *(You can't count them if you wanted to, there's that many. And new ones coming on line constantly.)*

I flickered. *(On line?)*

She rolled stronger. *(AA knew you would like it if I used that phrase.)*

I went with it. *(I would like to meet this AA face to face sometime. He knows more about me than I do myself.)*

She didn't respond, just rolled more strongly. I didn't think it was *that* funny. *(But are humans now in communication with other such, uh, civilizations?)*

She smoothed out. *(Not very much. There is some exchange, but it doesn't seem necessary or important.)*

(What about other, nonphysical energy systems?)

She lighted. *(Oh, those! We visit them as often as we can.)*

I threw a high hard one. *(To gather loosh?)*

She turned inward, then opened carefully. *(No. To sow it, to plant the seeds. That lets the, uh, ray have an ident to focus on.)*

Now I was the one who turned inward and closed. Her simple statement implied so much knowledge that made everything else no more than sophisticated monkey chatter. There was much monkey left in me, too much. But I had a sudden percept, and I knew I had to verify it.

I ran it smooth. *(Are you about to graduate?)*

She flickered. *(Yes.)*

(How do you know this?)

She vibrated. *(He told me you would ask the question, but you didn't ask it right. So I can't answer it.)*

I didn't have to ask who the "he" was. *(But you gave me you didn't have a percept what happened to graduates.)*

She smoothed nicely. *(I don't. But you do.)*

I blanked completely. Did she or INSPECS have it that I was to do the informing? A boy to do a man's job? I was so closed I almost missed the rest of it.

She was vibrating warmly. *(We've been expecting this, uh, an event to take place. Then we can leave!)*

I was ready to ask about who the "we" was, and the event, but I felt the familiar INSPEC signal and began to respond . . . and so did she! So did she! A great flood of percept ran through me and I had all the answers . . . I thought.

(We have to go back to the site now.) She was smooth, yet vibrating. *(Are you ready?)*

I closed . . . ident the knoll . . . reached and stretched.

CLICK!

I was over the knoll . . . about a hundred feet up . . . the ridges were off to the west, so I turned, looking past the fences . . . fences! And there were the Center buildings beyond, with their dark red roofs . . . the gravel road showed a cloud of dust as a car rolled past. I had made the wrong ident, back to 1982. A strange mixture of emotions surged through me, and I knew it would take much to sort them out, if I could at all. I had even returned to the second body without direction, which was unusual. It was old stuff to home in on the physical, slip in . . . open my eyes and move my arms and legs. I looked at the clock. Time: 2:40 A.M. Eight minutes! Only *eight* minutes?

16.
The Gathering

Days, weeks, and months passed by rapidly without any unusual OOB activity. I had grown away from the desire to investigate the local events that used to attract me so deeply. Occasionally, in the familiar early-morning hours, I would awaken out of habit and detach from the physical. I would wait for a strong ident INSPEC signal, but there was none. After a few moments, I would reenter the physical and go to sleep.

During this interim, I had no sense of isolation or deprivation whatso-ever. The absence of the signal in no way inferred to me that I was being ignored or abandoned. Instead, there was a complete sense of security, a full-fledged desire to continue and broaden my participation in physical life around me, a freedom to express my self-maligned curiosity rather than anxiety as to daily and upcoming patterns. I simply went back to the grazing principle—knowing what I found today would lead me to tomor-row, whatever tomorrow was. The signal would come when it was appro-priate.

And it did. One morning I began to get a feeling of needing to do something I had forgotten. At first, I wasn't sure but what it was indeed something I had failed to do in my physical activity. However, around eleven that morning I became exceedingly drowsy, so much so that I went into the bedroom to lie down for a short nap. I wasn't tired, but I did need to sleep. Within seconds after stretching out on the bed, I dropped into deep relaxation. At that point, I could perceive it clearly. The INSPEC signal was there, cleanly defined and strong. I succeeded in staying calm enough to develop the OOB pattern, roll out and into the second. Sliding out of the second was automatic, and I reached and stretched, homing in on the familiar ident.

The change was instantaneous, no sense of movement whatsoever. The bright glowing figure was in front of me. I was aware of the radiation, but it was quite comfortable.

(Very proficient, Ashaneen.)
And progress, too.
(There have been many changes. We believe you are ready for the next—how do you call it?—step.)
It was not a percept, but I wondered idly if that was a polite way to inform me I would no longer return to the physical. Well, I could go add some music to Charlie's sunsets, or . . .
(That is not the step we have planned. You will know when your physical body release is to take place. We will not need to inform you. Nor do we plan or participate in such release unless you request it. You have much to complete prior to such change.)
I received that information with mixed emotions, one great part of me yearning to get on with it, the other reaching back to physical earth and the deep, poignant emotions I was sharing there. I remembered many years ago, during a strong pressure point, when the option to stay or complete release from the physical was available to me—and I agreed to take the physical as long as it was operational, whatever the situation, because I wanted to find out what happened tomorrow. Curiosity!
(We have explained to you that it is one of your assets. Completion of this next step will provide you with many answers.)
There was very much a missing element in the pattern, and nothing in this world would prevent my curiosity from seeking the answer.
(Nor out of this world. You need no longer stay closed for the shift.)
I managed to stay calm, but expectant.

CLICK!

We were on the far rim of the outermost ring. I could recognize it from the very thin ambience of haze. The soft white forms were all around us. I could perceive my INSPEC friend was with me, but there was no glowing form.
(There is no need to distract their attention.)
I reached for any percept of Bill, then of Lou. I couldn't find either.
(They have, graduated, as you put it.)
That was to be expected, and I had a percept of their new address, as it were, but there was some factor involved that disturbed me, and I

couldn't bring it out. Then I became aware of the intent inward focus of
the entire outermost ring, the inhabitants thereof. There was a strong
radiation of expectancy, not concern, as if the star of the show was about
to make an entrance. I followed the line of their focus. It was the physical
planet earth, indistinct and nebulous from this perspective.

(Let us take another viewpoint.)

By all means, and the phrase does fit!

CLICK!

We were out in space somewhere between the earth and the moon,
indeterminate distance, fifty thousand miles plus from the surface of
earth. It was very clear and detailed, not as it was before. I turned to look
at the moon and blanked. No more than a thousand feet away, or so it
seemed, was an immense, solid-appearing object gray in color, long and
slender, conical-shaped with a hemispheric dome at the widest end—the
other end was somewhere in the distance, at least several miles. It appeared motionless, but I had the definite percept of M Band radiation
from it. A spaceship, a physical spaceship?

*(In your terms, that is correct. It is not a human construct. There are
many of such around the physical earth at this point. Their origins are of
your physical universe but not necessarily of your time reference.)*

"Many" could be five or five thousand. There was no point in trying to
find out. But why around our earth, was it . . .

*(They are focused on the planet earth and humans just as you observed
the others, and for the same purpose. Shall we move on? The answer will
come soon.)*

My curiosity accepted gladly.

CLICK!

My immediate percept of the earth was a pinpoint of reflected light in
the distance, no larger than a small star. From it came irregular waves of
energy, multidimensional, pulsing, intermittently broken by occasional
quick flares, a complex unorganized pattern composed not of light or
electromagnetic or gravitic structure, but of some other energy that I

couldn't define. I was so completely fascinated by the display that I did not at first notice the background. As far as I could perceive in all directions, with the earth at the center, was a host of forms, countless numbers, it seemed. Some had shape, others appeared as no more than a wisp of cloud vapor, all glowed in various degrees of intensity. From those nearest us, I had the same percept of expectancy, of waiting for the show to begin. It must be some big show to attract all of these . . .

(It is what we call the gathering. These have manifested from other nearby energy systems only to witness the big show, as you call it, just as those within the physical spacecraft and your final-process humans. This big show which is about to occur is actually a very rare event—the conflux of several different and intense energy fields arriving at the same point in your time-space. It is this rarity that has attracted so much attention. In terms that you can perceive, it may occur once every eighty-seven million of your earth years.)

Very long odds, and a long time to wait.

(This does not warrant that it will be produced at that frequency. There are random elements and variables in the format which cannot be predicted.)

So random that the event might not take place, perhaps. There would be a lot of disappointed . . .

(It is long past such point. It will occur. The interest lies in the result. It is best symbolized to you as a convergence of a great number of possibilities which emerge as several probabilities and few possibilities. One of such probabilities may alter not only your time-space but all adjoining energy systems as well. Therefore the wide interest. In human terms, still symbolized, the gathering is here to observe the possible birth of a new energy. Will it survive the birth process, and if so, what are the potentials inherent in such energy that will predict accurately the same at maturity? Or will the energy arrive stillborn, and all the possibilities remain no more than that— weak uncoordinated possibilities?)

Running a bit of my exquisite H+ rote made it quite clear. But my still in-human self looked at earth and the human system . . .

(There is a human oriental symbol for crisis which is composed of two subsymbols indicating danger and opportunity. The event in human and physical earth terms is definitely a point of crisis. It is quite valid that as to

human existence both danger and opportunity will be present in extreme degrees.)

Danger? Physical danger? Mental? The . . .

(Those are the possibilities, the exact nature of which will be determined by the event itself. Whatever your percept may be is one of the possibilities. One or several will occur.)

The other side, the opportunity.

(That is the key to the understanding of the event. It will offer human consciousness a rare potential to emerge rapidly into a unified intelligent energy system that will range far beyond your time-space illusion, creating, constructing, teaching as only a human-trained graduate energy is able to do.)

Our visit to earth in 3000 plus . . .

(A possibility that may become probable with the event. Your action is one of the minute random factors that may make it so.)

If the opportunity is missed . . .

(Humans will retreat as the dominant species on earth until they no longer survive as active consciousness, eventually in any form.)

I asked it directly. *(And you, all of you, what will you do if that takes place?)*

There was a beautiful warmth and a soft smile in the response. *(We would just have to start up some action on some other planet in time-space with new humans.)*

I turned inward and closed. There was not much I could think or do. I was hit hard emotionally and I didn't want to lose it, not now.

(There is one more process we have to perform, then you can return to your physical.)

I wasn't sure I could handle one more, but I knew that I would.

(Ident your friend BB and guide him here.)

The rote spread instantly. I had left him with Bill, and Bill wasn't there . . .

(You will locate him easily. There is a very special function he can perform for us.)

No questions were needed, and I reached ident BB and stretched.

CLICK!

I was getting better, or older. No sense of motion whatsoever. And I had very little surprise at the location. I was on the grass in front of Charlie's cabin. BB and Charlie were over to one side, busily engaged in something. I went over to them just as BB perceived me.

(Hey, RAM!) He vibrated loudly. *(Look what we're making!)*

Charlie was laughing. *(I keep telling the kid you can't have a sailboat and a hang glider all in one. Air and water aren't the same!)*

I flickered. *(You can see him now, Charlie, visually?)*

Charlie smiled. *(Oh, sure. Worked that out the first day he got here. He must have changed the ocean a hundred times before I got him stopped. Had it yellow with square waves. How about that. But he's smart, catches on fast.)*

I smoothed. *(Well, I hate to break it up, but I need BB here to do something for me.)*

BB opened. *(You name it, RAM!)*

Charlie waved. *(Come on back, kid.)*

BB rolled. *(Who's to keep me away!)*

Charlie shook his head and laughed, and I reached, stretched for the ident INSPEC . . .

CLICK!

BB was beside me. *(Hey, you sure tightened your skip. I would never have hung on except I was used to it from a game we played back in . . .)*

He cut short and closed tightly as he became aware of the brightly glowing form of the INSPEC. I should have warned him, I guess. Below us was the physical earth, about five hundred feet. It was night and occasional lights dotted the countryside. Almost directly under us was an area of water like a small pond or pool, and immediately beyond, a green pyramidlike structure with a light glowing inside. It had a strong point of familiarity, but I couldn't bring it back.

I turned to BB. *(Just open slow. It's a friend.)*

He did so carefully, then focused on the bright glow. *(Uh, hello.)*

(We appreciate your coming.)

BB had no cultural restraints. *(We had a curl back in KT-95 who claimed he met you or one just like you. We put it off as some more wild rote.)*

(It is understandable.)

BB went on. *(He kept throwing it at us and after a while he pulled a skip and never came back. So he was right, you're real.)*

(You are needed to perform a specific act, if you will.)

BB flickered. *(Uh, sure, sure.)*

(Let us move closer.)

The three of us moved down slowly, just over the top of the green pyramid and beyond, and stopped outside a small structure in the middle of a grove of trees. It was very familiar to me and for some reason I was becoming uncomfortable. It was as if I were encountering a resistance, something pushing me back the more I tried to move forward.

(Your friend AA is there. It is important that you help him at this point.)

BB blanked. *(AA?)*

(That is correct.)

BB focused and so did I. Inside the small structure, a man was lying on a bed or cot. The resistance I felt seemed to be emanating from him. It was exactly the same as the other times. It was AA, I was sure. The resistance was very strong and it made me vibrate.

BB turned. *(I guess it's him, all right. I get a part of his ident, not much. I'm getting some other with it that I know, too. But the percept is wild.)*

(It is important that you help him separate from his physical temporarily.)

BB lighted. *(You mean like RAM here?)*

(That is correct.)

He blanked. *(How can I do it?)*

(Just pull gently. Use the energy you apply when you skip.)

BB turned and moved in close to the man on the bed. I watched with fascination, wondering if this was the way it had started with me, if some nonphysical friend had been enlisted to help me move out of body during the early stages. But I didn't have any nonphysical friends back then— that I knew of.

Suddenly, the resistance grew much stronger and pushed me back. I held my position as best I could, feeling very uncomfortable. I turned inward and closed. The man was standing in the middle of the floor, and his physical body was on the cot. BB had backed away, flickering heavily.

He focused at the INSPEC. *(He's out, I got him out! But, uh . . .)*

(Inquire as to his purpose.)

The man responded, but all I was able to perceive was M Band scratching and screeching that indicated strong emotion. If it was his first time, I could understand and empathize with him.

(He stated he wished to serve humankind. Very noble goal.)

I managed to open somewhat. *(Why this resistance? It's there if I try to get close to his friend AA.)*

(A true paradox refuses to exist. You will understand soon.)

BB came in strong. *(He wants to go with us! Can he do that?)*

The resistance and screeching were so strong they hurt. Yet I knew I had the answer before the INSPEC gave it.

(Inform him he must stay and perform his designed function. He has no other choice at this point.)

In spite of the hurt, I tried to observe. After a moment, BB moved up and joined us. The man sank to his knees in the middle of the floor, and the screeching became so strong I had to close completely.

(Let us move to a point where it is more comfortable for you.)

I agreed eagerly.

CLICK!

We were just outside the thin haze of the Intermediate Area. In the distance were the rings with the indistinct form of the physical earth at the center. The M Band noises, especially the screeching, had faded completely. I opened in relief. The INSPEC was in front of me, BB off to one side, completely closed, which was strange.

(It is done. The pattern is complete.)

There was a point of finality in the statement that made me uneasy. It echoed back through me, triggering familiar emotional rote as it went, and I dealt with and diverted each one as it arose. This time it *was* different. I had far too much exquisite and precious rote to let it be otherwise. The uneasiness vanished.

I opened wide and smoothed. *(I understand about individuation. It is not necessary.)*

(You have learned your lessons well, Ashaneen.)

The brightly glowing form winked out. For now, I knew there would no longer be an INSPEC ident to follow, but I felt no sense of loneliness. I moved over to BB as he hovered motionless, still closed.

I focused. *(Hey, old buddy. I got to go back.)*

He opened slowly. *(Yeh, uh, RAM. I got to do something myself, anyway.)*

I had no doubt what it was. *(Well, you'll do fine. Just like pulling skips and playing games back on KT-95.)*

He lighted. *(Yeh, sure! A bunch of games!)*

I opened wide. *(You can do it, tiger! Keep my ident! And have fun!)*

I turned and started to reach but he stopped me. *(What's the push, BB?)*

He flickered. *(Uh, that last thing we did, me pulling AA out, uh, you don't have any percept on it, do you?)*

(No—except it was certainly AA. That same resistance stuff was there. Why? Something I didn't get?)

BB focused on me hard and I waited. Suddenly he lighted very brightly and started to roll strongly. It almost became human laughter, it was that strong.

I flickered. *(What's so funny?)*

(You *have fun, uh, RAM!)*

I watched as he moved in the direction of the First Entry Station, still rolling. When he disappeared inside, I turned and reached, ident physical body, and stretched gently. I moved slowly inward through the rings, feeling strong and sure, knowing I still had much human rote to pick up and go through. I entered the second and then into the physical, knowing one pattern had ended and another would begin.

But what was so funny? The green pyramid, the three of us, serve humankind . . . green, green pyramid roof, three on a beam . . . hey!

On a clear night before going to bed, I might go out and stand on the sun deck and look up. When I do, sometimes the stars disappear and there is nothing but blackness overhead. From beyond the black comes an unseen and eternal song that is hauntingly familiar, a reminder if needed, cutting sharply through the noise of local traffic. INSPEC, BB, Lou, Bill, her, all There, in the song. But *not* AA!

Then it fades, the stars return to the blackness, I take a deep breath, and go back inside.

Epilogue: End Game

With the calm that settled over me, I began to sort out and run the various rotes tossed me which I had simply tucked away for future reference. I did this not only to check what I may have missed but to lay the pattern down tightly, on the premise that someone, somewhere, as an individual or group, might seriously investigate the material—under the guise of philosophical, pathological, educational, or some other study. As before, if the following helps just one individual achieve a profound understanding of who and what he is, the purpose has been served.

Running a rote is much like trying to recall the memory of an event out of the past. The difference rests in the immediate clarity of every detail once the unrolling process begins. Best results appear to be obtained if one is in a relaxed state and isolated. It is important to remain completely awake physically, with your left-brain consciousness in the driver's seat. Then simply think of the ident—the subject of the rote—and wait. You can write down notes or dictate into a tape recorder as you attempt to convert the information into written or spoken words. If you feel you might have missed something, you can RESET and start again, either at the beginning or at any given serial point in the information/experience. You can hit a mental PAUSE button if the phone rings, although this often requires a complete rework back to the relaxation state if so interrupted. However, the rote will still be there—"open" at the point you left it. This takes time and patience, thus the need for isolation.

The early results came out in the following form, not very tight but perhaps more cogent:

Cruising the Rings

The first inner layer or ring was clear and more distinct from my non-physical perspective, and all seemed to be completely focused on the activities of the in-human physical condition. Any attempts to communicate or divert their attention were met with total unawareness at the least and, at the most, bewilderment, fear, or outright hostility. All were attempting to participate in physical life in one way or another with no success whatsoever. All seemed to have one common characteristic. They were completely unaware of any existence other than physical. Only through repeated observation at first hand was it possible to generally sort out and classify such near-earth humans into some semblance of order.

The Dreamers: This group has a distinctive vibration or radiation that indicates they are attached to a physical body somewhere in the current earth time-space. This infers but does not verify that they may be in an out-of-body state during sleep. They apparently are attempting to continue the activity they have been performing during their physical waking hours, or those they desire or fantasize. Some are simply going through the motions; others are trying to talk with those they know who are physically awake, or eating, drinking, working, playing, trying to perform sexual acts, acting out Mitty-like roles in the middle of Manhattan—all without fruition; all, with few exceptions, without any recognition of similar activities around them. What might be loosely termed evidence of their origin is that they suddenly "wink out" or disappear in the middle of an action. Are they awakening in the physical again, out of sleep? Dream analysts may be on the right track but with the wrong perspective.

The Locked-Ins: These are very similar to the previous category, and might be confused with them initially but for several key differences. This group is composed solely of those who have permanently exited their current physical body—dead physically but don't know it. Consequently, they are trying constantly to continue a physical existence to which they have become habituated. They often remain around physical locations, such as houses, and physically living persons to whom they have become attached. Some continue to attempt reentry into their dead physical bodies and to reactivate them, even into the grave—which may give credence to the strange radiation effects sometimes perceived in cemeteries. The anguish these must go through as they witness the cremation of their physical remains is certainly something to ponder.

As with the Dreamers, this group is totally and compulsively bonded to time-space materiality. Moreover, they appear to be deep into enveloping emotionally based fears and drives which they attempt to act out but never conclude. As a group, they are the major blockage in the flow of the human learning experience. Until they are reached and assisted or some glimmer of awareness occurs, they remain in this locked-in state for years, perhaps centuries. Their numbers increase constantly and will continue to do so as long as the physical human values that generate the condition remain unchanged.

The Wild Ones: Much lesser in number than the above but with the same motivating drives expressed in an entirely different manner. The reason is a slight shift in awareness. The Wild Ones do not realize they have lost the use of their physical bodies, and they do not perceive anything other than physical matter reality. However, they are very much aware that they are somehow different. They don't understand the whys or hows of it and have no desire to learn. All they realize is that such difference releases them from all of the restraints, obligations, and commitments that were a part of their physical lives. They construe this as absolute freedom and attempt to express themselves accordingly in the only way they know of—through replicas of physical activity. Thus their efforts to participate in physical human life—which they perceive as taking place all around them—take on many bizarre forms. The previously reported visit to the human sexual pile is a sample. There are implications that whenever a human physical consciousness in waking form becomes "loose" or shaky for whatever reason, it may provide an opportunity for one of these to "piggyback" just for the experience of it. The frequency of such incidents is not known, from my present perspective. Hopefully, very few. They can get mean at times.

There was much to be learned from these inner rings, most of it the hard way if your perspective is still heavily encased in human time-space illusions. It is pointless to recount the many attempted contacts with the inhabitants therein. You can do it yourself without bothering to enter the OOBE state. Interview and observe a cross section group of humans now living in any large city. The resulting data will be a restrained version and much easier to handle. The source of such preoccupation in every case seems to be extreme distortions of the original survival imprint.

Evidently there are methods by which rescues are achieved individually and on a relatively large scale—and the process is ongoing. I personally have been involved in only one or two that I can remember, and I am not particularly proud of my efforts. I did learn one or two minor items. First, awareness of the cacophony of discordant, undirected radiation engendered by human thought—identified as M Band noise (my label). Second, how to close down my perception to bring it to tolerable levels. The necessity syndrome again. It's a nice trick to have, even in the physical waking state.

The next ring outward is fairly straightforward. It is composed of those who do realize they are no longer in physical human life, but have no awareness or memory of any other possibility. Often they are stunned by the loss, and do no more than remain in a motionless, nonperceiving passive state, as if waiting for something to take place. They are usually easy to contact, instruct, and lead to a suitable outer ring. The population here is small, relatively, and remains more or less static due to the assistance supplied by the outer rings.

Moving outward, the next ring is the largest of all, and contains an apparently limitless number of sub-rings. However, they all come under a strong general category: At least, all residents here know they have passed through physical death. There may be vagueness and differing beliefs as to what and where they are at this point; hence the often sharply delineated sub-rings. Within this ring, approximately through the center, there exists what might be labeled a null point of a different variety yet quite perceivable from an external perspective. It is generated by the existence of two symbolized energy fields overlapping and exerting near-equal pressure/ influence without interaction between the two. There are no standing waves set up by frequencies beating against each other, for the two fields are not compatible. The analogy of a bar magnet with positive and negative fields meeting at the center of the bar does not apply. It would be better to picture a gravity field exerting attraction in one direction and the action of a sitcom on television in another.

On the inner side of such null point, the dominant force is HTSI, short for Human Time-Space Illusion, strongest at the innermost sub-rings and lessening inversely throughout the entire ring until it is quite insignificant on the outer edge. On the outer side of the ring, the dominant force is NPR, or Nonphysical Reality, which is as general as one can get if there is no accurate translation available for the little that is known of it. A mirror image in field strength, the NPR effect is greatest at the outermost edge, diminishing slowly to the null point, then exponentially to the inner edge of the ring.

The pattern of human passage through this particular ring is most fascinating, again from the external view. It is composed of energy in human experiential form moving in two directions, both inward and outward. The inward flow is composed of fresh energy from the NPR area first encountering the HTSI field, becoming more and more attracted by it through a series of in-human existences, passing through this particular ring more rapidly once the null point is crossed. From that point inward, the movement accelerates to the inner edge of the ring and through it, terminating usually in the lowest of the inner rings.

The outward flow, after release from or skirting the innermost rings, commences the haphazard-seeming yet meticulous path through this largest of rings. For some, the passage is relatively direct, with but a few in-human physical existences to provide the impetus. Others—the great majority—require up to several hundred in-human lifetimes and thousands of earth year cycles to complete the process. The reasons for this wide discrepancy are not obvious to me. However, one characteristic of the more direct route appears to be the careful selection of in-human life experiences, plus accomplishments in the face of what might be termed statistically impossible odds. The two routes both emerge at the outer edge of the ring and lead to the outermost ring.

The single outermost ring is composed solely of those who are preparing for their final in-human experience—the Last-Timers, or Seniors, whichever suits your perspective. They have lost their gray appearance and much of their humanoid form; they are nearly white in radiation with occasional sparkling patterns around them. They are tightly closed, and do not respond to any communication attempts except possibly among themselves. It is difficult to observe their final reentry into human experience. It is either too rapid or instantaneous. Their exit from the final cycle is represented by a sparkling glowing light which moves rapidly outward through the rings, with occasional pauses for some unknown reason. Upon passing this outermost ring, they suddenly disappear from perception, leaving no residual image or trace.

In some respects, the entire process resembles crudely the cycle of an innocent coping with an addictive drug or chemical such as alcohol. The first taste is scarcely palatable, but the effect is interesting, something new. When the opportunity arises, the neophyte takes two drinks just to see if the effect is enhanced—and it is. Uncontrolled, the pattern is all too familiar, all the way down to skid row. Nothing is more important to the wino, nothing occupies his thinking other than where the next shot or hit is coming from. Near-total amnesia is common, and more significantly, a lack of desire to change. He has forgotten who he is and couldn't care less. Reclamation and remembering is a slow and sometimes painful charade. Once achieved, however, the innocent has transformed into a state of being far different from the original first-taster. Where the analogy does not match: In the human life experience sequence, the change is permanent.

In serial form, the itinerary of human experience might be mapped something like this:

SITE	INWARD FLOW (read DOWN)	OUTWARD FLOW (Read UP)
ENTRY/EXIT INTERMEDIATE AREA	NPR First-Timer	Graduate
	To. In-Human Physical Time Full Spectrum	To. Home? NPR
AMBIENCE FIELDS (Awareness-Focus) NPR 95% HTSI 5%		
OUTERMOST RING		Last-Timer (Senior)
	Indeterminate	
AMBIENCE FIELDS (Awareness-Focus) NPR 80% HTSI: 20%		To. Final In-Human Time. Full Spectrum
MAJOR RING		

SITE	INWARD FLOW (read DOWN)	OUTWARD FLOW (Read UP)
OUTER QUARTER	First Repeaters, frequent	Long Repeaters
	To In-Human Physical	To Selected In-Human Physical
AMBIENCE FIELDS (Awareness-Focus)	Time Full Spectrum	Time Selected
NPR 60% HTSI 40%		Idents. Contemplatives, philosophers, certain religious groups, service-to-humanity devotees, helpers, guides, rescue workers, others
MAJOR RING		
UPPER QUARTER	First Repeaters, trace	Long Repeaters, intermittent
	To In-Human physical	To. Required In-Human
AMBIENCE FIELDS (Awareness-Focus)	Time Random	Time Coordinated
NPR. 50–55% HTSI. 45–50%		Idents Certain religious groups, quantum physicists, transpersonal psychologists, historical humanitarian leaders, specialists
MAJOR RING		
LOWER QUARTER		Long Repeaters, regularly

AMBIENCE FIELDS (Awareness-Focus)	To. Desired In-Human
	Time: Current
NPR: 30% HTSI 70%	Idents· Certain religious groups, friends and relatives, current, rest and recuperation facilities, rote- synthesized physical artifacts and activity including heaven and hell
MAJOR RING	
INNER QUARTER	Short Repeaters
	To. Desired In-Human
AMBIENCE FIELDS (Awareness-Focus)	Time Current
NPR 5% HTSI: 95%	Ident Refugees from lower rings, rehab centers, instructional classes, nonconformists, the guilty
WAITING RING	First-Timers, Short Repeaters
AMBIENCE FIELDS (Awareness-Focus)	To. Inner Quarter, Major Ring
NPR: 0 HTSI 0	Time: Indeterminate
	Ident: Total Spectrum

SITE	INWARD FLOW (read DOWN)	OUTWARD FLOW (Read UP)
INNERMOST RING		Short Repeaters, First-Timers
AMBIENCE FIELDS (Awareness-Focus)		
NPR. 0 HTSI. 100%		
DREAMERS		
LOCKED-INS		
WILD ONES		To. Stasis
		Time Indeterminate
SLEEPERS		
IN-HUMAN PHYSICAL	First-Timer	Repeaters
AMBIENCE FIELDS (Awareness-Focus)	To. Any Other Ring	Full Spectrum
	Time Full Spectrum	To. Various Outer Rings
NPR Trace HTSI 99 999999%		Time Full Spectrum

Another way to describe the process in contemporary terms: The Unit (the original you?) is attracted and drawn by the human earth energy field. The Unit decided to make a close-in pass-by through the field to obtain data and information. This reduces velocity in the Unit to a degree greater than that calculated to occur from friction, due to the unexpected adherence factor of the particles within the field. The reduction is so great as to fall below escape velocity, and the Unit moves inexorably into an elliptical orbit. At each apogee of the orbit, the Unit passes through the human earth energy field again and gathers additional adhering particles therefrom, causing greater reduction in velocity—which in turn lowers the perigee of the orbit. Finally, the orbit breaks down and succumbs to the now more powerful attraction of the field, and the Unit settles into the field itself, to become a part of it.

To launch and achieve escape velocity, the Unit must (1) remove the adhering particles that created the problem while retaining such information/data/experience so as to bring back Something of Value; (2) develop and store sufficient energy to achieve both launch and escape velocity, which infers a far greater amount than that available at the point of original entry under typical conditions, plus additional reserves to compensate for the extra payload on board.

The solution is made complex by the lack of efficient methods for proper detoxification and removal of adhered particles, as well as the availability of only the most primitive techniques for proper energy distillation and accumulation. Therefore, at best, extrication is a long and arduous process. The key is to begin first with ballistic trajectories, followed by elliptical orbiting, ever increasing the perigee until escape velocity is reached.

Thereafter, the Unit can return to its original base with its payload—or, with its increased energy, move on to greater exploration.

The foregoing is at best a generalization, specific only in the broad classifications indicated. It is a simplification of a very complex and intricate pattern of movements perceived from an external perspective. It is deliberately devoid of as much humanism as is possible by a human, in the belief that such starkness will gather the attention and understanding latent in the left-brain modality. However, the problem still remains—the need to express in a form remotely acceptable to in-human consciousness.

This, then, is a flow sheet of where the action is in which all of us are vitally involved. It could be identified as the Earth-Human Energy Environ, Human Time-Space Illusion. It is a summary based upon several hundred individual explorations, most of which are beyond literal translation. To chronicle each individually would consume an entire volume in itself, if indeed it were possible. Therefore, this baseline will have to serve for the moment. We might get lost, with or without it, but our chances are better with it.

Rote BHP-1
Compressed Learning—Category Human

The first point in consideration of human structure certainly should be the note that a small percentage have never been through the experience prior to the present sojourn in time. Some may have had physical life experience in other parts of time-space and in another physical form, but this is their first run as a human. Other first-timers have never been in a physical form of any sort.

Time-space—physical matter—and especially human existence on earth —is an interesting anomaly. It has some peculiar qualities that are unique in the development of intelligence and consciousness. As a result, human life has many attractions. To some it is like attending a vast amusement park with a multitude of different types of exciting rides to try—a playground where standard rules (non-earthly) are suspended for the moment. They desire human existence simply out of curiosity. They have received a rote on this interesting state, and want to find out what it is to be a part of it. Many, having observed the state at a particular point in human history, decide it is an ideal opportunity to try an experiment conceived in their periods of contemplation. The peculiarity of human existence at a given point in evolution provides an opportunity to try out the idea.

Still others find that the limitations imposed by physical incarceration as a human also engender concentration of certain energies available only in that state. This is the only point available to apply such energies.

By far the greatest motivation—surpassing the sum of all others—is the result. When you encounter and perceive a graduate, your only goal is to be one yourself once you realize it is possible. And it is.

Thus we "go to physical" because of what it is—an intense learning process, a school of a very unusual sort. It has the implication that an important part of that learning process is to force the admixture of two different types of energy modulation. One enters as male and the other as female. The drives, needs, enculturation, and other factors all may be designed to literally force the accommodation, melding, and understanding between these two systems of consciousness.

The conditions of entering physical life as a human are relatively strict. It is as if a detailed agreement is entered into. First, the energy form must agree that time-space truly does exist. Without this agreement, it is impossible to have primary human consciousness. The energy form must agree that there is a time, such as the 1980s or any other time frame by earth reckoning. It must be agreed also that there truly is a planet earth designed and created in the form that it is. It must further agree that consciousness expressed as a human has certain characteristics and limitations.

The blanking or sublimation of previous experience is a part of the process. This is to assure that there will be a minimum of interference in the performance as a human caused by previous life patterns, physical and in other realities. Bear in mind that this is all at the conscious perceiving level; it is not removed from the essence of the energy form accepting the agreement. Such experience will remain with the newly human energy form in a nonconscious state. This is important because such experience or purpose may well be the underlying motive that is the driving force behind the performance of such energy in human existence.

Once a decision or agreement has been reached, a propitious and probable birth entry point is selected, taking into consideration the genetic, environmental, social, political, and economic elements that may—not absolutely—ensure the realization of the purpose for such entry. Many times, due to the possibility that all factors may not be appropriate and suitable, some entries are made simply on the possibility or hope that the goals can be achieved. Often there are so many variables present that it in turn presents a most enticing challenge to simply try to beat the odds, as it were, or change them by thought and action. Some make it, some do not.

Another factor is that the demand or need for selective new points of entry far exceeds the supply. Thus, many may get tired of waiting, as it were, and will accept entry under the most marginal of circumstances.

A review of the learning processes and the absorption of information by a first-timer will provide a beginning overview. Upon entry (birth), the first-timer is surprised and shocked at the very severe constraints of the physical body. It can no longer move freely and easily at the mere thought or desire. Thus, much of the early weeks of existence as a human are taken up with conscious and frustrating efforts to obtain control of this new physical body. Simultaneously, it is overwhelmed by astounding demands for nourishment—a process that was an automatic function in previous existence. Add to that a massive battery of strong and chaotic signals pouring in from sensory sources never before perceived, the five physical senses, and one begins to get a better appreciation of the traumatic state that is undergone. There are indications that the effect would be much more severe were it not for the reinforcement received by the first-timer during nonconscious periods (sleep), from interested and concerned observers left behind in the reality outside of time-space.

From this beginning emerges the primary learning system that continues throughout human life. It is the focusing of conscious awareness. Pain or pleasure, as reported by the five physical senses, turns attention to the event being experienced, and such experience is then learned and stored. Further, if the element of emotion is involved, the storage process is enhanced greatly. Physical experience of an extreme nature also deepens the learning process. Simply stated, the depth of learning (retention, recall) is in direct relation to the intensity of the experience. Conversely, the more shallow the experience, the lesser the attention, which diminishes greatly the learning process.

Primary learning is the data base upon which we humans principally conduct our physical lives. Other learning processes affect our thoughts and actions, yet the fundamental pattern of performance is based upon this primary learning.

Secondary learning, another pattern which is present throughout human existence, takes place beyond what we call our level of consciousness. This is data received through our five physical senses in those areas where attention is *not* focused. This takes place during waking physical life and is stored and retained in the most minute detail. Due to the lack of attention, less than 20 percent of such secondary learning is ordinarily available for recall by the human conscious mind. Still, this entire spectrum of memory is called upon unknowingly by the individual as the need arises. It colors and affects our thoughts, decisions, and actions, and we are quite unaware of it.

A third form of learning occurs during our cyclic nonconscious state (sleep). At our waking conscious level, we remember very little of such activity although it becomes deeply embedded in and becomes a part of the memory-experience system upon which we base our life activity. Culturally, we have been trained to place the least importance upon those events we do not remember, and rarely recognize the influence these have upon our activities/experience. When examined from an external point of observation, automatic use of this learning process becomes quite visible.

The principal learning system devised by the various cultures in human history is the most widespread and accepted, yet the most unnatural. For the greatest part it ignores completely the in-place and operating primary and secondary learning processes. Thus its very artificiality, without natural means of focusing attention, requires a form of dedication and discipline generally unavailable to the average human conscious mind. Attention flickers, fluctuates, especially in low-order, repetitive experience, denigrating much of the learning that might take place. Crude as it may be, such learning methods are held in high esteem in human existence, and virtually all of it revolves around the knowledge, understanding, and control and application of physical matter, including the energy system so generated therein.

Most vital, this dominant yet artificial and limited system of learning operates entirely through input from the five physical senses. Because of this foundation, it has the effect of eliminating any last vestiges of origin-identity remaining in the individual. This is at once the heart of the problem and the major challenge to the naïve energy form.

As the first-timer lives his human life, he finds virtually nothing to guide his mentation in directions other than those directly related to time-space physical matter. Unfortunately for the human, this includes those organizations who purvey belief systems based upon individuals both present and in past history whose knowledge of origin-identity was operational during their human sojourn. In the retelling and conversion to verbal human communication, plus the erosion of many retranslations, only portions of the process remain. Sadly, such portions attempt to teach effects rather than causes. Only in very rare instances do these provide clear access to the source.

Therefore, as the first-timer moves through human physical life he picks up and absorbs many unsuspected attachments. The most powerful of these are emotional, or rather distortions thereof, which relate solely to expression only in time-space reality. These reach such magnitude as to be virtually impossible to achieve and experience in a single physical human lifetime. The results are a compulsive need to reenter and recycle to complete that which had been begun, to perform the purpose for which there had not been "time," to repay imagined "debts"—the list becomes endless.

In short, the problem can be stated very succinctly, which turns a first-timer into a repeater: human physical life is addictive.

There are two overwhelming factors that engender such addiction or decay of orbit, as you prefer. Put the two together and interweave them tightly, and it becomes easy to perceive just how difficult the Human Compressed Learning System can be, especially for the unaware and uninformed. This may in itself be part of the training. Any attempts to describe the methods are near-incomprehensible to those who have never been human, just as it is extremely difficult to explain postgraduate status to a human first-timer. The two factors involved are Survival Drive Distortion and Prime Energy Diffusion.

Survival Drive Distortion

Like animals, plants, and other organic life, physical man is heavily imprinted at birth with the will to continue to grow and live, to survive. This is expressed in two basic ways:

Body Protection and Maintenance

The first demand is the acquisition and consumption of food and water. This is followed by pressure to keep the body suitably warm or cool. Next comes the need to keep it safe from predation ranging from other humans and carnivorous animals through insects and down to the smallest virus. The fight-or-flee dilemma arises when two or more of such needs come into direct conflict as to priority.

Nothing controversial in that, so what's the problem? Most humans spend most of their waking hours taking care of these matters, one way or another. There's no choice in the matter. You're in the top .0001 percent of the human pyramid if you know without question these needs will be met tomorrow, the next week, the rest of your life—by your own action, your family, or "your" government.

There's also nothing new in the massive distortions that begin to occur beyond the basic needs. Storage of food or other assets just in case there may be a change in the future, endless varieties of food aimed not so much at nutrition as at taste and aesthetics, special food preparation and services. Entertainment "foods" in the form of alcohol, drugs, tobacco, etc., and back around the cycle to foods that are "good" for you, to keep you healthy. Clothes that not only keep you warm but are made correctly, of a desirable color or texture, made for a variety of occasions, and, of course, in rapidly changing style. Shelter that goes far beyond the hut in the hills, larger and/or in a desirable location, equipped and reequipped with newer furnishings, facilities, decorations, all catering to individual taste and current style primarily, far secondarily to comfort and overstated "need."

Some of these have been brought to the point where it is actually difficult to die. Extensive and expensive life-support systems in institutions are an example. Keep the body alive, never mind the details. In some "civilized" societies, it's a crime to take your own life. Whom will they prosecute if you're successful? All such extras and add-ons are stimulated and rationalized by countless inducements, few of which can stand up under intense scrutiny for validity. This is compounded by competition both to acquire and to dispense, which brings into full play the natural physical law of supply and demand.

To protect these accumulated items to serve the body which is you: locks on doors, fences around houses, doors and gates, laws and rules, medicines and drugs, guns, police officers in prowl cars, lawyers, doctors, nostrums ad nauseum, cities and nations, banks, armies and atom bombs.

Within this distortion lies the adhesive that binds the heavy particles to the energy form—which all began with the early agrarian cultures and tribes. Intense overkill by the survival drive—all physical. Nothing else is important. It had to happen, free will being what it is.

Sexuality-Reproduction

The most powerful of the survival drive imprints takes precedence over all others, and therefore has been subject to more major distortions than any other. The greatest among these has been, and is, the illusion that, as a creative act, it thus engenders automatically the creative emotion of love, ethereal and godlike. The results are attachments and commitments that are both irrational and restrictive, which not only distort severely any current physical life goals but continue beyond—illusory burdens of guilt, obligations, and a vast number of related memory patterns too potent to release. Further, the original motivating drive to reproduce has long since become secondary to the temporary sensory peak of the act itself. With few exceptions, it is doubtful if it has ever been otherwise with the male. Knowing this, the female with a propensity for perception has taken this manipulative advantage to broad extremes through hundreds of years of cultural evolution. Those females who succumb to the illusion of permanency have no choice but to lie back and take what is coming. Simply put, one fuck doesn't make a future. A baby maybe.

With increased objective knowledge of the influential power of the reproductive survival drive, the lures and blandishments thereto are used blatantly and consistently to distort even further the high sensory entertainment factor of the act itself—carefully omitting the slightest reference to its original purpose. Those using such enticements to irrationality range from the individual through major industries to governments themselves. The result is a cacophony of distortions, all aimed at increasing reproductive-act desire and need, the amplification of the problem without providing a sensible solution. All of which only adds strongly to the glue that binds the human in low orbit.

Prime Energy Diffusion

Consider what we call emotion in all forms to be unknowing expressions of our Prime Energy Drive, or the Creative Force inherent in each of us. There are no exceptions. Included are joy, sadness, anger, happiness, hate, friendship, nostalgia, possessiveness, loyalty, ego, greed, guilt, fun, worry, anxiety, among others. Add a few not ordinarily regarded as such: curiosity, ideas, equality, hope, loneliness—and, of course, love in a nonordinary connotation.

In this context, emotion is the key to and the driving force underlying every thought and action in human existence. The concept of unemotionalism is an illusion. Even the most extreme objectivity covers carefully an emotional agenda. Rationality and emotion go hand in hand when traced back to the source. If a human being is the product of a Creative Force, then being human is totally an emotional expression of such energy.

There has not been a single major act in human history that has not been driven and/or inspired by emotion. Astute politicians now recognize that voters emotionally elect presidents, that simple facts and figures contain emotional coloration. All great leaders throughout mankind's existence have had emotional appeal as their source of power. Motivation is an interim statement of emotion. Many studies, authoritative books, and hundreds of millions of dollars have been dedicated to the application of this concept during recent years—all apparently backing away politely from the fundamental source of the phenomenon, through either ignorance or rejection.

The result is a chaotic mixture of unchecked and misdirected energy that is and has been the human experience. Isolated attempts are made to act and think without emotion, which is an impossibility. Even in the laboratory, it is slowly being determined that any experiment is affected by the observer, inadvertently, unconsciously, and unobtrusively. Thus absolute replication can occur only under identical ambience—again an impossibility, considering the flickering thought-emotional patterns of the observer-experimenter. For a simple test, try recording each and every thought and emotion you have expressed during the past one minute. Then attempt the same recall for a minute one hour ago.

At the individual level, the generalization becomes specific. In every moment of existence, we are a seething brew of emotional response to both internal and external stimuli. Awake or asleep, the ever-changing mosaic of flowing energy continues to surge at assorted amplitudes and frequencies. We place value judgments on each and every portion, as determined by our own experience and impressed upon us by the culture in which we now exist. When the two conflict, we usually choose the latter as a sop to expedience. Thus we attempt to let full expression of the "good" emit from us and try to suppress and repress the "evil," hide it from view. For the vast majority of us, this is the extent of our efforts to control this mighty and most vital energy that is our true heritage. At best, we are only partially successful using an incorrect standard of measurement.

We make decisions in blind anger and resent the results. We hope and become disappointed. We laugh in joy and become depressed when the moment fades. We hate when a person, place, or thing does not fit or meet our concept of what it "ought" to be. We think we "love" and break our hearts when we discover it just isn't so, we were mistaken. The list is endless, and we keep trying because we can't help ourselves and we don't know any better. We ride the waves of our emotions through the peaks and the valleys until some of us become cynics—neatly neglecting the obvious, that cynicism is itself an emotion. The mess gets messier when we do perceive that effective and achieving left-brain decisions are made ultimately by some emotional factor, hidden and disguised as it may be. This propounds the old can't-live-with-it, can't-live-without-it syndrome. Free will is no longer free and hasn't much will, buried under a swarm of emotional encumbrances.

By far the largest accumulated heavy load is the emotional mass loosely held as the human ego. Originally a probable sprout from the survival imprint, it requires and consumes constantly immense amounts of reinforcing emotional patterns, all of which are by their very nature distorted and distorting. Ego exploits the concept that it is needed to exist and achieve, that the emotion of confidence cannot exist without ego support, that happiness is satiated ego. Ego can bring forth hundreds of irrational emotional reasons to justify its existence—sidestepping the fact that emotion and irrationality are not synonymous. It steadfastly maintains that there would be no human personality were it not for the ego.

At least, the ego is correct in one premise The human is an emotional being. It's simply a question of utilization, of application.

The epoxy that locks the whole heavy load onto the unit and makes orbit decay inevitable: The heavy preponderance of such emotions are directly related or attached to time-space physical matter earth events, things, and relationships; as such, they are not applicable to nor can they exist in any reality other than their point of origin.

There is one exception. It is the only clear and accurate representation of the original Prime Energy, and cannot be generated at will. It is a synthesis of other emotional thought and action, brought into expression and thenceforth indestructible. Most important, it is not peculiar to the time-space continuum and the existence of it is not contingent upon such environs. As such, it is not part of the load factor. Instead, it is the source of power to obtain lift-off, reach orbit, and establish escape velocity.

The major—if not the only—reasons for attending the human experience school are first, to learn to translate such energy into a discernible form, and second, to become a first-order generator thereof. This is no easy task if you don't know what it is, if you don't know how to express it, and if you can't knowingly generate it. How does a person learn to sing if he's never heard a song, doesn't know of words, melody, and pitch; worse, if he doesn't know he has vocal cords or even a voice?

Clues may lie in the common mislabeling and misconstruing of emotions akin to but definitely not the same. To avoid confusion, call it Super Love (SL). Knowing the difference is the key, as the ident love has been used so broadly as to have lost any significant meaning. Try this crude overlay for starters: SL is indestructible, as stated. Once activated, no subsequent thought, emotion, or event can have any effect upon it. SL is not in any way dependent upon manifestation in physical matter, or activity therein. SL has no object, animate or inanimate, although such may be one of the catalysts to trigger the generation thereof. SL is a continuous radiation, totally nondependent upon like reception or any other form of return whatsoever. SL is.

A very complex and rugged curriculum, this Human School of Compressed Learning. Parris Island at its peak was a teatime social by comparison. There, at least, you had a reasonably clear idea of what you were doing and your probable destination. Knowing this, it was worth it.

My very deeply dedicated response: Among the very few seniors and graduates I have encountered, there was not one who would not repeat the in-human learning system again and again, no matter how many times —knowing the indescribably magnificent result. My fleeting glimpses support totally this perspective.

Preparation: Launch and Lift-off

Here is what might be euphemistically called a crib sheet for the course —presumably offered with the knowledge and consent of the instructors. Like all such aids, it doesn't give all the answers and there is no guarantee as to accuracy. The best that can be said is that it was hurriedly copied from the instructors' manual with their permission and cooperation. Distorted and poorly filtered as it may be, perhaps this cup of murky water is indeed better than none at all to the parched and thirsty runner. At least it's water and it may help cross the finish line jogging lightly and happily.

Detoxification/Load Reduction/Purging

The design calls for a continuation and expansion of physical life activity in all forms—physical, mental, and emotional. There is no inference that a lessening or retreat must occur, as this will extend the process rather than shorten it. The change lies in the perception, control, and redirection of the energy forms that are you, just as coherent light produces far more effective results as a laser. Start with these fundamentals as a baseline.

Reality Is That Which Is Perceived

As a participant in time-space, you perceive it and it is a reality to you. If you have not perceived any other energy systems, they are not real to you. However, you must consider that you have done so but they are not within your present awareness. It then becomes simply a matter of remembering.

Energy Does Not Exist Until Expressed

We are expressions of energy. The energy that we transform or generate has no reality until we express it. An idea has no reality until we transmit it or put it into practice. Knowledge and information are nothing without dissemination and/or application. A single thought is not real unless it is instilled into or acts upon another or is acted upon itself. Think and do is the operating productive combination, either mentally or physically, in one or more energy systems. Inhibit, restrain, or block the flow of any such energy and it ceases to exist.

Energy Focused Is Exponential

Just as a lens can concentrate solar radiation to a temperature many times greater than normal, so other energies can be transformed and modified. This is particularly valid within the energy spectrum available to human consciousness. The fact that we exercise them randomly and unknowingly for the most part, specifically in the nonphysical categories, does not invalidate such potential.

Consciousness Is Focused Energy

In particular, human consciousness is widely focused into time-space physical matter. This is not the totality of energy consciousness involved, as other forms of the same consciousness are active concurrently in divergent systems of reality. Two inferences may be drawn from such multiplicity: The human aspect can be adjusted in focus to a much more concentrated point, offering potentials of power and action too immense and unfathomable to be considered lightly. Second, the other, nonhuman forms of the same energy system might be drawn upon if the need arises.

With the above tucked away, it is possible to get to the "hands on" phase. Although the following notes are presented in a sequential manner, it is quite appropriate to refer to any portion that may serve a given need. There is no fixed pattern or order common to all of the human learning experience. An event early in the life exercise of one may surface years later in another, if at all.

Establish Grazing Principle

Instead of actively seeking out needed changes, deal with each as it appears in your daily life. Live and be just as you have until you perceive an emotion or attachment that is so obvious you can't ignore it.

Live a Twenty-four-Hour Day

Become aware of what you do and think at all times, in all activities, and examine the emotional factors that appear to be the strongest, that attract your attention. Include your sleep periods with their NVC-dream content. Explore these by asking yourself why, repeating the probe until you reach each source. It is then easy to detach and release the energy for other purposes. Start with the small and work into the large.

Begin Ego Diet Regimen

A frontal attack on this most entrenched and concentrated center of distorted emotion is contraindicated as not feasible. Much too many lose that battle, most never begin it. The trick is to start a cutoff of the emotional power feeds that are vital to its existence, modify and redirect the energy therein. Bear in mind that you are bombarded constantly with ego gratification ploys aimed at modification of your behavior for the benefit of others. The problem is in your emotional response, not in the blandishment itself and the consequential acts you perform. If you want to drive a luxury car simply because you enjoy doing it, that's fine. If it makes you feel more important, or you like to be seen driving it, if you have to put "my" in front of the identification, you've found an ego power feed. Keep this perspective and apply it when the need arises, and act accordingly.

The second source of ego-emotional power feeds is internally generated. It is generally accepted that ambition and the drive for achievement are primarily ego-gratifying processes. To determine if this is valid or such motivation comes from a more profound origin, conduct this test: Will these needs be happily met if you in no way receive any public or private credit for your success? Are they absolutely essential to your physical survival? If the answer is affirmative to both, you're further along than you realize. Even with fame, fortune, and adulation, your load will actually lighten. If both come out negative, start unplugging the feed by asking why.

At a point in your unplugging process, you will find glimmers of Prime Energy radiation which provide any justification you may desire. The more emotional energy you so release, the greater such energy you will perceive.

Divest Survival Sex Ties

Due to the need to protect and maintain until physical maturity the offspring of the reproductive act, many cultures have attached certain obligations thereto. While this is generally a purely physical requisite, many have taken the position or inference that far more is involved. The reproductive act is first and foremost a very powerful response to purely sensual stimuli. The response is not in itself an emotion, although the depth of the experience often causes fantasizing that it is exactly that and of much greater import. To confuse the issue further, sexual union is one of the significant ways to express the SL emotion found in the Prime Energy.

The load reducer is to understand the difference. There is no right or wrong engendered either way, only difference. Recognize that, from the perspective of solely a physical act, any emotional attachments thereto relate only to time-space reality. As a procreative act, it is physical in nature. Unless other energy patterns emerge as a result, enjoy it but don't get hooked on it. You don't need to take it with you, because there's better in the original form—what you experience here sexually is a very weak imitation of a part of a totality. No male or female "owes" the other an obligation to copulate. Sexual attraction and attractiveness are elements of a survival drive which is purely physical and no more. Yet these are enough to alter drastically individual life patterns. Load is induced when more is made of it than it is.

Sexuality is not love, if love is defined as an expression of Prime Energy, but may well be a procedure through which the individual eventually learns of its existence. If this does indeed take place, keep the love and release the sexuality, then no load exists.

Release Value Judgments

With the distortion of time-space as a baseline, it is impossible for anyone to discern accurately the quality of any thought or action; good-evil, right-wrong, exist only as illusion. In orbit, there is no up-down. As a point of expediency, it may be necessary to adhere to the concepts of the culture in which we exist temporarily. Without a solid overview, we cannot understand the ultimate value of what we do. Therefore, follow your own design, lighten the load by refusing to bond lasting emotion onto any physical act or the action of others.

Detach Matter-Emotion

Physical things, places, etc., are units within time-space, to be enjoyed and to be used as tools in the learning experience. None is "ours." We don't own or possess any thing or person, nothing belongs to us. Even the matter we use for our physical body is "borrowed," as it were. Store the memory and the experience, leave the emotion behind.

You Are Your Responsibility

We like to lay this one off wherever and however we can, blame conditions and/or anyone else for what we do and are when there seem to be mistakes, take credit when everything is great. As exercisers of free will, we do our own instigating. Calmly accepting the results will get you lift-off points. An old folk song with the title "Ain't Nobody's Fault but My Own" says it very well. Look it up.

Free Will Is Fantasy

Within time-space, the very constraints thereof preclude any such theory. At physical birth, we are bound not only by our previous experience, whatever it may be, but by the genetic structure of the physical body we inhabit. From that point on, we have no choice but to be bonded into the flesh for that lifetime, long or short. We are bound to maintain and operate our physical bodies within the limitations they impose. The set and setting of our physical existence is controlled, initially at least, by others. What remains, colored and modified as it is, might be considered free will. Exercising this upon another only increases the load. Off-loading is accomplished by maximizing this remainder in nonphysical areas and accepting without emotion the limitations so imposed.

Laughter Is a Purging Process

As a direct expression of the Prime Energy, when in doubt let it out. An inadvertent smile is part of the same spectrum. It's one of the best of emotions, but must be spontaneous to produce results. Seeing and enjoying the humor in life is something not to be missed. It relaxes, de-tunes the ego, puts any event into its proper perspective.

Pain-Pleasure (PP) Is a Learning Curve

Consider these as a waveform originating within the survival imprint, and therefore signals relating only to time-space physical matter. They are essential tools that can be used for measurement. Think of it as a sine wave, with pain below the baseline and pleasure above it. The amplitude of each is an indicator of intensity, which can be controlled. Step one: Sort out and remove all emotional energy adhered to your PP accumulated memory. Step two: Begin control of each portion of the waveform so that you can increase or decrease the amplitude at will. You are approaching escape velocity status when you can reduce your PP waveform to a near-perfect straight line.

Maximize Your Sleep Periods

This is the most neglected and misunderstood portion of our existence. Freed temporarily of the restrictions placed upon us by our left-brain organization and the press of physical input, the sleep segment offers a great opportunity to advance in many areas. Any of the previous suggestions can be initiated and developed during the sleep state. Consistency and frequency are important. You may not get the results the first, third, or fifth time, but eventually you will succeed. Begin by stating the affirmation:

I am more than my physical body. Because I am more than physical matter, I can perceive that which is greater than the physical world.

Therefore, I deeply desire to expand, to experience: to know, to understand, to control, to use such greater energies and energy systems as may be beneficial and constructive to me and to those who follow me.

Also, I deeply desire the help and cooperation, the assistance, the understanding of those individuals whose wisdom, development, and experience are equal to or greater than my own. I ask their guidance and protection from any influence or any source that might provide me with less than my stated desires.

Say it first as words in your mind just as you are drifting off to sleep. Convert as early as possible to nonverbal communication (NVC), stating the affirmation in mental action rather than words. After you are well established with the technique, add specific needs such as information, health care, problem solving, communication, or any of the procedures listed previously, using NVC. The answer will come usually not in words, but in pictures, sound, living action in your mind. There is no limit to the ways you can use this method provided you do not impinge upon the will of others. If you need help, ask for it by NVC. You will receive it, perhaps not immediately, but you will, often in the most astounding serendipitous and synchronistic ways. Be sure that you qualify your need and that you can handle the answer or result.

Measure Your Load-Energy Ratio

At physical birth, we enter physical life into a presumed innocent consciousness. The path to adulthood and your progress along it can be termed a loss of such innocence, scaled by the number of responsibilities you have willfully assumed, as created by your authoritative acts. Maturity, which is not the same, is calculated by totaling the percentage of illusions you have released and discarded—deliberately, not forced disillusionment. Wisdom—the lightest and most valuable of payloads—and your progress along the interstate highway thereto are reflected in your willful action, mental and physical, as the result of your release of such illusions.

The Detoxification/Load Reduction/Purging process can be interpreted as simply the sequence of these three, adulthood, maturity, and wisdom. You ultimately are your own instructor and you will fill out your own report card.

Building Escape Velocity Energy

It will begin to generate automatically as the result of the human learning experience, more than enough to achieve a tangent to your previous orbit when you graduate. It is the understanding that the actions suggested here may help in such production. Then no longer will you reflect and transform the Prime Energy as in the past, but create it in and of your own and radiate it in all ways, in all forms—call it loosh/love or whatever label fits—without need for subject or object.

"Pas de Lieu Rhône que Nous"

A language professor father, now in another reality, used this to wake up students in his class in French, claiming it was an old and famous French proverb. Some worked earnestly for hours trying to solve the enigma. It may be very appropriate here, too. To find the solution, say it in your mind or vocalize it using a French accent. Listen to what you are saying.

See you in Home—or along the way.

Appendices

I. The Out-of-Body Experience:
Most Frequently Asked Questions and Answers

QUESTION: HOW DO YOU KNOW IT ISN'T JUST A TYPE OF
DREAMING?

Most individuals do dismiss the experience when they encounter it as nothing more than a vivid dream. At most, it may be categorized by some as what is identified as a "lucid" dream. In the latter, the dreamer is apparently aware that he is dreaming, and can control the content of his dream, even to the point of changing the event, the participants, and the outcome.

In the OOBE, the individual is near-totally conscious, as our civilization defines the state. Most if not all of your physical sensory perception is replicated. You can "see," "hear," and "touch"—the weakest seem to be smell and taste. Your perspective is from a position outside your physical body, near or distant. In a near state, it is usually from a location impossible for you to "be" with your physical body, such as floating against the ceiling. In a far location, it could be in Paris when you know you are in New York physically. You can observe events taking place, but you cannot change or significantly affect them. You can verify the authenticity of such events subsequently if you so desire. You cannot participate to any major degree in this physical activity because you are not "physical." It is the extreme reality of the OBE that sets it apart from a dream. It is as "real" as any physical life experience.

QUESTION: CAN ANYONE GO OUT OF BODY?

Several studies made during the past ten years indicate that some 25 percent of adult humans remember having at least one spontaneous OOBE. Many were unaware of what had happened to them until the phenomenon was described to them. As stated earlier, we take the position that everyone goes into the OOBE state during the delta or deep-sleep state, as a natural process and in varying degrees. Therefore, one step may be to begin to remember the OOB patterns you have or are performing each night when you sleep. Further, after specific psychological and/or philosophic preparation, we believe that anyone can indeed consciously move into OOB states.

QUESTION: WILL DELIBERATELY GOING OOB HURT YOU?
COULD YOU DIE FROM IT?

After twenty-five years of investigation as well as personal exploration, there is no evidence to support either possibility. There is no doubt as to the emotional impact upon discovery of the reality of the OOB state. The major adjustment of one's belief systems is often traumatic and must be dealt with carefully Physiologically, there seems to be no effect, including any depletion of energy.

QUESTION: DO DRUGS OR ALCOHOL HELP OR BRING ON AN OOBE?

There is some data to indicate that hallucinogens may be producing an uncontrolled OOBE. The drug experience in and of itself has not been studied in depth as to this possibility. Alcohol, as a depressant, tends to inhibit a conscious OOBE, or at least the memory thereof. There is some support to the concept that anesthetics are no more than chemical triggers to produce deep OOB states, e.g., unconsciousness. Experimental slow administration of these under nonthreatening conditions as well as the medical descriptions of the various "planes" of anesthesia are the basis for this premise.

QUESTION: IS THE OOBE SIMILAR TO THE NEAR-DEATH EXPERIENCES THAT HAVE BEEN WRITTEN ABOUT IN SEVERAL RECENT BOOKS?

It is very similar. More pointedly, with allowances for cultural connotation and uncontrolled action-reaction due to a high-stress ambience of the moment, they appear to be one and the same Most if not all of the elements found in the near-death reports have been replicated repeatedly with various laboratory subjects using the Hemi-Sync process. The difference lies in the perception of the events and situations encountered. Without anxiety and stress, armed with objective observation, another perspective of the same state/condition is forthcoming.

QUESTION: ARE SUCH THINGS AS WEATHER CONDITIONS, MOON PHASE, LYING NORTH-SOUTH IMPORTANT IN ACHIEVING THE OOBE?

We have no hard data to support the premise that any of these have a significant effect on the OOBE. There are a few indicators that lying in the north-south position does have some effect, which would infer that the earth's magnetic field may have some bearing on the process. Because it was easily done, the new isolation booth in our laboratory is aligned in a magnetic north-south position. By setting up artificial magnetic fields within the booth, we will be able to equalize or produce a "null" magnetically, much as the astronauts experienced in their moon exploration. Subsequent studies therefore should provide partial answers, at least.

QUESTION: IF I LEAVE MY BODY TEMPORARILY, CAN'T SOMEONE ELSE GET IN IT WHILE I'M GONE?

If our premise is correct, there is no more possibility of this taking place than there would be during normal sleep If there could be statistics worked up on such possibility, the odds against an occurrence of this sort are far greater than those of your being killed in an auto accident during the coming year. Over the past fifteen years, working with laboratory subjects and program participants, there have been no incidents that remotely could be construed as "possession" or something destructive or uncontrollable.

QUESTION. IN YOUR PREVIOUS BOOK, YOU GAVE AN "ANGLE" METHOD FOR GETTING OUT OF YOUR BODY, BUT I CAN'T MAKE IT WORK FOR ME. IS THERE SOMETHING I AM NOT DOING RIGHT?

The method described was a very early technique that worked at that time. We have since discovered the many other vital factors that are involved in the process. Also, we currently use other techniques that are easier to understand and perform. Briefly put, it is not quite as simple as envisioned earlier.

QUESTION: WHAT DOES IT MEAN WHEN YOU GET STRANGE ACHES AND PAINS IN YOUR HEAD AND VARIOUS PARTS OF YOUR BODY WHEN YOU TRY TO GO OOB?

Generally, it infers unconscious anxieties and concerns that must be sought out and addressed before you can go on to the OOB state. If you are able to get behind or perceive the reason for each one at the level they exist, then release the emotion attached, these physical signals will disappear.

QUESTION. CAN YOU GET BACK INTO THE WRONG PHYSICAL BODY BY MISTAKE?

"Can" implies the ability for such incident to take place. It can happen, as it did to me in the early days. How often is another matter. In our current civilization, there are no means to understand this possibility even on a speculative basis. It has never happened to our laboratory subjects or those who have trained with us. We use a simple homing device to ensure return to "your" physical body. To return neatly and in a hurry, all you need to do is to think of one part of your physical body—such as a big right toe—and attempt to move or wiggle it. This brings prompt results. Because there is no data and the "wrong body" incident has occurred (to me), it does presume the possibility that it might happen with an untrained novice. If that is your possibility, remember the "wiggle big toe" signal. It will save much fear and worry.

QUESTION: WHAT ABOUT ANIMALS IN THE OOB STATE? HAVE YOU MET ANY? COULD YOU COMMUNICATE WITH THEM?

The only ones recognizable to me have been domestic cats which have been a part of our household family. They evidently have at least a second body, too, which can be perceived if they are asleep when you are out of body and you go to investigate. Of recent interest to me, during the departure phase, I encountered three cats just outside, sitting relaxed and observant. In greeting them, I was surprised to find they were the three of our favorite cats who had died physically during the past three years. In retrospect, why I was surprised I don't know.

QUESTION. WILL YOUR SOUNDS ON YOUR AUDIO CASSETTES
                 OR THOSE ON ANY OTHER SOUND CASSETTE IN-
                 DUCE THE OOB STATE?

It would be very rare if at all. Certain other factors must be approached first—such as the fear barrier, reappraisal of belief systems, among others. It is the extreme exception that balance has been reached sufficiently to move that easily into the OOB state.

QUESTION: WHAT ABOUT FLYING DREAMS? IS THIS AN OOBE?

We generally recognize that the flying dream, with or without an aircraft, is a rationalization of an OOBE which is unacceptable to the belief system of the conscious mind. Later data suggests that the dream of getting out of your "car" and performing some act falls into a similar category. Have you ever dreamed that you forgot where you parked your "car"! Also, the falling dream often becomes reentry into the physical when practiced in "slow motion."

QUESTION: HOW IS REMOTE VIEWING DIFFERENT FROM AN
                 OOBE?

Remote viewing, or the ability to "see" events taking place at another physical location, employs a trained state of consciousness that is effective while still very much within the physical body. Usually only one form of perception is utilized which translates as visual. In the OOB state, there is no awareness of the physical because you are "away" from it. Also, perceptions other than visual are invariably present. There are other differences, but these are the basics.

QUESTION: CAN AN OOBE BE INDUCED BY HYPNOSIS?

There are a number of reports that this has taken place, and it may be possible. We have no direct experience with it. The weakness of this technique from our perspective lies in the fact that the OOB individual is not in control of the activity —which seems to be quite important in the process

QUESTION: WHEN YOU FIND YOURSELF OOB WHILE STILL PER-
                 FORMING A PHYSICAL ACT SUCH AS DRIVING A
                 CAR, WHAT SHOULD YOU DO? HOW DO YOU CON-
                 TROL IT?

Get back as fast as you can! Use the quick-return method described earlier. This has not happened to me personally, but I understand it does occur infrequently.

QUESTION: IS IT EASIER TO GO TO A PLACE OR A PERSON WHILE IN OOB?

Usually to a person, easiest to someone who is close to you emotionally. There are some who can go to places, but it requires a specific "address" or ident.

QUESTION: IF YOU MEET A BEING WHILE OOB, HOW CAN YOU TELL IF IT IS MALEVOLENT OR BENEVOLENT?

An unqualified reply to this one is difficult. Often what is perceived as vicious or evil is simply a very impersonal energy you have encountered which you interpret as aimed at you personally. A sudden undertow at the beach may seem frightening and deadly, and it is your fear and the unknown potential of it that makes it so. The undertow itself doesn't know you exist and cares less. These can be avoided if you consciously limit your input "frequency," as it were, allowing only those on your "wavelength" to communicate and/or make contact with you. At best if there is a question, pat it on the shoulder and tell it to go home. At worst, you go back to the physical and regroup. Otherwise, say hello and enter into some form of communication.

QUESTION: CAN ONE GO FORWARD AND BACKWARD IN TIME WHILE OOB?

Very much so because the true OOB is not a time-space state or condition. It is not as productive as one would imagine, for several complex reasons. Most important is to use a strong home ident to get back in your original start-point. Such ident must include not only place, but time. Practice near-time runs before tackling the "long" ones.

QUESTION: WHAT IS MY "FORM" WHILE OOB?

Think of your second or immediate nonphysical body as much like gelatin that has been removed from a mold. It "remembers" the human form and thus is near-identical. The longer one is separated from the physical, the weaker the memory becomes unless reinforced. Time-distance also seems to be a factor. The farther "away" from the physical, such memory or its effectiveness becomes less. If left to its own devices, you may become a ball, a teardrop, a small cloud, or just a "blob." All of this can be bypassed by slipping out of the second body immediately after separation, and becoming clear undiluted energy. You can always "grow" a hand and arm if you need one.

QUESTION: WHAT ABOUT THE REINCARNATION PROCESS? ARE PHYSICAL LIFETIMES SEQUENTIAL, SIMULTANEOUS, OR WHAT?

First, they are not sequential in time. They may indeed be simultaneous. It is a question of "who is doing the perceiving?"

QUESTION: WHY WOULD SUPER BEINGS AS YOU DESCRIBE NEED TECHNOLOGY?

They don't. Putting their activities and ability within this context appears to be one possible way for our left-brained culture to begin to understand what they are doing. Such "technology" is as natural to them as our autonomic system is to us. We don't think about our gastrointestinal tract, our circulation system, or our lungs as technology. We just use them without conscious effort, although we now understand much of the technology involved. Their technology is much the same, relatively, except that they deliberately apply it and control it.

QUESTION. IS OUR HUMAN TECHNOLOGY A RESULT OF COMMUNICATION WITH SUCH SUPER BEINGS?

There is much to support this premise, especially when key figures and events in human history are objectively studied with this prospect as an alternative to our present belief system.

QUESTION. DO CERTAIN TYPES OF FOOD, COFFEE, SMOKING, SUGAR, ETC., AID OR INHIBIT OOBS?

There is no direct correlation either way, based solely upon those laboratory subjects and program participants active with the Institute We are not aware of any reliable in-depth studies on the matter Moderation may be the common factor, if any.

QUESTION: WHAT WOULD YOU SAY IS THE NATURE OF GOOD AND EVIL?

They exist only in the mind of the perceiver, due to ignorance and lack of understanding plus an immersed viewpoint.

QUESTION: CAN ONE LIVE TWO LIVES SIMULTANEOUSLY RELATIVE TO TIME?

This question has been asked of our nonphysical friends, who report that it is not only possible but does take place frequently. We have no further information about it, how or why it occurs, except that I personally was given the name and location of a "second life" I am living—but I have not had the time or the courage to verify it, if possible.

QUESTION. HAVE YOUR RELIGIOUS BELIEFS CHANGED AS A RESULT OF YOUR OOB ACTIVITIES?

Yes.

II. The OBE Psychophysiology of Robert A. Monroe
By Stuart W. Twemlow, M.D., and Glen O. Gabbard, M.D.

Robert Monroe is a businessman from Virginia, now in his sixties, who is one of the most widely known gifted subjects in the OBE literature. He has written a book cataloguing his out-of-body exploits,* and has founded a private institution devoted to the study of such phenomena: the Monroe Institute of Applied Sciences in Faber, Virginia. He voluntarily submitted himself to in-depth psychiatric and psychological evaluation several years prior to the publication of this book. He underwent intensive psychiatric interviewing and a battery of different psychological tests. Monroe has never had psychiatric treatment of any form. He has performed at a high level of functioning throughout his career as producer, businessman, and entrepreneur.

As we delve into his background, we find that he did not have out-of-body experiences until the age of forty-two. He had an orthodox Southern upbringing with high-achieving and successful parents. From an early age, Monroe had a fascination with flying. He built model planes as a little boy and learned to fly airplanes when he was only in high school. Later, he became an accomplished glider pilot. He was also preoccupied with the thrill of *movement* and has wonderful memories of riding on trains. Tolpin (1974) has related such intense developmental vicissitude to the grandiose fantasy which she calls "the Daedalus Experience." She takes this name, of course, from the myth of Daedalus and Icarus, who longed to fly over the sea and created wax wings for themselves to accomplish this task. Icarus, the son of Daedalus, became intoxicated with his ability to fly and flew too near the sun. The sun melted the wax on his wings, and he plunged into the sea as his father, Daedalus, continued on his way. Tolpin postulates that this myth and the fascination with flying is intimately connected with a certain developmental period when the infant experiences an ecstatic primal pleasure at being flung about by his mother and father and doting relatives. This archaic grandiose fantasy of defying gravity and flying through the air is normally tamed in the process of maturity and channeled into high achievement and other kinds of sublimatory activities. Tolstoy, for example, leapt out of a window at the age of

* *Journeys Out of the Body*. Garden City, N.Y.: Doubleday & Company, Inc., 1971; Anchor Press edition, 1977.

nine in an attempt to fly and suffered a concussion. However, he almost never relinquished the literal belief that he could fly He had ecstatic notions about merging with the moon, which Tolpin relates to the fantasy of mystical merger with his mother, whom he lost at the age of two. This early grandiose notion was, of course, channeled into extraordinary mastery and creativity in the area of writing. Winston Churchill had a similar background, and at eighteen jumped off a bridge onto treetops. This early grandiosity was gradually transformed from the realm of action into the realm of thought, as in his stirring speeches, e.g., "We shall never surrender." Tolpin provides another example of a six-year-old child who leapt off a merry-go-round in an effort to fly and became furious with his mother because he could not. This wish to fly was later transformed into a wish to fly an airplane.

The fascination with out-of-body "travel" seen in Monroe is likely an adult derivative of this Daedalus fantasy. His childhood grandiose wish is transformed not only into out-of-body experiences as an adult but also into the creation of an institute devoted to the study of these and other esoteric experiences. Hence, in Monroe we see perhaps a more direct translation of the childhood wish to fly into an adult form of the grandiose wish. However, he has used this interest adaptively and productively rather than in a self-destructive or counterproductive way. It may be that this persistent grandiose wish to fly is more likely to be operative as a determinant in those subjects who have the esoteric variety of out-of-body experience, i.e., travels to distant locations and through other realms which are fantastic and inexplicable. This determinant may not apply to the more mundane experiences where one simply finds himself floating on the ceiling above his body.

If one of the determinants of Monroe's out-of-body experience is this persistent wish to escape the shackles of the earthbound physical form, what are some of the others? His history indicates that he was free from childhood trauma and in fact somewhat indulged with creature comforts. His mother, a dynamic and successful physician, had a certain outlook on life which tended to avoid ugliness and unpleasantness. This attribute also emerges in an analysis of Monroe's personality. Both Monroe and his mother used the defenses of denial and avoidance to a significant extent. These hypomanic defenses against aggression, tragedy, and destructiveness were further demonstrated in projective psychological testing. The Rorschach tests indicated that Monroe was a man who avoids many aspects of his internal life. He has strong defenses against dealing with sexuality, defensive feelings, and especially aggression, all areas of his psyche that he prefers to keep out of his awareness. He has a pervasive tendency to avoid and detach himself from feelings which shows itself in his patterns of thinking, his use of language, and his interpersonal relations. He often simply steers off, away, and tangential to the way others think, feel, perceive, and express themselves. These personality inclinations contribute to the content of what he saw on a particular inkblot, which is often seen as a bat or a bird. Monroe saw this as "a flying unit, with wings, in the shape of a bird or the body of a butterfly or insect, flying upwards toward the top of the card." Thus, the out-of-body experience in Monroe also serves the function of avoidance of conflict. By transcending the prison of his body, it allows him to steer clear of such potential conflict areas as sexuality, depression, and aggression.

Observations of Robert Monroe were made by one of us (SWT) and a colleague, Dr. Fowler Jones of the University of Kansas Medical Center, over a thirty-minute time period when Monroe was monitored by a Beckman polygraph with left and right occipital EEG electrodes. He was observed by us through a one-way window (Twemlow, 1977). Most striking was Monroe's spasmodic breathing with periods of apnea. After these apneic periods, the breaths were gulping. Simultaneously, Dr. Jones and SWT turned to each other and reported the impression of a heat wavelike distortion beginning at Monroe's waist, so that it was difficult to get a clearly focused picture of his upper body, although his lower body *was* in clear focus. Previously, Monroe had stated that he would be able to get out of his body quickly but could not signal it, although he could signal within five seconds of return. This distortion disappeared rather suddenly a little before he roused himself. At that time his EEG showed a shift in high amplitude patterns to the right hemisphere with a low amplitude in the left occipital lead.

He seemed to wake without anxiety, although he was moderately disoriented in space for about thirty seconds, with slight slurring of his speech. He could not recapture his experience immediately. His GSR level during the session showed an increase in arousal of approximately 150 microvolts, marked by the total absence of either specific or nonspecific responses during his out-of-body phase. At one point, when a technician entered the room to check electrodes, Monroe appeared to be unaware of his presence, and there was no fluctuation in GSR. The skin of his arm and forearm were dry and warm to the touch. At that time rapid fluttering eye movements were noted (although eye movements were not measured).

Sections of Monroe's EEG during this reported out-of-body experience were analyzed for frequency differences both within and between hemispheres. An analysis of variance was run, with the data divided into beginning, middle, and end sections, each section having 29 values for a total of 290 seconds. Two groups were analyzed: right and left hemispheres. There seemed to be no significant frequency differences between hemispheres, although the amplitude differences were obvious. There were significant differences between the beginning and middle, the middle and end, and the beginning and end sections of Monroe's EEG in each hemisphere. This latter difference $(F = 41\ 47$ and $F = 59.08;\ p < .001)$ showed that the "before" and "after" OBE frequencies were much higher than the "during" OBE frequencies. Standard deviations were also significantly smaller with the middle section as compared to the beginning and end sections. A power spectral analysis of OBE periods showed power peaks at 4–5 Hertz with very little activity above 10 Hertz.

What are we to conclude from this experiment? Although the observational findings were more provocative than the EEG findings, they are less easily explained. Clearly, Monroe was in a state of deep relaxation. In addition, when in his out-of-body state there is a frequency slowing, with an interesting shift in power to a 4–5 Hertz range in the theta-delta transitional zone. This electrophysiological borderline state correlates closely with Tart's findings and Harary's reference to borderline sleep-wakefulness states

III. The Out-of-Body Experience: Phenomenology
By Stuart W. Twemlow, M.D., Glen O. Gabbard, M.D., and Fowler C. Jones, Ed.D.

Paper Presented at the 1980 Annual Meeting of the American Psychiatric Association, May 5–9, in San Francisco

Dr. Twemlow, formerly Chief Research Service, Topeka V.A. Medical Center, is now in the private practice of psychiatry, 2145 S E. Maryland, Topeka, Kans. 66605. Dr. Gabbard is Staff Psychiatrist, The Menninger Foundation Dr Jones is Assistant Professor of Psychiatry, University of Kansas Medical Center.

The authors would like to acknowledge Robert Ellsworth, Ph.D , for questionnaire analysis and interpretation; Gary Clark, Ph.D., and Lolafaye Coyne, Ph.D., for statistical consultation.

The project was supported in part by the Monroe Institute of Applied Sciences, Faber, Va.; University of Kansas Medical Center, Department of Psychiatry; The Menninger Foundation, Topeka, Kans.

Précis
Descriptive data is presented from 339 subjects who reported out-of-body experiences in response to an advertisement. The data was analyzed according to preexisting conditions, phenomenological features, and impact of the experience. Questions are raised about the etiology of this phenomenon and its meaning to the individual.

Introduction
In his 1979 presidential address to the American Psychiatric Association, Dr. Jules Masserman noted that one of man's three ultimate seekings is "a system of values and mystic beliefs to provide metapsychological serenity." He noted that there was a growing interest in what he called "metapsychiatry, reflecting a parallel

preoccupation in the general public with esoteric faiths and transcendental seekings for the ultimate." There is scant recognition of such areas in the traditional psychiatric literature although periodic case reports appear, for example, a case study of "self-induced depersonalization" by Kennedy.[1] It is true that increasing numbers of patients who are involved in movements, such as Transcendental Meditation, report experiences traditionally classified as psychopathological. These movements emphasize that some of these symptom complexes should not be *treated* in the way that a symptom is usually treated (e.g., interpretation, medication), but that many of these phenomena should be viewed by the unfamiliar treating physician with "benign neglect" and referred back to the meditation teacher for management. This is because a number of them are usual and expected accompaniments of changes in cognition, perception, and affect modulation that are expected to occur and are desirable.[2,3]

Our two papers summarize a study of one such phenomenon, the out-of-body experience (OBE).

The goal of our study is to address the following questions: (1) what is the continuum of phenomenological features which is the "out-of-body" state; (2) how does it compare with certain other states of consciousness such as dreaming, life-threatening experience, sensory deprivation states, and mystical religious experience; (3) how does it relate to pathological states; for example, depersonalization, autoscopy, and psychosis; (4) what are the short- and long-term effects on the individual and what does the experience mean to him; (5) what, if any, are the implications of this phenomena for the practice of psychiatry?

Definition of the term "out-of-body experience"

For the purposes of our survey we chose to define the experience in a very general way since review of the literature clearly revealed that there is little, if any, agreement about what characterizes the state phenomenologically, physiologically, in terms of personality structure, or in terms of significance to the individual. We chose the following definition "An experience where you felt that your mind or awareness was separated from your physical body." As with Palmer[4] we felt that the only theme in the literature which distinguishes these experiences is a sense of location of the total sense of self at some place other than in the physical body. We did not feel that it was wise to restrict our definition further at this point until the experience had been more thoroughly studied. Such a definition, however, does reflect certain biases on our behalf, explicitly, there are. (1) a belief that with the current state of knowledge, *the subject* is in a better position than the investigator to decide whether or not he had an out-of-body experience; (2) we wanted to emphasize the sense of location of self-awareness rather than the complex and extremely variable visual and auditory experiences reported in the anecdotal literature;[5] (3) whether or not there is objective laboratory demonstration of a separation of self-awareness from its normal location in the brain seems not relevant to the study of the phenomenon *from a psychiatric point of view.* Although some take the position, for example, Osis,[6] that such a criterion should be *fundamental* to the experience, we feel it peripheral to an understanding of its psychological impact and its meaning to the individual, particularly in terms of his value structure and the organization and functioning of his ego. For now, we feel that the experience should be subjectively defined. However, we are very aware of the vast literature on perceptual illusion suggesting that such research is enormously subject to bias; for example, Orne[7] demonstrated that experimental results are directly affected by the experimenter's personal belief system.

Attempts such as those of Tart[8,9] and Twemlow[10] to obtain psychophysiological correlates of such an experience cannot be said to characterize it even partially adequately, not unlike, for example, trying to describe a whole person using only an EKG. Reported laboratory studies show no stable features, but are suggestive. In our own studies[10] of the gifted subject Robert Monroe, and in a time series study of 11 Ss conducted to examine his OBE facilitating technique, one naïve subject did show some unusual EEG changes, an occipital EEG pattern most similar to an occipital slow wave of sleep variant. Tart[8,9] notes, as we do, that EEG measures in general show a dramatic reduction in neuronal energy in the alpha and theta band with some unusual patterns *not* characteristic of REM sleep or other normal sleep stages

The term "out-of-body experience" was coined by Tart in 1960 primarily to avoid the judgmental alternative names present in the literature which implied some nonexistent exact knowledge of etiology of the experience, for example, such terms as astral projection, ESP projection, doubling, astral travel, etc. Some writers feel that out-of-body experience is a specific form of depersonalization, a point to be addressed in the third paper of this series. Others such as Ehrenwald[11] emphasize not only the sense of separation but also the visual accompaniments of what is seen by the self located "outside" the body.

Following Tart's generally widely accepted definition of an altered state of consciousness as a "qualitative alteration in overall pattern of mental functioning, such that the experiencer feels his consciousness is radically different from the way it functions ordinarily,"[12] an adequate definition of OBE might include the following points: *an altered state of consciousness in which the subject feels that his mind or self-awareness is separated from his physical body and this self-awareness has a vivid and real sense about it, quite different from a dream.*

To flesh out this rather abstract definition, a letter was selected from one of approximately 700 describing such experiences received by one of the authors (SWT). This report is an example without many of the dramatic trappings of those reported in the parapsychological and theosophical literature and is given by a 52-year-old retired government employee living in Puerto Rico. He says, "When I was approximately ten years old I was living together with my older brother at my uncle's house, a major in the U.S. Army Medical Corps. One day I was reclined on my bed quite awake and was looking at the ceiling beams of the old Spanish building where the living quarters were located. I was saying to myself many questions such as what was I doing there and who was I. All of a sudden I get up from the bed and start walking toward the next room. At that moment I felt a strange sensation in me; it was a sensation of weightlessness and a strange mix of a sense of a feeling of joy. I turned back in my steps in order to go back to bed when to my big surprise I saw myself reclined on the bed. This surprising experience at that very small age gave me the kind of a jerk which, so to say, shook me back to my body." This example, particularly well exemplifies the ordinary, even mundane, content of the experience, its vivid emotional impact, the sense of a complete functioning self located outside the brain and the considerable surprise when the physical body is seen, and the way this anxiety triggers the delicate balance of the alteration of consciousness causing a restitution of the normal cognitive set of "in-body state."

Taxonomy of OBEs

As might be expected, all possible classification approaches have been applied to such experiences and each generally begs the question because there is no agreement as to what constitutes the OBE. Four possible approaches suggest themselves:

1. A classification by natural clustering of phenomena, that is, subjective reports, the approach addressed in this paper.

2. Classification by precipitating agents or stressors, that is, the conditions existing at the time of the experience, although a cause-effect relationship has never been established (discussed in this paper).

3. Classification by psychosocial and psychopathological variables, suggested only anecdotally and being addressed in the second paper in this series. For example, Eastman[13] reports OBEs associated with fearful states of mind, states of loneliness, and states of extremely positive mood (ecstatic states).

4. Classification by analogy. Here is suggested a state of sensory deprivation, peak and plateau experiences, and psychopathological states (schizophrenic body boundary loss, autoscopy, depersonalization, etc., being addressed in our third paper).

A correct taxonomy may make use of all four approaches, in an attempt to define pathognomonic features of the experience. Naturally the ultimate value of a taxonomy would depend on what it can explain. Many features of OBEs are most likely explainable by the idiosyncratic effects of precipitants (for example, drugs), personality and defensive constellations, and cultural factors, including belief systems.

Surveys of OBE

Few surveys of the incidence of OBEs exist; the earliest was by Hart in 1954.[14] He asked 155 students whether they had ever had an OBE. 27.1% of them said that they had, most of them having had more than one experience. This result is not inconsistent with the results of several later surveys. In 1968 Green[15] reports the results of asking 380 Oxford undergraduates: "Have you ever had an experience in which you felt that you were out of your body?" Of these 34% replied affirmatively. Palmer and Dennis in 1975[16] published the first survey using a *randomly* selected group of 1,000 students and townspeople in a small town in Virginia 25% of the students and 14% of the townspeople reported having had an OBE. A rather original approach to the study of OBEs was that of Shiels,[17] who collected data on belief in OBEs from nearly 70 non-Western cultures. Despite cultural differences the beliefs were strikingly similar. Shiels felt that this was indirect evidence for an account of a *genuine* event, the OBE. It is quite well known, for example, that many cultures attribute to shamans the capacity to fly out of the body.[18] In fact, a shaman cannot be anointed as such unless he has that capacity. According to Eliade, such flights express "intelligent understanding of secret things, metaphysical truths, symbolic meaning, transcendence, and freedom." A South African study,[19] analyzing 122 accounts in response to a press request, found that the OBE occurred often while the subject was asleep, relaxed, or dozing, and that over 50% of the subjects claimed to have been in a normal mental state when the phenomenon occurred.

Anecdotal accounts exist from people already convinced of the veracity and validity of such experiences.[5,20-24] All contain vivid and exciting descriptions based on the assumption that an objective separation and independent existence of mind from body is possible. Many of the reports are interested in what other dimensions of reality can be explored under these conditions. Eastman[13] reported the first summary of conditions under which OBEs occur, for example, before, during, and after sleep, during hypnotic trance (not supported subsequently in the literature), during illness, drug states, and after shock or accident. The sparse psychiatric literature[11] provides elaborate frameworks to explain the experience based on, for example, psychoanalytic theories which usually emphasize defenses against the imminence of physical death and various ways to deal with infantile omnipotence. Thus OBEs are often seen as unconscious attempts to portray aspects of man's eternal quest for immortality. Literature from philosophical and psychic sources, however, use the OBE to classify people as more or less spiritual (which usually means psychologically healthy and/or with ESP ability) based on the type and nature of their OBE.[25]

Method

On February 15, 1976, one of the investigators (SWT), in an interview with a national periodical (circulation 15 million on the North American continent), solicited letters from people who thought they might have had an out-of-body experience. Of about 1,500 responses, 700 subjects reported experiences in which they thought their consciousness was separated from the physical body. About one year after the interview two multiscale questionnaires (Profile of Out-of-Body Experiences, POBE, and Profile of Adaptation to Life, PAL) were sent to the individuals and 420 people returned valid questionnaires. 339 reported OBE experiences, while 81 people did not have such experiences, but expressed a strong interest in learning more about them, and for the purposes of this study were used as a comparison group, controlling for high interest in esoteric phenomena.

On the POBE questionnaire, items relating to phenomenology were selected from the following sources: reports of near-death experiences, mystical religious literature describing transcendent states, philosophical-occult psychic literature describing OBE experiences, psychoanalytic and psychiatric data describing states of depersonalization, psychotic, autoscopic, and hysterical-dissociative states, and dreaming.

Five psychological test scales described in our second paper were included to distinguish the psychopathological conditions and states traditionally connected with a tendency toward alterations in consciousness, for example: "attention absorption."[26]

Demographic data focused on previous experience with consciousness-altering drugs, hypnosis, and meditative experiences and to determine some of the background belief systems, including religious background and types of reading material.

In addition, the PAL questionnaire,[27] a well-validated psychological health scale, was sent to the subjects. This instrument is one of the few available tests of psychological health suitable for use in nondisturbed populations. Its health criteria are largely based on concrete behavioral measures rather than subjective assessment of mood states.

Results

Of the 339 subjects who reported an experience, 228 (66%) have had more than one such experience, while 117 (34%) have had only one. 74 subjects have had more than 10 OBEs.

A. PRE-EXISTING CONDITIONS

Table 1 summarizes the conditions remembered to exist at the time OBE occurred. Of course, no cause-effect relationship necessarily occurs between these conditions and the experience itself, although such has been implied by a number of authors.[28] An overwhelming majority of the sample were in a relaxed and calm state of mind (79%), and the variety of emotionally stressful conditions (23% of the sample), and states of physical pain, drug and alcohol intoxication, childbirth, and general anesthetic accounted for much smaller percentages of the sample. The finding that this experience is not usually associated with illness or stress compares with similar findings by Crookall,[28] who found four out of his five subjects normal and well. He attempted to classify OBEs based on those occurring under stress (physical or mental) and those occurring under nonstressful conditions. Comparing these findings with those of Green,[15] those who had one OBE only were characteristically people under some identifiable stress prior to the experience, especially physical trauma. In our sample, an analysis of the top and bottom 25% for frequency of OBEs utilizing univariate independent group t-tests failed to find any precondition reaching the level of $p < .01$. The bottom 25% of the sample reported more spontaneous OBEs, that is, those occurring without effort to leave the body, significantly more frequently than the top 25% $(df = 62, p < .01)$. A small but intensive study of 10 subjects* reports that states of mental calm were mentioned 20 times more frequently in subjects with multiple OBEs. Single OBE subjects reported psychological stress only three times in the sample. Most of the pundits of parapsychological literature recommend a physically relaxed state[10,22] from their own personal experiences. OBE occurring during dreaming is distinguished emphatically by subjects as being "more real than a dream" in the majority of cases. Flying and falling dreams, quite common in childhood, comprise a majority of the dreams occurring at the time the OBE is noted. It was of interest to us the certitude with which the subjects emphasize that they knew the difference between a dream state and an OBE state.

Subjects who were in a state of mental calmness at the time of the OBE tended to have a significantly greater proportion of meditators $(df = 178, p < .0001)$ than those who were not in such a state of mental calmness; otherwise no other preconditions significantly separated this group. Subsequent multivariate analyses of this data will be conducted to determine any cluster emerging from the preconditions listed. Life-threatening experiences as described by Stevenson and Greyson[29] have given rise to a prevalent opinion in the literature that OBEs are frequently associated with severe illness, threat to life, either internal (psychotic) or external (physical). Can such near-death experiences be separately characterized from out-of-body experiences? Another study will summarize this in more detail.† However, certain characteristics of the out-of-body experience itself allow a discrimination between nonstress OBE and those that occur while under stress (emotional and that posed by imminent death). A Chi† test of associations showed that the following experiences are more common in combined subjects (near death and under emotional stress): (1) experience of going through a dark tunnel $(p < .05)$; (2) brilliant light experience $(p < .001)$; (3) observation of a border or limit $(p < .002)$; (4) a sense of some attachment to the physical body $(p < .05)$; (5) a panoramic vision of images of dead relatives and friends $(p < .05)$.

The use of drugs and alcohol had a low incidence in this population. A study of marijuana users[30] showed that 44% of the marijuana users had had at least one OBE. Our population is a lot older (mean age 45 years) than Tart's, and the drugs reported used by our subjects were not classifiable, ranging from antihypertensives through vitamin pills and antibiotics. Only four subjects reported using psychedelic drugs (LSD and marijuana) at the time of the experience.

Individual descriptions of the type of emotional stress totaled 74 reports. Striking were the themes of loss, mourning, and loneliness represented in 21 of the subjects; threats of death, including illness, being in a war zone, pre-surgery, and cancer in 20; marital and family problems in 12; and the remainder miscellaneous, including unspecified tension states. When the descriptions were reviewed from the point of view of those who had had one OBE only $(n = 33)$ and those who had more than one $(n = 41)$, 21.7% of the one OBE sample reported stress involving loss, mourning, and loneliness, compared with 34.2% of those who had had more than one OBE. Similarly, Eastman[13] reports the sense of loneliness as quite frequent at the time of OBE and such findings may be seen to support theories that place emphasis on defensive methods of adapting to threat of loss or damage to the ego.

A question was asked to explore why the individual wanted to have an OBE and revealed some interesting findings. Of 91 classifiable responses, 19 (20.9%) were simply interested for curiosity or fun, 21 (23 1%) were members of a psychical research or study group, 23 (25.3%) were involved in personal, existential explorations associated with major developmental stages, and in 28 (30.7%) the experience was entirely spontaneous and unexpected. Only 10% of the sample had previously attended workshops on OBEs and it was significant that approximately one-third of the sample had not expected in any way to have such an experience and did not admit at least to expecting or even knowing about such experiences.

B. NATURE OF THE EXPERIENCE

Table 2 summarizes a number of phenomenological features of the experience. The first six features, occurring in more than 50% of the subjects, do not show the more esoteric aspects described in the literature but describe a simple subjective perceptual experience of great vividness and reality, showing not only a sense of separation of the total self from its normal location in the head but also being aware that this self exists in the same environment as the physical body, which can be clearly seen and is associated with a feeling of unusual "energy" and a desire to return to the body.

As might be expected, some of the more vivid and detailed phenomenological features were overrepresented in the top 25% of the sample. For example, using independent group t-tests, the following features were more common in the top 25%: a sense of energy $(df = 94, p < .0005)$, noises, particularly roaring noises $(df = 39, p < .0005)$, vibrations $(df = 97, p < .01)$, seeing the body from a distance $(df = 97, p < .005)$, a sense of being able to pass through objects $(df = 93,$

$p < .00006$), awareness of the presence of nonphysical beings $(df = 96, p < .005)$, and seeing a brilliant light $(df = 96, p < .002)$.

These findings show some differences from the major surveys reported in the literature. For example, Crookall,[31] in an analysis of anecdotal reports from 380 subjects, found a high representation of people who felt connected to their bodies by a cord, who see other apparitions during the experiences, and who demonstrate ESP during the experience, none of which were significantly represented in our population. However, some of his major findings—for example, the subject being able to see his own body from a new and spatially independent vantage point, finding himself in a form similar to his physical body, and feeling the "other body" tends to float—were supported in our study. Our findings correspond more closely with those of Celia Green,[15] who found that practically none of her correspondents saw a cord.

C. IMPACT OF THE EXPERIENCE

As seen in Table 3, a majority of the subjects had remarkably positive experiences. What is striking is the use of superlative adjectives in the reports. By no means was this experience ordinary and in 60% of the sample was life-changing. Even those who experienced the OBE as extremely frightening, or giving sensations of great power, on a Chi† test of association were not significantly related to mean scores on the Hysteroid and Psychoticism scales, suggesting that the experience itself neither occurred in particularly sick people nor had a pathological impact. 85% termed it "a very pleasant experience."

T-tests revealed, as would be expected, that those who were in a state of mental calmness at the time of the OBE experienced more positive moods both during and after the experience. Mood states such as joy $(df = 304, p < .01)$, freedom $(df = 309, p < .008)$, calm, peace and quiet $(df = 90, p < .0002)$ were experienced much more frequently than in those who had feelings of fear during the experience. T-test comparisons also revealed the fact that those who were mentally calm had more detailed and vivid experiences than those who experienced fear at the time of the OBE, for example, senses of energy $(df = 312, p < .02)$, vibrations $(df = 322, p < .01)$, feelings that people not out of the body were aware of their presence $(df = 155, p < .008)$. In the mentally calm group the experience was seen as having a more lasting and dramatic impact on life; for example, it was described as a spiritual or religious experience $(df = 302, p < .01)$, an experience of great beauty and lasting benefit $(df = 301, p < .0003)$, and effected a change toward a belief in survival after death $(df = 313, p < .01)$.

The data is quite reminiscent of the categories used to describe peak and plateau experiences[32] and mystical religious experiences:[33] for example, the sense of unity, transcendence of time and space, sense of objectivity and reality, a noetic and sacred quality, a deep positive mood state, and a quality of ineffability.

Subjects who described a sense of purpose to the experience in general indicated that the experience enabled them to obtain closure on some of the major existential questions, for instance: "to show me everything is possible," "to show me new possibilities or new realities." These accounts reflected a preponderance (85%) of subjects who were dealing with issues associated with major life changes and requiring much introspection, review, and assessment of personal strengths and weaknesses.

DISCUSSION

Even without reviewing the widely recognized defects of the questionnaire approach, this study has a number of added defects, including the fact that many of the experiences are remembered from many years before. Structuring the questionnaire in a directive way added forced-choice features; however, the questions were forced-choice to aid in quantifying data but the sacrifice, of course, is obvious. Although a large number of questions were asked, this approach suffers from a lack of detailed individualized protocols. In an attempt to remedy this defect, extensive psychological testing has been done on a selected sample of 100 of these subjects, a random cross section of whom will be personally interviewed and reported in future studies. The generalizability of this data is aided by the semi-random nature of the study and the anonymity of respondents. The study population is highly representative of the general population at large; separate research, for the Profile of Adaptation to Life Scale, compared a number of different populations, including college students, Transcendental Meditators, professionals, and psychiatric patients to arrive at norms for the test. It was found that our OBE group was the "norm" group, representing a broad range of educational age and geographic characteristics as well as having a good psychological and physical adjustment.[27] The 280 nonrespondents to the questionnaire cast some doubt on how generalizable our data is even to the OBE population. However, about 100 of the questionnaires were undeliverable and there was a one-year unavoidable time delay between the published interview and the mailing of the questionnaires.

As one reviews our results as an attempt to delineate the phenomenology of the OBE, this study adds a number of major features to the understanding of the experience An old theosophical tract[34] used the concept of "thought form " In the general case the OBE is a typical "thought form," the question really being. What form does this thinking take? We have elected not to address the issue of whether mind *really* separates from the physical body, but our research has raised in our minds fundamental questions about the nature of what is "really real." In addition to the sense of separation of mind from body, what becomes apparent from the survey is that total mind, perhaps best referred to as *"sense of whole self,"* is separated. There is visually no self-awareness in the body. The whole self, including observing *and* experiencing ego functions, is located at a point in perceptual space other than the brain, with the physical body being seen as inert and "thoughtless." There is no clouding of consciousness as is reported in hypnogogic, hypnopompic, and dream, including lucid dream states; in fact, consciousness is felt to be quite clear. A most striking finding reported by subjects is the absolute certainty that they were not dreaming, whether or not the experience occurred when quite aroused; for example, when in severe pain or, as in the majority of cases, in a resting state. Those who are fearful, frightened, or in pain when they have this experience tend to have a much more negative reaction to it and, as might be expected, utilize it for much less extensive attitudinal change, and the experience remains less vivid in the memory. Future studies will further differentiate the latter group, which might be experiences of depersonalization. Far from being primarily attributes of illness, painful or toxic states, the majority of these experiences occur often when the person is least expecting them and when quite relaxed. Theories such as those of Palmer[35] emphasize the importance of reduction in proprioceptive input in the physically relaxed state akin to sensory deprivation. As the brain receives less proprioceptive and other sensory input, the ego theoretically becomes able to relax reality testing. Regressive components of the OBE seem to occur in the 22% of patients who are reminded of childhood experiences, thus it is tempting to invoke the psychoanalytic concept of regression in the service of the ego. But the question remains: What is the service, both from a defensive as well as an adaptive synthetic viewpoint? There is no need to find a single cause for OBEs. Multideterminism is a widely accepted concept in psychiatry. Thus our approach to the etiology of OBE is to consider there to be contributions from different *levels of explanation*.

Each OBE experience might thus be determined by a number of factors (psychopathological, toxic/organic, evolutionary, developmental, and perceptual-cognitive), each making a contribution. The same individual would likely have a different etiological combination under different circumstances and the experience would have a different impact. This concept is elaborated in a paper we have in preparation.‡

In the *Republic*, Plato delineates four levels of experiential reality: imaginary, physical, conceptual, and direct transcendental cognition, which he calls direct seeing or "the Good." In the story of Er *(Republic,* 616–17) the story is told of a valiant man, Er, who died in battle and who later revived and told a story whereby his soul had departed from him. Plato claims something utterly alien to the modern mentality; he says that only after death, when we are free of bodily influence, shall we know the whole crux of being. Plato feels that freeing the psyche from the body is an essential condition for the philosophic journey to ultimate wisdom. As indicated by Grosso,[36,37] monistic materialism has collapsed the architecture of being to a one-level affair, the really real world of sense experience. The middle kingdom, the unreal domain of dreams, the flimsiest form of epiphenomena, perhaps the collective asylum of artists and the mad, may teach us to be less dogmatic in the way we toss about epithets like "real." It may help us to open up to more multilevel ontologies.

References

1. Kennedy, R. B. "Self-induced Depersonalization Syndrome." *Am. J. Psychiatry,* 133: 1326–28, 1976.
2. Twemlow, S. W. Discussion of *A Psychoanalytic Theory of Altered States of Consciousness* by Erika Fromm. *Bull. Menninger Clinic,* 42(6): 538–40, 1978.
3. Twemlow, S. W., and Bowen, W. T. "Psychedelic Drug-Induced Psychological Crises: Attitudes of the 'Crisis Therapist.'" *Journal Psychedelic Drugs,* 11(4). 331–35, 1979.
4. Palmer, J., and Vassar, C. "ESP and Out-of-the-Body Experiences: An Exploratory Study." *J. Amer. Society for Psychical Research,* 68(3): 257, 277, 1974.
5. Muldoon, S., and Carrington, H. *The Phenomenon of Astral Projection.* New York: Samuel Weiser, Inc., 1970.
6. Osis, K. "Perspectives for Out of Body Research." In W. G. Roll, R. L. Morris, and J. D. Morris (eds.), *Research in Parapsychology.* Metuchen, N.J.: Scarecrow Press, 1973.
7. Orne, M. T. "On the Social Psychology of the Psychology Experiment: With particular reference to demand characteristics and their implications." *American Psychologist,* 17: 776–83, 1962.
8. Tart, C. T. "A Psychophysiological Study of Out of the Body Experiences in a Selected Subject." *J. Amer. Society for Psychical Research,* 62: 3–27, 1968.
9. Tart, C. T. "A Second Psychophysiological Study of Out of the Body Experiences in a Gifted Subject." *International Journal of Parapsychology,* 9: 251–58, 1967.
10. Twemlow, S. W. In *Journeys Out of the Body* by Robert A. Monroe. Garden City, N.Y.: Anchor Books, 1977, pp. 275–80.
11. Ehrenwald, J. "Out-of-the-Body Experiences and the Denial of Death." *J. Nervous & Mental Disease,* 159(4): 227–33, 1974.
12. Tart, C. T. "States of Consciousness and State Specific Sciences." In R. E. Ornstein (ed), *The Nature of Human Consciousness.* San Francisco: W. H. Freeman, 1973.
13. Eastman, M. "Out-of-the-Body Experiences." *Proceedings of the Society for Psychical Research,* 53(193): 187–309, 1962.
14. Hart, H. "ESP Projection: Spontaneous Cases and the Experimental Method." *J. Amer. Society for Psychical Research,* 48: 121–46, 1954.
15. Green, C. *Out-of-the-Body Experiences.* London: Hamish Hamilton, 1968.

16. Palmer, J., and Dennis, M. "A Community Mail. Survey of Psychic Experiences in Research in Parapsychology" Metuchen, N.J.. Scarecrow Press, 1975.

17. Shiels, D. "A Cross-cultural Study of Beliefs in Out of the Body Experiences." *J. Amer. Society for Psychical Research,* 49 697–741, 1978.

18. Eliade, M *Shamanism: Archaic Technique of Ecstasy* Princeton, N.J.: Princeton University Press, 1972.

19. Poynton, J "Results of an Out of the Body Survey." In J. Poynton (ed.), *Parapsychology in South Africa* Johannesburg: South African Society for Psychical Research, 1975.

20. Landau, L "An Unusual Out of the Body Experience." *J. Amer. Society for Psychical Research,* 42: 126–28, 1963.

21. Muldoon, S., and Carrington, H. *The Projection of the Astral Body.* London: Rider & Co., 1929.

22. Muldoon, S. *The Case for Astral Projection.* Chicago: Aries Press, 1936.

23. Stratton, F J. M. "An Out of the Body Experience Combined with ESP." Letter to the Editor, *J. Amer. Society for Psychical Research,* 39: 92–97, 1957.

24. Whiteman, J. H. "The Process of Separation and Return in Experiences Fully Out of the Body" *Proceedings of the Society for Psychical Research,* 50· 240–74, 1956.

25. Crookall, R. "Astral Projection." *Light A Journal of Psychic Studies,* 194–200, 1970.

26. Tellegan, A., and Alkinson, G. "Openness to Absorbing and Self-Altering Experiences ('Absorption'). A trait related to hypnotic susceptibility." *J. Abnormal Psychology,* 53: 368–77, 1974.

27. Ellsworth, R. B. *Profile of Adaptation to Life Holistic Scale.* Institute for Program Evaluation, P.O Box 4654, Roanoke, Va. 24015, 1979.

28. Crookall, R. *The Study and Practice of Astral Projection.* New Hyde Park, N.Y.· University Books, Inc., 1960.

29. Stevenson, I, and Greyson, B. "Near-Death Experiences: Relevance to the Question of Survival After Death." *J.A.M.A.,* 243(3): 165–67, 1979.

30. Tart, C. T. *On Being Stoned: A Psychological Study of Marijuana Intoxication.* Palo Alto: Science & Behavior Books, 1971.

31 Crookall, R. *Out of the Body Experiences: A Fourth Analysis.* New Hyde Park, N.Y.: University Books, Inc., 1970.

32 Maslow, A. H *Religions, Values and Peak Experiences.* New York The Viking Press, 1970.

33. James, W. *The Varieties of Religious Experience* New York: Crowell-Collier, 1961.

34. Besant, A, and Leadbeater, C. W. *Thought-forms.* New York, London, and Benares: The Theosophical Publishing Society, 1905.

35. Palmer, J. "The Out-of-Body Experience: A Psychological Theory." *Parapsychology Review*, Sept.–Oct., 19–22, 1978.
36. Grosso, M. "Plato and Out-of-the-Body Experiences." *J. Amer. Society for Psychical Research*, 69: 61–74, 1975.
37. Grosso, M. "Some Varieties of Out-of-Body Experiences." *J. Amer. Society for Psychical Research*, 70: 179–93, 1976.

Table 1 Pre-existing Conditions

| | Frequencies | | |
Attribute	Present	Absent	% Present
Physically relaxed	263	70	79
Mentally calm	261	69	79
Dreaming*	117	211	36
Meditating	88	241	27
Under emotional stress	74	250	23
Unusually fatigued	51	279	15
Near death	34	298	10
Cardiac arrest	17	313	5
Drug	26	300	8
General anesthetic	20	312	6
Severe pain	21	307	6
Childbirth†	14	316	4
Accident	13	318	4
High fever	11	320	3
Sexual orgasm	11	322	3
Alcohol	5	328	2
Driving a vehicle	8	324	2

* In 97 S, (83%), the dream was described as a "flying or falling" dream.
†52.5% sample were female.

Table 2 Nature of the Experience

Attribute	Frequencies Present	Absent	% Present
More real than a dream	315	19	94
Form similar to physical body	232	73	76
Same environment as physical body	197	123	62
Sense of energy	177	145	55
Wanted to return to body	164	138	54
Saw physical body from distance	171	162	51
Passed through objects	155	157	50
Vibrations in body	128	204	38
Heard noises in early stages*	71	123	37
Part of awareness still in body	120	203	37
Awareness of presence of nonphysical beings†	121	209	37
Change in time sense	107	220	33
Brilliant white light‡	96	225	30
Presence of guides or helpers	85	238	26
Tunnel experience	85	242	26
Attached to physical body	68	259	21
Able to touch objects	54	251	18
Person not out of body aware of presence	45	277	14
Sense of border/limit	44	279	14
Panoramic vision	14	313	4

* A variety were reported, the most common being buzzing (29%), roaring (19%), music or singing (16%).
† In 19% were people close to the subject, but who had already died.
‡ 46% sample found the light strongly attractive; 33% felt it was a being.

Table 3 Impact of the Experience

During	Frequencies		
	Yes	No	% Yes
Calm, peace, quiet	281	90	72
Freedom	215	103	68
Sense of purpose	182	115	63
Joy	173	139	55
No special feelings	91	161	36
Fear	111	209	35
Power	89	218	29
Sadness	39	267	13
Going crazy	15	294	5
Immediately After			
Became interested in psychic phenomona	266	46	85
Talked about it to others	242	85	74
Curious	232	95	71
Felt life changed	188	127	60
Spiritual experience	174	145	55
Felt he possessed psychic abilities	136	180	43
Ordinary event	120	195	38
Confused	87	233	27
Kept it secret	77	237	25
Upset and frightened	80	242	25
Forgot about it	20	295	6
Going crazy	15	304	5
Longer-Term Effect			
Like to try again	284	34	89
Developed greater awareness of reality	281	47	86

| | Frequencies | | |
	Yes	No	% Yes
Very pleasant	273	47	85
Lasting benefit	240	67	78
Change toward a belief in life after death	215	109	66
Great beauty	208	112	65
Like traveling to far-off land	165	149	53
The greatest thing that ever happened	136	177	43
Reminiscent of childhood experiences	68	248	22
Disappointing	20	299	6
Like being drunk or high	20	297	6
Mentally harmful	7	313	2

Notes

* Ironson, D. S. "An Investigation into the Preconditions, Characteristics, and Beliefs Associated with the Out-of-the-Body Experience." Unpublished doctoral dissertation, 1975.

† Gabbard, G. O., Twemlow, S. W., and Jones, F. "Do Near Death Experiences Occur Only When Near Death?" Submitted for publication 1980; preprint available from the corresponding author.

‡ Twemlow, S. W., and Gabbard, G. O. "The OBE as an Overdetermined State of Consciousness." Manuscript available from the corresponding author.

About the Author

Robert Allan Monroe is a man of many talents. More important, he has the ability to explore and experience these different facets that make up an unusual personality.

The son of a college professor and a medical doctor mother, he received his degree from Ohio State University after studies in engineering and journalism, and entered the radio broadcasting industry as a writer and director of programs. In 1939 he went to New York, where he was the creator and producer of some 400 radio and TV network programs in the ensuing twenty-year period. In addition to directing and writing, he composed all of the orchestral music for his programs, much of which is still in use in television and motion pictures.

His first radio network program was *Rocky Gordon,* a railroad adventure series which for several years preceded the famous Lowell Thomas–*Amos 'n' Andy* program block on NBC. Some of the other network program series he created and produced were *High Adventure* (George Sanders), *Nightmare* (Peter Lorre), *Starlight Theatre* (Madeleine Carroll), *Scramble* (Bob Ripley), *M-G-M Screen Test,* and the quiz shows *Take a Number* and *Meet Your Match.*

After an early sojourn at Donahue and Coe, Advertising, he formed Robert Monroe Productions, which at the peak of its operations was producing as many as twenty-eight radio network shows weekly. He later became vice-president of programs and director of Mutual Broadcasting System, Inc., a position he held until mid-1956. He then became president of Laury Associates, which brought him into ownership and operation of radio stations in North Carolina and Virginia. He also formed Jefferson Cable Corporation, which, as president, he guided in the construction and operation of cable-TV systems in Charlottesville and Waynesboro, Virginia—a position he held until April 1976.

Mr. Monroe's major avocation in recent years has been exploration and research into practical methods of accelerated learning through expanded forms of consciousness. To augment such activity, he founded the Monroe Institute of Applied Sciences in 1973, with facilities and laboratories at Afton, Virginia. With his long and varied experience in sound, it was natural that he utilized this medium for his investigation. One of the results of his work was a method and technique of inducing relaxation and sleep, which was granted a generic patent in 1975. The technique employs a system of audio pulses which create a frequency-following response in the human brain. By this method, it is now possible to hold and maintain specific stages of sleep for any depth and duration in the average person. A later development at the Institute has utilized the same methods and technique in a form of "binaural beats" to create synchronization of both left and right hemispheres in the human brain. The unique coherent brain state that results is known as hemispheric synchronization, or "Hemi-Sync." This discovery also permits external control of the degree of activity of either right or left brain. These two patterns, when employed in an ordered sequence to achieve specific effects, offer a significant gateway to new understanding and application of human thought and endeavor. Along with others, the Monroe Institute (now located in Nelson County, Virginia) is exploring the potentials of such methods in all areas of individual and cultural activity.

Mr. Monroe, as executive director and founder of the Institute, still plays an active part in this educational-research organization. He is author of the book *Journeys Out of the Body* (Doubleday & Company, Inc., 1971; Anchor Press edition, 1977), which has been published in five languages worldwide. With his family, he lives on his farm in Nelson County, Virginia, near the Institute headquarters.

P.O. 0005447867 20240216